ROYAL HISTORICAL SOCIETY

STUDIES IN HISTORY

New Series

GENDER, CRIME AND JUDICIAL DISCRETION
1780–1830

GENDER, CRIME
AND JUDICIAL DISCRETION
1780–1830

Deirdre Palk

THE ROYAL HISTORICAL SOCIETY
THE BOYDELL PRESS

First published 2006

A Royal Historical Society publication
Published by The Boydell Press
an imprint of Boydell & Brewer Ltd
PO Box 9, Woodbridge, Suffolk IP12 3DF, UK
and of Boydell & Brewer Inc.
668 Mt Hope Avenue, Rochester, NY 14620, USA
website: www.boydellandbrewer.com

ISBN 0 86193 282 X

ISSN 0269–2244

A CIP catalogue record for this book is available
from the British Library

This book is printed on acid-free paper

Printed in Great Britain by
Biddles Ltd, King's Lynn

Contents

List of Tables

Acknowledgements

The origins of this book lie in my PhD thesis completed in 2002. My journey to that point, and beyond it to this book, has not followed the usual pattern and has been a particularly lonely one. Returning as a mature student to historical research and reflection and at the same time following a long career in a profession with no links with history or academic life, dependence on my own interior (and economic) resources has at times been more daunting than I would have wished. However, I retained a strong feeling that there were useful and interesting issues arising from my research which needed to be incorporated in a book which could be shared with other social historians, in particular historians of crime and of women. In addition, non-historian friends wanted me to write, in an accessible way, about the experiences of 'ordinary' people caught up with the late eighteenth- and early nineteenth-century English criminal justice system. I hope that my attempt to be both academically rigorous and generally accessible has been successful.

The loneliness of the journey has been significantly relieved by a number of people to whom I owe grateful thanks: to a group of inspired women who returned to historical study with me to complete a master's degree in women's history at Royal Holloway, University of London, and whose continued sisterhood and support have been important – Sara Bailey, Meg Irving, Linda Massie, Julie Peakman, Diana Peschier, Stephanie Spencer; to my supervisors during my doctoral research, Peter King, Joanna Innes, Alison Oram for their encouragement, guidance and challenging demands on my researching and writing abilities; to the staff of various record offices, libraries and archives, especially the archivists at the Bank of England for their considerable help and interest; to Randall McGowen for sharing some of his developing work; and to David Eastwood and Christine Linehan of the Royal Historical Society. The greatest gratitude, however, is due to Richard Palk, partner, best friend and fellow-historian, without whose encouragement and forbearance over the dozen or so years this project has been in gestation, this book would certainly never have seen the light of day; it is to him, radical critic, kind suggester of improvements and as familiar with every page as I am myself, that this book is dedicated.

My debt is also to the men and women who people this book. I have been closely involved with them, and have used their stories and their words, and so have changed their history. I trust I have been fair to their memories and have not dealt them any further injustices.

Deirdre Palk,
Auxerre, France
January 2006

This book is produced with the assistance of a grant from Isobel Thornley's Bequest to the University of London

Abbreviations

TNA   The National Archive
BECLS   Bank of England Law Suits Committee
BEFP   Bank of England Freshfields' lawyers papers
OBSP   Old Bailey Sessions Papers
CLRO   Corporation of London Records Office
HO   Home Office
PRO   Public Records Office
PP   *Parliamentary papers*

AJLH   *American Journal of Legal History*
BJC   *British Journal of Criminology*
CJH   *Criminal Justice History*
EcHR   *Economic History Review*
EHR   *English Historical Review*
G&H   *Gender and History*
HJ   *Historical Journal*
HWJ   *History Workshop Journal*
JBS   *Journal of British Studies*
JLH   *Journal of Legal History*
JSH   *Journal of Social History*
JWH   *Journal of Women's History*
LHR   *Law and History Review*
P&P   *Past and Present*
WHR   *Women's History Review*

1

Gender and the Criminal Justice System

Four people ordered for execution, one for forgery, one for burglary, two for beating and robbing a man in a house of ill-fame. There was a woman engaged, who was spared on account of her sex, but she was the most guilty of all.[1]

A journey through the criminal justice system

Amy Steele was fifteen years old when she was sentenced to death for robbery in 1821 at the Old Bailey court. This looks like an example of the terrifying harshness of the 'bloody code' of criminal justice which operated in England at this time. Yet, four years later, the same Amy Steele was back at home with her parents, free and pardoned of all wrong-doing. Steele's story was not a freakish aberration of the justice system in the early years of the nineteenth century. Rather it was an example of what very often happened in a country where 'the entire legal fabric, from prosecution to punishment, was shot through with discretion'.[2] So, was Steele's good fortune a result of being female, the outcome of persistent paternalistic leniency shown towards women through history? Or was the reason more complicated than this?

If Steele's story is carefully followed through the judicial records, issues other than her gender emerge. After the pronouncement of the terrible sentence, appeals for royal mercy came from her parents, mercy for their 'child' who had never offended before, and who had the potential to become a respectable member of society. The judge who sentenced her then reported doubts over the facts of her case, and summed her up as 'a bad character . . . but from the mildness and feebleness of her manner one would not expect her to be engaged in an outrage of this sort'. Royal mercy was extended to her, and she was conditionally pardoned – instead of being executed, she should be transported to Australia for the rest of her life. But Steele did not leave England. The next decision made about her future – another conditional pardon – despatched her to prison in the General Penitentiary at Millbank to serve ten years there. When a cholera epidemic hit Millbank in 1824, she was transferred to a hulk on the Thames, and shortly found herself on a list of

---

[1] Lord Colchester (ed.), *A political diary, 1828–1830, by Edward Law, Lord Ellenborough*, London 1881, entry for 12 June 1828, 154–5.
[2] J. Brewer and J. Styles (eds), *'An ungovernable people': the English and their law in the seventeenth and eighteenth centuries*, London 1980, 18.

women granted free pardons and sent home, only two and half years after she was sentenced to death.[3]

Steele's story presents an intriguing and complex mix of reasons for judicial leniency. In this book some answers are suggested to questions about the effects of gender in a number of capital property crimes (shoplifting, pickpocketing and forged Bank note circulation in London and Middlesex) and in the operation of the English criminal justice system in the late eighteenth and early nineteenth centuries. Were offenders against the criminal law treated differently in accordance with their sex, and if so, why and how? These questions have, as yet, been only partially faced by historians. Some have presented what appears to be a more lenient pattern of treatment of women offenders (at least where serious crimes are concerned);[4] but the attempt to discover why this should be so has proved a much more difficult task.

The same attempt to explain the 'mismeasure' of justice between men and women exercises modern criminologists. Here, there is no dearth of theory, reflection and analysis.[5] One of the most interesting of these modern criminological studies showed how men and women coming before the courts said different things about themselves, and about what they had done, but there was no 'gendered' difference in the ways they sought to justify themselves. There was significant gender difference, however, in how the courts made judgements about their characters, and therefore in the sentencing thought appropriate.[6] Another valuable study, published in 1997, started from the proposition that a 'superficial examination of the criminal statistics suggested that, for virtually every type of offence, women were treated more leniently than men'. It went on to show that the leniency which emerged from sentencing patterns for shoplifting, violence and drug offences in 1991 was more in the nature of different rather than lighter sentences. Interviews with

---

3   TNA, PRO, HO 17/53/1Ih02; HO 17/53/2/Ik8.
4   See particularly P. King, 'Gender, crime and justice in late eighteenth- and early nineteenth-century England', in M. Arnot and C. Usborne (eds), *Gender and crime in modern Europe*, London 1999, 44–74, and *Crime, justice and discretion in England, 1740–1820*, Oxford 2000, 259–96; and G. Walker, *Crime, gender and social order in early modern England*, Cambridge 2003.
5   Since the literature is vast, only a selection is mentioned here: D. Farrington and A. Morris, 'Sex, sentencing and reconviction', *BJC* xxiii (1983), 229–48; F. Heidensohn, *Women and crime*, Basingstoke 1985; L. Gelsthorpe, *Sexism and the female offender*, Aldershot 1989; A. R. Edwards, 'Sex/gender, sexism and criminal justice: some theoretical considerations', *International Journal of the Sociology of Law* xvii (1989), 165–84; L. Gelsthorpe and A. Morris, *Feminist perspectives in criminology*, Milton Keynes 1990; K. Daly, *Gender, crime and punishment*, New Haven, Conn.1994; S. Edwards, *Sex and gender in the legal process*, London 1996; C. Hedderman and L. Gelsthorpe (eds), *Understanding the sentencing of women*, London 1997. C. Smart, *Women, crime and criminology: a feminist critique*, London 1976, is still useful although it shows its age; the 'silence' of which it speaks in relation to women's crime is no longer entirely relevant.
6   Daly, *Gender and crime*.

magistrates showed clearly the influence of gendered attitudes on their deci-sion-making, both conscious and subconscious.[7]

Only relatively recently has writing on the history of crime and the crim-inal justice system in England broached the difficult question of the relation-ship between gender and law-breaking, and gender and judicial decisions in the early modern and modern periods.[8] Despite the growth of the study of women's history and the increasing interest in social history over the last thirty years, there is still insufficient research and writing on the criminality of women and their encounter with the criminal justice system. In particular, the voices of those on one side of the unremarkable, daily drama of the system of criminal justice – the men and women who were tried, judged and punished – remain largely unheard. Those on the other side – prosecutors, juries and judges – rarely gave reasons for their decisions which determined the fate of the poor and the obscure. Nevertheless, the decisions which were made at all stages of the criminal justice system were not as arbitrary and illogical as they might at first seem; they were the result of rational choices made within a system which frequently demanded that choices were made.[9]

Historians currently researching and writing on women, crime and the courts in the early modern and modern period [10] are beginning to discard the traditionally presented picture of women as law-abiding and not worth consideration in crime and criminal justice history.[11] The study of crime and the criminal justice system requires that the many women involved in crime, tried and punished, are taken more seriously. The motives of those with judi-cial power over them need to be better understood.

[7] Hedderman and Gelsthorpe, *Understanding the sentencing of women*.
[8] P. King, 'Female offenders, work and life-cycle in late eighteenth-century London', *Continuity and Change* xi (1996), 61–90, and *Crime, justice and discretion*, 196–207, 235–7, 279–88; Arnot and Usborne, *Gender and crime*; C. Emsley, *Crime and society in England, 1750–1900*, 2nd edn, London–New York 1996; J. Kermode and G. Walker, *Women, crime and the courts in early modern England*, London 1994; Walker, *Crime, gender and social order*; L. Zedner, 'Women, crime and penal responses: a historical account', in M. Tonry (ed.), *Crime and Justice: a Review of Research* xiv (1991), 307–62, and *Women, crime and custody in Victorian England*, Oxford 1991; C. Conley, *The unwritten law: criminal justice in Victorian Kent*, Oxford 1991; U. Rublack, *The crimes of women in early modern Germany*, Oxford 1999. Relevant earlier works include J. M. Beattie, 'The criminality of women in eighteenth-century England', *JSH* viii (1975), 80–116 [repr. in D. Kelly Weisberg (ed.), *Women and the law: the social historical perspective*, Cambridge, Mass. 1982], and *Crime and the courts in England, 1660–1800*, Oxford–Princeton 1986; and C. Z. Wiener, 'Sex roles and crime in late-Elizabethan Hertfordshire', *JSH* viii (1975), 38–64.
[9] N. Landau (ed.), *Law, crime and English society, 1660–1830*, Cambridge 2003, 4–6.
[10] See, for instance, King, 'Female offenders'; Kermode and Walker, *Women, crime and the courts*; Walker, *Crime, gender and social order*; Zedner, 'Women, crime and penal responses', and *Women, crime and custody*; Conley, *Unwritten law*; Rublack, *Crimes of women*.
[11] L. Pike, *A history of crime in England*, London 1876; C. Lombroso and W. Ferrero, *The female offender*, New York 1895; O. Pollack, *The criminality of women*, New York 1961; J. J. Tobias, *Crime and industrial society in the nineteenth century*, London 1967. Similar views to those expressed in these works on female criminality can be found in much earlier writings: see Zedner, 'Women, crime and penal responses'.

Addressing the questions

The questions that will be addressed in this book are crucial ones about men and women's involvement in three selected crimes: shoplifting, pickpocketing and circulation of forged paper currency. All three of these crimes were felonies which attracted the death penalty. The questions are about the life-style, the social status and the occupations of those charged with these felonies, and how such factors may have motivated their actions. They are also questions about male and female means and techniques of participation in such criminal activities, and whether their methods differed from each other. If there were differences in the ways that men and women committed their illegal acts, might that, in itself, have resulted in differing judicial responses and decisions? Were juries and judges, as they came to decisions about men and women charged with identical offences, comparing identical or different behaviours?

The decisions which were made about these offenders will then be addressed, not only at the stage of the criminal trials, but at all the stages of the justice system, an endeavour so far barely attempted by historians. The result of a trial and the handing down of a sentence by the judge were only the first moves in the long journey that many men and women took through the criminal justice system. There were many opportunities in that system for them to escape to lesser sentences, even to freedom, and at all these points it is possible to ask how the gender of the offender affected what happened.

The three capital property crimes and the men and women caught up in them have been scrutinised in order to see whether this might provide answers to the questions outlined above. The study centres on the men and women from London and Middlesex who appeared before the court of the Old Bailey Sessions, charged with stealing privily in a shop (shoplifting), stealing privily from the person (pickpocketing) and circulating (uttering) forged Bank of England currency notes. These offences were selected for three reasons. They involved a significant proportion of women, and this allows a more balanced consideration of the questions posed.[12] They attracted the death sentence, which permits those convicted to be followed through the subsequent stages of the judicial system. Their capital status gave the offences added significance in the eyes of contemporaries. The enquiry is mainly confined to London and Middlesex. This region provides a rich setting since it is the only part of England where there are full trial reports to give the kind of qualitative evidence which is important in providing an

---

12 Women were involved in a wide range of property crimes, but their numbers in some of them were small. Horse, cow, and sheep stealing, burglary, housebreaking, and highway robbery, for instance, involved very low overall numbers of indicted females: King, *Crime, justice and discretion*, table 6.4 (for Essex) at p. 196, and 'Gender, crime and justice', table 2.1 (for Old Bailey and Home Circuit) at p. 45.

insight into the life-style and behaviour of the accused.[13] The enquiry is set between the 1780s and the 1830s, a time of significant change and development in the English system of criminal justice. Debates about punishment, in particular the death penalty, the possibility and purpose of transportation and the growing use of prison, were at their height and the judicial and penal system was under strain from vastly increasing criminal business.[14]

Following the men and women involved in these crimes through the various stages of the criminal justice system is a particularly important feature of the enquiry. The following description aptly captures the complexity of the system and provides a striking metaphor for the way in which the criminal justice system worked in England:

> Those accused of property crimes . . . found themselves propelled on an often bewildering journey along a route which can best be compared to a corridor of connected rooms or stage sets. From each room, one door led on towards eventual criminalization, conviction, and punishment, but every room also had other exits. Each had doors indicating legally acceptable ways in which the accused could get away from the arms of the law . . . Each room was also populated by a different and socially diverse group of men and women, whose assumptions, actions and interactions, both with each other, and with the accused determined whether or not he or she was shown to an exit or thrust on up the corridor.[15]

So, the three crimes, and the men and women involved, have been considered not only crime by crime, but also in stages, reflecting their journey through the justice system. The first question addressed is to what extent English law itself was structurally gendered. Then comes analysis of the evidence from the public trials at the Old Bailey, the verdicts and sentences of the court, together with evidence about how the crimes were committed and who the defendants were. Subsequently the less public arena of the

---

[13] See appendix below for details of the sources used, the specific dates for detailed analysis and the methodology for the research.

[14] Views on the debate about punishment can be found in Beattie, *Crime and the courts*, 520–615; S. Devereaux, 'In place of death: transportation, penal practice and the English state, 1770–1830', in C. Strange (ed.), *Qualities of mercy: justice, punishment and discretion*, Vancouver 1996, 52–76, and 'The criminal branch of the Home Office, 1782–1830', in G. Smith, A. May and S. Devereaux (eds), *Criminal justice in the old world and the new: essays in honour of J. M. Beattie*, Toronto 1998, 270–308; V. A. C. Gatrell, *The hanging tree: execution and the English people, 1770–1868*, Oxford 1994; M. Ignatieff, *A just measure of pain: the penitentiary in the industrial revolution, 1750–1850*, London 1978; and R. McGowen, 'The image of justice and reform of the criminal law in early nineteenth-century England', *Buffalo Law Review* xxxii (1983), 89–125, and 'A powerful sympathy: terror, the prison and humanitarian reform in early nineteenth-century Britain', *JBS* xxv (1986), 312–34. There is evidence of administrative overload in Home Office records: HO 17, petitions archive from 1819; HO 19, register of petitions; HO 26, criminal registers, 1791–1823.

[15] King, *Crime, justice and discretion*, 1–2.

appeals system and the pardoning process is examined to see if light can be shed on what happened there, and the role of gender in this part of the journey.

The approach of historians so far

It has been the accepted view that the entire English criminal justice system was driven by and operated through the exercise of discretion on the part of those who had power within it.[16] However, the role of gender in this discretionary process in the late eighteenth and early nineteenth centuries went unremarked until recently.

For as long as systematic records of crime have been kept, the sex of offenders has been recorded. Over time, certain trends and patterns in female criminality have been observed and commented upon by historians. Amongst long-term patterns are the accepted facts that women commit a minority of all recorded crimes; and that their crimes are categorised as less serious and less 'professional' than those of men.[17] It is usually said that, in the eighteenth century, women accounted for a relatively small proportion of (property) offences, and were less likely than men to be accused of capital crimes or of property crimes involving violence. This generalisation, based largely on research which counted and compared indictments without any qualitative approach, limits what can be known about context and other issues such as the occupation, age and status of defendants and their relationship to the victim of crime.[18] A picture of continuity seems to emerge, if overall criminal statistics over a long period provide the only view. The ratio of men to women indicted for felony/serious offences appears to remain relatively constant from the Middle Ages onwards,[19] with an increase in the

---

[16] Brewer and Styles, *Ungovernable people*, 18; D. Hay, 'Property, authority and the criminal law', in D. Hay, P. Linebaugh and E. P. Thompson, *Albion's fatal tree*, London 1975, 17–63; P. King, 'Decision-makers and decision-making in the English criminal law, 1750–1800', *HJ* xxvii (1984), 25–58; J. Langbein, 'Albion's fatal flaws', *P&P* xcviii (1983), 96–120.

[17] F. Heidensohn, 'Gender and crime', in M. Maguire, R. Morgan and R. Reiner (eds), *Oxford handbook of criminology*, Oxford 1994, 998.

[18] King, 'Female offenders', 61–2.

[19] See, for example, J. Bennett, *Women in the medieval countryside: gender and household in Brigstock before the Plague*, Oxford 1987; K. Garay, 'Women and crime in late-medieval England: an examination of the courts of gaol delivery, 1388–1409', *Florilegium* i–ii (1979/80), 87–103; J. Given, *Society and homicide in thirteenth-century England*, Stanford 1979; B. Hanawalt-Westman, 'The female felon in fourteenth-century England', *Viator – Medieval and Renaissance Studies* v (1974), 253–68, and *Crime and conflict in English communities, 1300–1348*, Cambridge, Mass. 1979; A. L. Klinck, 'Anglo-Saxon women and the law', *Journal of Medieval History* viii (1982), 107–21; S. Mercer, 'Crime in late-seventeenth-century Yorkshire: an exception to a national pattern?', *Northern History* xxvii (1991), 106–19; Beattie, 'Criminality of women'; and Wiener, 'Sex roles and crime'.

women's share occurring only in the later twentieth century.[20] Few historians seriously challenge this long-term view.[21] However, when criminal records can be consulted in much more detail, when different classes of crime are observed and the exploration covers the whole range of the criminal justice system, the 'universal truth' – that women commit much less crime than men and are more leniently treated when they do – looks questionable.

As late as 1996 it was possible to say that historians of crime in England in the eighteenth and early nineteenth centuries had given little attention to the role of gender, and had 'found it remarkably difficult to give their work a properly contextualised gender dimension'.[22] Through the 1980s and into the 1990s many text books on crime in the eighteenth and early nineteenth centuries contained no index reference to women or gender, other than to women as victims of crime, or with reference to infanticide or prostitution.[23] Some historians of crime now include considerations of women and of gender in their work, and by 1996 it was possible to say that

> It is not simply that historians and criminologists have begun to explore the role of women in criminal activity . . . and the experience of women enmeshed in the various elements of the criminal justice system, but, more importantly, there is a recognition that gender is central to economic, political and social relations, and as such it contributes to the ways in which communities, institutions and states formulate their regulations and their laws as well as to the ways in which these regulations and laws are interpreted and enforced.[24]

One historian of the English criminal justice system, John Beattie, has carried out groundbreaking work over the last few decades, which has led to growing

[20] A. Morris, *Women, crime and criminal justice*, Oxford 1987, 19–20; Heidensohn, *Women and crime*, 5, and 'Gender and crime', 1001.

[21] Exceptions to views of the constant nature of the global statistics for female involvement in crime until the twentieth century are M. Feeley and D. Little, 'The vanishing female: the decline of women in the criminal process, 1687–1912', *Law and Society Review* xxv (1991), 719–57, and M. Feeley, 'The decline of women in the criminal process: a comparative history, *CJH* xv (1994), 235–74. However, P. King, 'Gender and recorded crime: the long-term impact of female offenders on prosecution rates across England and Wales, 1750–1850', ch. vi in his *Crime and law in the age of reform*, forthcoming 2006, makes a persuasive argument against the views of Feeley and Little.

[22] King, 'Female offenders', 61.

[23] J. A. Sharpe, *Crime in early modern England, 1550–1750*, Harlow 1984, and *Judicial punishment in England*, London 1990; G. F. E. Rudé, *Criminal and victim: crime and society in early nineteenth-century England*, Oxford 1985; C. Emsley, *Crime and society in England, 1750–1900*, 1st edn, Harlow 1989; J. Briggs, C. Harrison, A. McInnes and D. Vincent (eds), *Crime and punishment in England: an introductory history*, London 1996 (a very few references); A. Barrett and C. Harrison, *Crime and punishment in England: a sourcebook*, London 1999.

[24] C. Emsley, 'Introduction', to Arnot and Usborne, *Gender and crime*, pp. vii–viii. Emsley added 'Mid-point assessment, I: Crime and gender', to the 2nd (1996) edn of *Crime and society*. See also idem, 'Albion's felonious attractions: reflections upon the history of crime in England', in C. Emsley and L. A. Knafla (eds), *Crime history and histories of crime: studies in the historiography of crime and criminal justice in modern history*, London 1996, 67–85.

interest in the study of crime and the criminal courts in the early modern period. With his quantitative reviews of crime in Surrey and Sussex between 1660 and 1800, he laid solid foundations for future historical work. Reflection on the effect of gender was not his main purpose, but, here and there in his work, the curtain was tentatively raised on the involvement of women as defendants in the criminal justice system. However, his scope was too broad to allow for the systematic qualitative work needed to show how gender operated in the prosecution and punishment of crime.[25] Some other historians of the early modern period have shown what can be achieved if qualitative approaches are pursued.[26] In particular, Garthine Walker, considering women's involvement in property offences, showed that men and women had different patterns of thieving activity – in the type of goods they stole and in their choice of partners in crime.[27]

Such a qualitative approach can unmask the role and presence of women. If the details in the stories of the encounters of men and women with the criminal justice system are systematically interrogated and analysed, striking differences in male and female behaviour can often be observed. This will emerge as the strongest theme in this book. The wide-ranging scale of difference of behaviour strongly suggests reasons for differences in judicial decisions. The dynamics of female criminality offer a far more complex and instructive view of gendered experience than historians of crime have hitherto acknowledged.

It is possible to draw conclusions from careful analysis, both quantitative and qualitative, of information in the pardoning archive, considering the effect of gendered strategies in appeals for mercy and pardon, as well as the effect of age, family background, poverty and other factors put forward by those appealing.[28] More recent study of female offenders, their work and life-cycle change, has shown the importance of a contextualised and qualitative account of those offenders, and has linked the discussion about women's crime with the debate on women's work. This has highlighted the complex relationship between female offenders, work and life-cycle change as central

---

[25] In later work Beattie has not significantly pursued the issue of gender; there is limited mention of women or gender in, for instance, *Crime and the courts*, and 'Scales of justice: defense counsel and the English criminal trial in the eighteenth and nineteenth centuries', *LHR* ix/2 (1991), 221–67; nor is there in 'London crime and the making of the "bloody code", 1689–1718', in L. Davison, T. Hitchcock, L. Keirn and R. Shoemaker (eds), *Stilling the grumbling hive: the response to social and economic problems in England, 1689–1750*, Stroud–New York 1992, 49–75; and only slight consideration in 'Crime and inequality in eighteenth-century London', in J. Hagan and R. D. Peterson (eds), *Crime and inequality*, Stanford 1995, 116–39.

[26] Kermode and Walker, *Women, crime and the courts*; Walker, *Crime, gender and social order*; Rublack, *Crimes of women*.

[27] G. Walker, 'Women, theft and the world of stolen goods', in Kermode and Walker, *Women, crime and the courts*, 81–105, and *Crime, gender and social order*, 159–97.

[28] King, 'Decision-makers'. It has been possible to extend the 'factors mentioned' approach first used by King to include gender issues: see chapter 7 below.

to any attempt to explain patterns of female crime.[29] The conclusions in this book will allow modification and refocusing of Peter King's crucial findings.[30] This comes about through a more precise use of the crime categories to show differences between men and women on trial for ostensibly the same offences, through the use of a wider range of sources from the whole of the judicial process and through a continuation of the search for the operation of gendered decisions within and after the pardoning process.

Apart from the work of Beattie, King and Walker, qualitative historical research on crime and the criminal justice system, and the place of gender as an explanatory force in the late eighteenth and early nineteenth centuries, has been thin, often tangential and unfocused. However, on more specific issues, historians are continuing to add depth to the picture which emerges about gender, crime and the criminal justice system.[31] For later in the nineteenth century, there have been contributions to the crime and gender discussion, although none has engaged sufficiently with the crucial questions about the extent to which gender affected trial outcomes, and why.[32]

Links with broader debates on gender history

The behaviour of men and women who committed crimes and their encounter with the system that sought to judge and punish them are located in the wider context of debates on gender history, women's history, the construction of masculinity, femininity and sexuality, and discourses on issues such as 'public and private', 'separate spheres', 'golden ages' and 'continuity and change'. However, care needs to be taken to ensure that the links with wider debates do not mask the experiences and materiality of the lives of women who were involved in crime and tried by the justice system. They have been hidden for so long that the recovery of their important experience requires a strongly focused effort. There is a prime need for 'retaining a focus on the collective and individual experiences of flesh-and-blood women',[33] at

---

29 Idem, 'Female offenders', and 'Gender, crime and justice'.
30 Idem, 'Decision-makers'.
31 Among these is work by Australian historians on the backgrounds of those transported to New South Wales at the end of the eighteenth and during the first half of the nineteenth century which is achieving a more balanced view of the convicts sent to New South Wales than the previously stereotyped male and female pictures of the mid-1960s. Other qualitative work relates to the death penalty, to the lives of those who were hanged in London, and to the place of gender in the summary and quarter sessions courts, and in vagrancy, prostitution and violence.
32 Zedner, 'Women, crime and penal responses' poses, but does not engage with, the question of how far attitudes to women affected judgements at their trials. The case is similar in her *Women, crime and custody*, on women's treatment in prison. Conley, *Unwritten law*, focuses on typically 'female' activities, in summary courts.
33 L. M. Newman, 'Critical theory and the history of women: what's at stake in deconstructing women's history', *JWH* Winter (1991), 58–68.

the same time as being aware of how the concept of 'gender' works to construct the changing meanings associated with terms such as 'male', 'female', 'masculine', 'feminine', 'womanly', 'manly' and so on, which appear in the judicial sources, in order to articulate the inter-relationship between 'experience' and 'meaning'.[34]

There is now a plethora of work from historians who see the eighteenth and early nineteenth centuries as times of significant change in attitudes to gender and sexuality. Each defines the period they write about as 'revolutionary' or 'seminal', but bows to a 'continuity' argument, leaving many unanswered questions.[35] The eighteenth century may indeed have witnessed a sexual revolution which transformed attitudes, resulting in the creation of a phallocentric, increasingly heterosexual, culture.[36] On the other hand, as others argue, it was a time of increasing male participation in 'polite society'; yet others suggest that it was a time of increase in male aggression.[37] The question also arises as to whether definitions of 'public' and 'private' really changed, with women increasingly confined to the private and domestic; or were the critical changes not so much a confinement of women to a private sphere, as the growth of the public sphere to which men had nearly exclusive access? Perhaps, to the contrary, women were enjoying the benefits of a changed share in the nation's work and wealth – something that touches on the tendency to break the law.[38]

[34] A good synthesis and summary of the development of feminist, Marxist and psychoanalytical approaches to gender history is to be found in K. Honeyman, *Women, gender and industrialisation in England, 1700–1870*, Basingstoke–London 2000. A less detached view is expressed in most of the essays of J. W. Scott, *Gender and the politics of history*, rev. edn, New York 1999, and in L. Davidoff, *Worlds between: historical perspectives on gender and class*, Cambridge 1995, especially 'Regarding some "old husbands' tales": public and private in feminist history' at pp. 227–76, and in M. Maynard, 'Beyond the "big three": the development of feminist theory into the 1990s', *WHR* iv/3 (1995), 259–81, in particular her comments on 'The importance of a historical dimension' at p. 267.

[35] It is therefore useful to have a synopsis over a longer historical period, as in S. Kingsley-Kent, *Gender and power in Britain, 1640–1990*, London 1999.

[36] T. Hitchcock, *English sexualities, 1700–1800*, Basingstoke 1997; T. Hitchcock and M. Cohen (eds), *English masculinities, 1600–1800*, London–New York 1999, 1–21.

[37] Hitchcock and Cohen, *English masculinities*; G. J. Barker-Benfield, *The culture of sensibility: sex and society in eighteenth-century Britain*, Chicago 1992; H. Barker and E. Chalus (eds), *Gender in eighteenth-century England: roles, representations and responsibilities*, Harlow 1997; P. Carter, *Men and the emergence of polite society, Britain, 1660–1800*, Harlow 2001.

[38] K. von den Steinen, 'The discovery of women in eighteenth-century English political life', in B. Kanner (ed.), *The women of England from Anglo-Saxon times to the present*, London 1980, 231–58; L. Davidoff and C. Hall, *Family fortunes: men and women of the English middle class, 1780–1850*, London 1987; V. Jones (ed.), *Women in the eighteenth century: constructions of femininity*, London–New York 1990; S. Walby, 'Women's employment and the historical periodisation of patriarchy', in H. Corr and L. Jamieson (eds), *Politics of everyday life: continuities and change in work and the family*, London 1990, 141–61; B. Hill, *Women, work, and sexual politics in eighteenth-century England*, London 1989; L. Klein, 'Gender, conversation and the public sphere in early eighteenth-century England', in J. Still and M. Worton (eds), *Textuality and sexuality: reading theories and practices*, Manchester 1993,

Discourse presents various scenarios of change. However, engagement with the lives of men and women of the 'labouring class', 'the poor', those who were the majority embroiled with the criminal justice system, shows gender structures which changed little or which may even have resisted change. Notions of sexual polarisation, said to represent changed attitudes, were mainly expounded in medical, and prescriptive and didactic writings and were not a description of actual social relations. Such polarised notions may have taken hold, or strengthened, amongst the aristocracy and the 'middling sort', especially as the latter sought to 'better' themselves. However, much that was said and written could have been 'a shrill response to an expansion in the opportunities and ambitions of Georgian and Victorian women – a cry from an embattled *status quo*, rather than the leading edge of change'.[39] Amongst the poor, persistence of unchanged social relationships between men and women is likely to have been more significant than change.[40] Few historians have penetrated the lives of the truly poor. Ignorance of the way in which the poor might have been affected by the perceptions of domesticity apparently held by the 'middling sort' remains almost total. Discussion of the 'appropriate' spheres of activity for poor and labouring men and women has hardly begun.[41] The language of 'domesticity' may have sounded more loudly during the eighteenth century, and a notional division between public and private may have had considerable hold on eighteenth-century imaginations, but, as Amanda Vickery points out, 'even the most cursory sweep of Georgian usages reveals that the public/private

100–15, and 'Gender and the public/private distinction in the eighteenth-century: some questions about evidence and analytic procedure', ECS xxix (1995), 97–109; J. Brewer, 'This, that and the other: public, social and private in the seventeenth and eighteenth centuries', in D. Castiglione and L. Sharpe (eds), *Shifting the boundaries: transformations of the language of public and private in the eighteenth century*, Exeter 1995, 1–21; A. Fletcher, *Gender, sex and subordination in England, 1500–1800*, London 1995; R. Shoemaker, *Gender in English society, 1650–1850: the emergence of separate spheres?*, London 1998; P. Sharpe (ed.), *Women's work: the English experience, 1650–1914*, London 1998; J. Rendall, 'Women and the public sphere', G&H xi (1999), 475–88; E. Chalus, 'Elite women, social politics and the political world of late eighteenth-century England', HJ xliii (2000), 669–97.

39 A. Vickery, *The gentleman's daughter: women's lives in Georgian England*, New Haven, Conn.–London 1998, 7.

40 Vickery's much quoted article, 'Golden age to separate spheres? A review of the categories and chronology of English women's history', HJ xxxvi (1993), 383–414, provides a useful overview. Although she is preoccupied with women of the middling and genteel sort, the introduction to her *Gentleman's daughter* takes sides effectively in the debate.

41 See T. Hitchcock, *Down and out in eighteenth-century London*, London 2004, esp. pp. 238–40, for perceptive comment on the 'refocussing away from the experience of the poor and onto the words of the middling sort'. See also T. Hitchcock, P. King and P. Sharpe (eds), *Chronicling poverty: the voices and strategies of the English poor, 1640–1840*, London 1997, and A. Clark, *The struggle for the breeches: gender and the making of the British working class*, Berkeley 1995, in which her focus is 'the working class', with a culture different from the poor, often out-of-work, people who were the majority of those who found themselves in court in London between 1780 and 1830.

dichotomy had multiple applications, which only sometimes mirrored a male/female distinction, and then not always perfectly'.[42]

The lives of the men and women who found themselves embroiled with the criminal justice system of the country demonstrate continuity in life-style, occupation, status and attitude more than change at this period. However, shifting notions of appropriate male and female behaviour would have significantly affected the views of the decision-makers – men of authority, elite and middling, who operated the criminal justice system – officials, magistrates, juries, judges, parliamentarians and government servants, thus impacting on the lives of some of the poorer folk.

It is also important to include in the equation the differences of life in London from life elsewhere in the nation. The capital was not affected in the same way as other areas of the country by industrialisation. The work of men and women, particularly of women, was marked by a solid continuity. Women remained locked into the marginal, seasonal, part-time, poorly remunerated areas of service, commerce and small manufacturing enterprise.[43] On the other hand, whilst the material circumstances of the poor may have changed little, changes in London from the late seventeenth century significantly affected their lives. Between 1700 and 1820, London's population increased from about 675,000 to around 1,300,000 and the area it covered grew to about twelve square miles. The industrial districts grew to the east and south of the City, while to the west, around Westminster, there flourished more elegant and wealthy districts. London was an important European capital, a 'colossus' in comparison with other English towns.[44]

This rapidly growing commercial city was home, on the one hand, to polite culture and the increasingly comfortable material lives of propertied individuals, with their various networks of authority over the materially less well-off. On the other hand, London was home to multitudes of the poor; it provided extensive employment opportunities for domestic servants, a degree of anonymity for those with something to hide and care for many with illegitimate children. There were endless temptations, and opportunities for crime – in crowded streets, in shops full to overflowing to meet the rapidly increasing consumer desires of men and women of property, and at leisure activities and entertainment where wealth was on display.[45] Women in the

---

[42] Vickery, Gentleman's daughter, 288–93.

[43] P. Earle, 'The female labour market in London in the late-seventeenth and early-eighteenth centuries', EcHR 2nd ser. xlii (1989), 328–53; cf. S. Alexander, 'Women's work in nineteenth-century London: a study of the years 1820–1850', in J. Mitchell and A. Oakley (eds), The rights and wrongs of women, London 1976, 59–111, which provides a view of continuity in women's work and lives, and M. Ginsberg, 'The tailoring and dressmaking trades, 1700–1850', Costume vi (1972), 64–71.

[44] There are useful brief descriptions of the growth of London in R. Porter, English society in the eighteenth century, London 1982, 60–1, and P. J. Corfield, The impact of English towns, 1700–1800, Oxford 1982, 8–9, 66–81.

[45] L. Weatherill, 'Consumer behaviour and social status in England, 1660–1750', Conti-

metropolis formed a higher proportion of those accused of criminal activities than their rural counterparts, perhaps because of their often wretched and irregular work opportunities, as well as their greater personal freedom.[46] Women without strong support networks would frequently opt for earning their livings illegally, as part of London's extensive receiving networks, or in the prostitution trade.[47]

Behind the various debates which have gender at their core, there are the patriarchal assumptions operating in the criminal justice system. Such assumptions were (and are) changing, shifting, but pervasive.[48] The law was constructed, interpreted and administered by men for a society ruled by men, and embodied these assumptions. Women's access to the courts as prosecutors was highly constrained. Their appearance as defendants in most crimes and misdemeanours remained significantly less than men's. There have been many generalised suggestions as to why this should have been so. Women may have preferred to prosecute using less formal methods, such as in the courts of summary jurisdiction. There may have been a reluctance to prosecute women because they were seen as less legally responsible for their actions. Men may also have had more difficulty in perceiving female criminality in a system where activities defined as criminal related to a male view of acceptable behaviour, both male and female.[49] The law itself adopted a highly gendered approach to all the matters it addressed, as will be discussed in chapter 2. Although it may be impossible to answer the question as to how the law was capable of dealing equitably with women, nevertheless the male-created system placed issues of gender at the centre of decision-making. Therefore, at each stage of the justice system, there are crucial questions to be asked as to how decisions were made about guilt or punishment for individual

nuity and Change i/2 (1986), 191–216; P. Langford, *A polite and commercial people, England, 1727–1783*, Oxford 1989; D. Kent, 'Ubiquitous but invisible: female domestic servants in mid eighteenth-century London', *HWJ* xxv (1989), 111–27; C. Walsh, 'Shop design and the display of goods in eighteenth-century London', *Journal of Design History* viii (1995), 157–76; T. Hitchcock and H. Shore (eds), *The streets of London from the Great Fire to the Great Stink*, London 2003; Hitchcock, *Down and out*.

46 King, *Crime, justice and discretion*, 198–9. In the early 1790s women were about a quarter of the offenders tried at the Old Bailey, compared with an average of 11.3% in the five Home Circuit counties, a differential too large to be accounted for by women forming a higher proportion of the London population.

47 Beattie, 'Criminality of women', *Crime and the courts*, 239–40, and 'Crime and inequality'; King, 'Female offenders', 67; T. Henderson, *Disorderly women in eighteenth-century London: prostitution and control in the metropolis, 1730–1830*, London 1999.

48 Walby, 'Women's employment'; J. Bennett, ' "History that stands still": women's work in the European past', *Feminist Studies* xiv (1988), 269–83, and 'Women's history: a study in continuity and change', *WHR* ii (1993), 173–84; cf. B. Hill, 'Women's history: a study in change, continuity or standing still?', *WHR* ii (1993), 5–22.

49 For a synopsis of the gendered nature of law and crime see Shoemaker, *Gender in English society*, 291–304; Beattie, 'Criminality of women', passim; Zedner, *Women, crime and custody*, 27; and M. Hunt, 'Wife-beating, domesticity and women's independence in eighteenth-century London', *G&H* iv (1992), 22.

women and men, and how far the decisions were surprising and contradictory, working in favour, rather than against many women.

Criminal justice in social and legal environment

It is beyond the scope of this book to deal in any detail with the changes and continuities of the period which had a significant impact on the commission of crime, and on attitudes to crime and to offenders. The effects of war and subsequent periods of peace between 1780 and 1830, together with fluctuations in the prices of basic foodstuffs, and the availability of employment – in particular for men returning from military service, with London as a focal point – made their mark in increasing property crime figures. It is reasonable to suppose that an increasing proportion of poor people turned to theft when times were hard. However, the proportion of theft victims prepared to prosecute exerted more influence on indictment levels as anxieties increased amongst those with property and goods to protect. Periods of war, in general, led to a reduction in indictments, whilst the establishment of peace increased them. Post-war increases in crime were often anticipated before they happened, in the form of a 'moral panic', often provoked by newspapers. The relationship between poverty and crime cannot be ignored when considering the effect of gender on legal decisions.[50]

The system of administration of justice was, at the same time, the subject of fervent debate, change and upheaval – all of which could be expected to influence and inform the decisions of prosecutors, juries, judges and government servants as they dealt with the men and women accused and convicted of crime. The merits and effectiveness of the 'bloody code' were coming under debate, both as part of a humane reforming agenda and, on a more bureaucratic level, as an attempt to retain the effectiveness of capital punishment at a time when it was being less and less carried into effect.[51] Concern

---

[50] D. Hay, 'War, dearth and theft in the eighteenth century: the record of the English courts', *P&P* xcv (1982), 117–60; King, *Crime, justice and discretion*, 145–68.

[51] S. Romilly, 'Observations on the criminal law of England as it relates to capital punishments and on the mode in which it is administered', *Law Tracts, 1801–2*, London 1810; Gatrell, *Hanging tree*; B. Hilton, 'The gallows and Mr Peel', in T. C. W. Blanning and D. Cannadine (eds), *History and biography: essays in honour of Derek Beales*, Cambridge 1996, 88–112; P. Jenkins, 'From gallows to prison? The execution rate in early modern England', *CJH* vii (1986), 51–71; McGowen, 'The image of justice'; 'A powerful sympathy'; 'The body and punishment in eighteenth-century England', *Journal of Modern History* lix (1987), 651–79; 'The changing face of God's justice: the debates over divine and human punishment in eighteenth-century England', *CJH* ix (1988), 63–98; 'Punishing violence, sentencing crime', in N. Armstrong and L. Tennenhouse (eds), *The violence of representation: literature and the history of violence*, London 1989, 140–56; 'Making the "bloody code"? Forgery legislation in eighteenth-century England', in Landau, *Law, crime and society*; and 'The problem of punishment in eighteenth-century England', in S. Devereaux and P. Griffiths, *Penal practice and culture, 1500–1900: punishing the English*, Basingstoke 2004,

about the English system of justice tended to express itself in some circles as an attack on the gallows, rather than on other punishments. Even so, the range of secondary sentences was under scrutiny – again for both reformist and pragmatic reasons. The judiciary, in 1780, had recourse to a wide range of punishments for serious offences, particularly hanging, transportation, incarceration, whipping, branding, forced hard labour, despatch to the armed services and fines. Juries often returned partial verdicts which avoided the death penalty. Judges were able to select certain capital convicts and certain types of offence for more lenient treatment, and, for Old Bailey convicts, the Home Secretary, through the King-in-Council, had discretion over the outcome and some choice over the substitute penalty. By the end of the period, repeal of the capital statutes was under way; transportation was approaching its demise; women convicted of murder or coining were no longer burned at the stake; they were no longer flogged, and men were less likely to be flogged or sent to the armed services. Imprisonment became the state's main punitive weapon.[52] To all these changes can be added the developments in the Home Office as it responded to the overloading of the administration of criminal justice. This in turn changed the nature of the pardoning and appeals system by the 1820s.[53] The process of policing was changing in some places from a reactive to a more preventative mode,[54] and court proce-

210–31; H. Potter, *Hanging in judgement: religion and the death penalty in England from the bloody code to abolition*, London 1993.

52 Emsley, *Crime and society*, and 'Repression,"terror" and the rule of law in England during the decade of the French Revolution', *EHR* xiii (1985), 801–26; V. A. C. Gatrell, B. Lenman and G. Parker (eds), *Crime and the law: the social history of crime in western Europe since 1500*, London 1980; V. A. C. Gatrell, 'Crime, authority and the policeman state', in F. Thompson (ed.), *Cambridge social history of Britain, 1750–1950*, III: *Social agencies and institutions*, Cambridge 1990, 243–310; L. Radzinowicz, *A history of English criminal law and its administration from 1750*, II: *The clash between private initiative and public interest in the enforcement of the law*, London 1956; Rudé, *Criminal and victim*; King, *Crime, justice and discretion*; R. Campbell, 'Sentence of death by burning for women', *JLH* v (1984), 44–59; A. D. Harvey, 'Research note: Burning women at the stake in eighteenth-century England', *CJH* xi (1990), 193–5; Devereaux, 'In place of death', and 'The making of the Penitentiary Act, 1775–79', *HJ* xlii (1999), 405–33; S. Nicholas (ed.), *Convict workers: reinterpreting Australia's past*, Cambridge 1988; W. Oldham, *Britain's convicts to the colonies*, Sydney 1990; Ignatieff, *A just measure of pain*, and 'State, civil society and total institution: a critique of recent social histories of punishment', in D. Sugarman (ed.), *Legality, ideology and the state*, London 1983, 183–209.

53 Devereaux, 'Criminal branch'.

54 J. Styles, 'The emergence of the police: explaining police reform in eighteenth- and nineteenth-century England', *BJC* xxvii (1987), 15–22; D. Hay and F. Snyder (eds), *Policing and prosecution in Britain, 1750–1850*, Oxford 1989; R. Paley, ' "An imperfect, inadequate and wretched system"? Policing London before Peel', *CJH* x (1989), 95–130; D. Taylor, *The new police in nineteenth-century England*, Manchester 1997; E. A. Reynolds, *Before the bobbies: the night watch and police reform in metropolitan London, 1720–1830*, Stanford, CA 1998; J. Beattie, *Policing and punishment in London, 1660–1750: urban crime and the limits of terror*, Oxford 2001; A. T. Harris, 'Policing and public order in the City of London, 1784–1815', *London Journal* xxviii/2 (2003), 1–20.

dure was accommodating and responding to increased use of defence counsel.[55]

The day-to-day administration of criminal justice in London and Middlesex was similar to that in the rest of the country, although in certain respects it differed from it. Pre-trial procedures were identical to those in most other parts of the country. There was the same 'layer upon layer of negotiation opportunities and discretionary choices'[56] as victims of crime decided whether or not to bear the costs and trouble of pursuing a case, taking the alleged perpetrator before a magistrate or justice of the peace in the summary stage of proceedings.[57] If he decided to do so, the magistrate would hear the facts of the matter, take depositions in writing from the victim and his witnesses, examine the accused and decide whether to let them go, or grant bail or commit them to jail, either for three days for further examination, or for a longer period to await trial in a higher court.[58] In the City of London, the Lord Mayor and aldermen sat as magistrates at the Mansion House and the Guildhall; and in Middlesex, from the 1750s, public police offices, where there were frequent sittings of magistrates, developed, notably the busy office at Bow Street, and others, for instance at Queen Street and Marlborough Street.

The higher court of referral could be the quarter sessions courts, held four times a year at locations throughout the country. The range of cases heard by these courts changed considerably up to and during this period, and there was no national homogeneity. In general, they heard most of the lesser crimes (misdemeanours) and many serious, though usually non-capital, crimes. The more serious crimes, including the types upon which this book focuses, were tried at the assize courts. Outside London these were held in each county town (or other main town) twice a year only (in Surrey four times a year), and were presided over by peripatetic circuit judges drawn from the central courts at Westminster. However, in London, the assize level of court was the Old Bailey Sessions, which met eight times a year, and was presided over by more locally-based judges. The Old Bailey court dealt with crimes committed

55 Beattie, 'Scales of justice', and 'Garrow for the defence', History Today (Feb. 1991), 49–53; D. Bentley, English criminal justice in the nineteenth century, London 1998; D. Hay, 'The criminal prosecution in England and its historians', Modern Law Review xlvii (1984), 1–29; J. Langbein, 'Shaping the eighteenth-century criminal trial: a view from the Ryder sources', University of Chicago Law Review l/1 (1983), 1–136, and The origins of adversary criminal trial, Oxford 2003; S. Landsman, 'The rise of the contentious spirit: adversary procedure in eighteenth-century England', Cornell Law Review lxxv (1990), 497–609; A. N. May, The Bar and the Old Bailey, 1750–1850, Chapel Hill, NC 2003.
56 King, Crime, justice and discretion, 125.
57 From 1792 in metropolitan London, these could be stipendiary magistrates. For the effect of these new arrangements see N. Landau, 'The trading justice's trade', in her Law, crime and English society, 46–70.
58 There were matters that were dealt with in the courts of summary jurisdiction and not referred elsewhere; over the period of this study, such cases increased: Emsley, Crime and society (1st edn), 142.

in the City of London and in the county of Middlesex, with separate juries appointed for each location. At all assizes, indictments against prisoners were first scrutinised by a grand jury, which decided if there was a case to answer, and, if a 'true bill' was found, the accused would appear for trial before judge and petty jury.[59]

Differences in London were significant beyond the trials in court. When appeals against sentences were being considered, it was usual for the Home Secretary to call for reports from the assize judges who had sat in judgement in various towns all over the country. Their reports provided a useful source of information about defendants. However, written reports were rarely called for from the London and Middlesex judiciary. The proximity of the Old Bailey to the seats of royal and bureaucratic decision-making meant that reports were likely to be given orally at the 'Recorder's Report', a private meeting of monarch, senior cabinet members, the judicial bench and the chief sentencing officer – the Recorder. Verbatim court reports were also consulted.[60]

The variety of decision-makers

As men and women passed through the many 'rooms and winding corridors' of the criminal justice system, they encountered a variety of 'doorkeepers' or decision-makers, who allowed some of the offenders the chance of escape, or of a lighter punishment. It is useful to define who these 'doorkeepers' were who exerted choice and influence at critical points. The criminal justice system at this time can be described as essentially a 'personal' system. The initial accusation and complaint was made to the magistrates by the individual who was the victim of the offence. If a decision was made to pursue the wrong-doing through the justice system, the victim then became the person who prosecuted in the higher court of law (rather than an official prosecutor, 'The Crown', of later days).[61] That individual had many official supporters.[62] In property crime cases support came from constables and justices of the peace, and, in the City of London, from peace officers and men of the watch. Each had a part to play in deciding how far the alleged offender would

[59] Langbein, 'Shaping the eighteenth-century criminal trial'; Beattie, *Crime and the courts*, 268–377; King, *Crime, justice and discretion*, 222–31; Emsley, *Crime and society* (1st edn), 138–60. For the operation of grand juries in London and Middlesex see May, *The Bar and the Old Bailey*, 17.

[60] S. Devereaux, 'The City and the sessions papers: "public justice" in London, 1770–1800', *JBS* xxxv (1996), 466–503, and 'Peel, pardon and punishment: the Recorder's report revisited', in Devereaux and Griffiths, *Penal practice and culture*, 258–84.

[61] However, for the development of notions of public and private, civil and criminal, state and personal in English law see, for example, D. Lieberman, 'Mapping criminal law: Blackstone and the categories of English jurisprudence', in Landau, *Law, crime and society*, 139–61.

[62] Langbein, 'Shaping the eighteenth-century criminal trial'.

journey through the system. The major escape of offenders from the justice system was permitted by the failure of victims to press charges. There were many reasons for this. A victim may have thought a theft was trivial, may have felt compassion for the offender, or may have wished to avoid the time, trouble and expense involved in going to court. It was not unknown for rough justice to be meted out on the spot and the matter to be concluded then and there. Many a shopkeeper preferred to avoid prosecuting as this might be seen as bad for trade. Many a victim of a pickpocket would rather have kept quiet about the circumstances of a theft. If an indictment could lead to a capital sentence, a victim might be reluctant to set off down this path. Police and peace officers at different times had different motives for seeking to apprehend offenders and to bring them before the magistrates. Magistrates, with their own sentiments about crime in the metropolis, had to make a further sift, and decide whether there was *prima facie* evidence of an indictable offence which could properly be passed to the higher court. In times of war, an escape route for significant numbers of young males, particularly those accused of indictable property offences, would be provided by immediate enlistment in the armed forces.[63]

If offenders passed through these first sets of 'rooms' and found themselves at the Old Bailey, first the grand jury could open and close doors to the accused.[64] Then, at the trial stage, many escape doors were opened. The victim, who had had further time to think about the situation, frequently failed to turn up in court to prosecute, despite the possibility of losing money put up as a recognisance to see the case through. In these circumstances the trial could not proceed and the prisoner would be acquitted of the offence. If all the required actors were in place, the petty jury had to listen to the evidence, and make the crucial decision of guilt or innocence, or decide to find the prisoner only partially guilty of the charge and subject to a lesser category of punishment. The judge frequently guided the jury and on occasions interjected to assist the prisoner make his or her case. Some prisoners were aided by lawyers, who could also change the course of events. After the judge had pronounced sentence on the prisoner, the victim and the jury could ask for mercy to be shown, and, at the end of the sessions, the judge could remit or change the sentences of as many convicts as he saw fit.

Beyond this public stage of the process, the decision-maker for London and Middlesex convicts was technically the King-in-Council, where the royal prerogative of mercy could be exercised. The Home Secretary and his Home Office servants took the lead in this stage of the decision-making,

---

63 P. Griffiths, 'Introduction', to Devereaux and Griffiths, *Penal practice*, 5–31; P. King, 'War as a judicial resource: press gangs and prosecution rates, 1740–1830', in Landau, *Law, crime and society*, 97–116. For a useful and detailed description of pre-trial processes see King, *Crime, justice and, discretion*, 17–81.

64 See Beattie, *Crime and the courts*, 318–31, for a description of the composition and task of grand juries.

handling the papers of all capital convicts, and all appeals from convicts sentenced to other punishments, sometimes consulting the Old Bailey judges and the City of London Recorder, following up factors raised in convicts' appeals.[65] They were also responsible for a growing number of bureaucratic decisions about the release of prisoners from overcrowded incarceration facilities. Even beyond this point, decisions could be made which could make life more bearable for some offenders after sentence.[66]

The journey

The men and women of London and Middlesex, charged with shoplifting, pickpocketing and forged Bank note crimes undertook a long journey through the rooms and corridors of the criminal justice system. This book aims to follow them all the way. However, before beginning the examination of their journeys, chapter 2 will consider the law itself, asking whether men and women started out as equals in its eyes, expecting equality of judicial treatment. The next three chapters focus on their public trials at the Old Bailey and examine the stories told in court, the verdicts and the sentences in order to see whether differences emerge between men and women committing ostensibly the same crime and, if so, to what extent this affected the decisions taken about their future.

Chapter 6 looks beyond the public trials, verdicts and initial sentences, and considers whether the justice system, in its later stages, became more or less gendered. As far as possible the men and women tried for the three selected crimes are followed, to find out what happened in the end; then to ask whether leniency was exercised in a gendered way and, if so, reasons for it. In chapter 7 the examination is extended to see how the men and women sentenced for serious crime used the appeals and pardoning procedure, or sought other ways to obtain mercy, or to make their lives more tolerable.

The core question at all stages is: what part did gender play, in the crime itself and in the decisions which were made about justice? Through systematic scrutiny of the men and women involved in the three selected groups of illegal activity and their journeys through the justice system to their final outcome, it is possible to see how decisions could be affected not only by the over-riding paternalistic assumptions of those in powerful positions, but most strongly by the diversity of male and female behaviour. In chapter 8 the conclusion is that the effects of gender in judicial decisions, particularly towards the end of the journey through the system, have to be seen against a wider background – with male and female convicts held hostage to the needs

---

65 Devereaux, 'Criminal branch', 'City and the sessions papers', and 'Peel, pardon and punishment'.
66 The Bank of England's 'compassionate' relationship with those convicted of forged Bank note offences who were awaiting transportation is described in chapter 5 below.

of the state and being the objects of more complex reasoning. The crimes and the offenders have to be seen through three important filters: of different gendered behaviours, of the patriarchal construction of the system of criminal justice and of the entirely pragmatic needs of the state to adjust sentencing and punishment. Each filter provides a view of a highly gendered process.

2

Gender and the Laws of England

So great a favourite is the female sex of the laws of England.[1]

As an essential first step to understanding the place of gender in crime and the justice system, and before seeking to discover whether the men and women who came to their criminal trials in London were treated differently 'on account of their sex', it is important to consider the nature of English law itself. 'Law makes claims to neutrality, to objectivity, and to universality. Law speaks for us all', but 'what if discretion, prejudice, opinion and sentiment are an inevitable part?'[2] Was the sex of the offender a matter for discretion, prejudice, opinion and sentiment? Or was there fairness and equality between men and women, was the law 'gender-blind' in its neutrality, objectivity and universality?

The three crimes under the spotlight – shoplifting, pickpocketing and circulating forged Bank of England notes – were selected for study because they were not, on the face of it, 'gendered' crimes. Many crimes and misdemeanours were specifically gendered – for instance, infanticide, witchcraft and prostitution, where women were vastly more numerous as defendants; or crimes like rape, murder, burglary, robbery, horse- and cattle-stealing which involved very few women. The selection of 'non-gendered' crimes is an attempt to avoid an obvious gender bias. If there were a level playing field at the start of the journey through the judicial process, these three crimes might reflect some kind of gender equality. An examination of the law of England should help to determine whether equality existed at the very start of the process.

Non-existent wives and coerced women

From at least the twelfth to the early twentieth century, English lawyers sought to explain and justify the disabilities and subordination of women, particularly of married women, which were visible all around them. The eighteenth-century legal commentator, William Blackstone, discussing the theory of 'marital unity', wrote that 'we may observe, that even the disabili-

1 W. Blackstone, *Commentaries on the laws of England in four books*, i, 5th edn, London 1773, 445.
2 Edwards, *Sex and gender*, 1–2.

ties, which the wife lies under, are for the most part intended for her protection and benefit. So great a favourite is the female sex of the laws of
England'.[3] Edward Christian, who edited and annotated Blackstone's
Commentaries between 1800 and 1830, disagreed. In 1830 he inserted a
printed exclamation mark in the margin of the work at this point, noting that

> Nothing, I apprehend, would more conciliate the good will of the student in
> favour of the laws of England, than the persuasion that they had shown a par-
> tiality to the female sex. But I am not so much in love with my subject as to be
> inclined to leave it in possession of a glory which it may not justly deserve . . .
> and I shall leave it to the reader to determine on which side is the balance, and
> how far this compliment is supported by truth.[4]

Christian set out several disabilities of a married woman,[5] and concluded:
'From this impartial statement of the account, I fear there is little reason to
pay a compliment to our laws for their respect and favour to the female sex.'[6]
 The following much-quoted passage from Blackstone has often been used
uncritically:

> By marriage, the husband and wife are one person in law: that is, the very
> being or legal existence of the woman is suspended during the marriage, or at
> least is incorporated and consolidated into that of the husband; under whose
> wing, protection and cover, she performs everything; and is therefore called in
> our law-french a *feme-covert, faemina viro co-operta*; is said to be *covert-baron*,
> or under the protection and influence of her husband, her *baron*, or lord; and
> her condition during her marriage is called her *coverture*.[7]

The common law practice of *coverture* or the concept of marital unity, which
Blackstone describes, does not directly explain gender discrimination in cases
brought under the criminal law, such as the crimes dealt with in this book.
The description, with its powerful thinking about women and their rights
and duties, legitimated and justified a system of male-dominated economic
and social control, deeply embedded in the English way of life, a system
which can properly be described as patriarchal.[8] This system, in practice,

3   Blackstone, *Commentaries*, i (5th edn), 445.
4   E. Christian (ed.), *William Blackstone's commentaries on the laws of England*, i 17th edn,
London 1830, 444 n. 23.
5   For instance, Christian states, in relation to common and criminal law, that if a woman
is killed by her husband, it may be held as if she was a stranger; that her punishment for
treason is more severe than for a man; that she is denied benefit of clergy [this was not so in
practice] and that in civil law she is subjected to multiple property, testamentary, inheritance and personal disabilities.
6   Christian, *Blackstone's commentaries*, i (17th edn), 445.
7   Blackstone, *Commentaries*, i (5th edn), 442.
8   I use the wide definition of 'patriarchy' offered by G. Lerner in *The creation of patriarchy*,
New York–London 1986: 'The manifestation and institutionalisation of male dominance
over women and children in the family and the extension of male dominance over women
in society in general. It implies that men hold power in all the important institutions of

shifts and changes its structure and function, and adapts to various pressures and demands. However, it is essentially hierarchical, depending on the subordination of subject to monarch, servant to master, religious inferiors to their superiors, son to father, women to men and, in particular, wives to husbands. It defines both public and private relationships. However, understanding of the way in which English law created, justified or described the position of women in society was by no means unanimous. For instance, the concept of marital unity did not receive universal support, and was not universally applied in legal and judicial settings.

Whether the concept was myth, fiction or mere description of daily-observed inequalities, its dogma could be applied through the common law in civil, property matters. It was not directly applicable in common law or statute criminal matters, and was modified in equity law. Although at this time the separate notions of criminal and civil law were not as clearly defined as they have become today, there was a general or abstract conception of an area of law which might be called 'criminal'.[9] In the imprecise area of criminal law, a different form of legal protection – that of 'marital coercion' – might, in specific, narrow circumstances, be available to married women, because of their 'civil subjection' to their husbands. It was a legal excuse which could be used if there might have been 'civil subjection or compulsion by another to perform a criminal act'. It is appropriate to consider 'marital coercion' in criminal cases, where *coverture* and concepts of 'marital unity' are not strictly applicable. The excuse of marital coercion, as a defence presumption, could be used only in limited situations. In the crimes studied in this book, the excuse was rarely attempted in court, and gave married or cohabiting women little protection.[10]

The power of the myth of marital unity

It is hardly likely that powerful men – lawyers, judges, juries, government servants, members of parliament, or any man with some property and a wife – would, consciously, separate the discriminatory legal devices relevant to common, civil law, from those relevant to the criminal law. The theoretical

society and that women are deprived of access to such power' (p. 239). The continuing debates about, for instance, whether it is correct to call a system of male domination 'patriarchal' (in view of, for example, race and class oppression) have been taken into consideration. This book does not enter those debates but, in a consideration of the institutionalising of the dominant system through law, 'patriarchy' is the appropriate term to use. See arguments in Scott, *Gender and politics*; Kingsley–Kent, *Gender and power*, esp. pp. 5–54; M. Mies, *Patriarchy and accumulation on a world scale: women in the international division of labour*, London 1986, esp. pp. 36–8.

9 Lieberman, 'Mapping criminal law', 140–2.

10 Blackstone thought that matters of 'rights' between master and servant, or husband and wife, were restricted to 'private, oecumencial relations': *Commentaries*, i (5th edn), 160.

powerlessness of married women, sanctioned by law, was taken for granted as the model for all women, single, married, widowed, young or old, rich or poor.[11] *Coverture*, the collective label for women's legal disabilities brought about through wifehood, was a system which could affect all women, married or not. Systems of economic and social organisation, of course, change with time and the needs of society. The English system throughout most of the Middle Ages was based on a military covenant, putting women at a disadvantage. Although the system was modified in practice by the eighteenth and nineteenth centuries, it needs to be considered in order to understand the position of women and the law. Land had been gifted, and protection and other rights bestowed, by a land-holding feudal superior, in return for provision of armed service on the part of a man. The effective working of such a covenant depended on physical strength, year-round availability and freedom from other responsibilities. None of this could women unequivocally offer. If women were given undisputed rights to inherit land, the hierarchical system would collapse, with power dispersed and uncertain. Such a system also required that men had control over familial reproduction to establish male primogeniture. This system, monarchic and patriarchal, prevailed, with legal extensions and modifications from time to time.[12] A means of giving legal justification to a husband's power was effected through the dogma of marital unity.

In England, the concept of marital unity can be traced at least to the twelfth century. It has featured in the writings of every major common-law commentator since.[13] It underwent changes over the years to fit the needs of the times,[14] but proved remarkably persistent. At the end of the nineteenth century some legal historians dismissed the idea as a useless, meaningless abstraction, at odds with legal reality.[15] In the twentieth century it was held to be a doubtful legal principle, sheltering or concealing the invalidity of certain strictures held to be rules of law.[16] Yet there has never been an official renunciation of the concept, although, in 1981, the Court of Appeal held that it should no longer be regarded as an effective part of the common law of England.[17]

---

[11] M. Doggett, *Marriage, wife-beating and the law in Victorian England*, London 1992, 34–99.

[12] P. Strohm, 'Treason in the household', in his *Hochon's arrow: the social imagination of fourteenth-century texts*, Princeton 1992, 121–44.

[13] F. Pollock and F. Maitland, *History of English law before the times of Edward I*, Oxford 1895, i. 465–8; ii. 397–434.

[14] For instance, for Bracton's views of marital guardianship and his more relaxed attitude to wifely disabilities and criminal excuses see *On the laws and customs of England*, iii, ch. xxxii, trans. S. E. Thorne, Cambridge, Mass. 1968.

[15] Pollock and Maitland, *History of English law*, i. 465.

[16] M. Lush, *The law of husband and wife within the jurisdiction of the Queen's Bench and Chancery Divisions*, 4th edn, London 1933.

[17] *Midland Bank Trust Company Ltd. v. Green* (No.3) (1981) 3 All E R 744.

Favoured by the law

William Noy's legal textbook, much used in the eighteenth and nineteenth centuries, demonstrated how lawyers constructed advice on legal principles.[18] He set out forty-eight maxims of the English law. Among them: 'the law favours some persons . . .; the law favours a thing which is of necessity; the husband and wife are one person . . .; all that a woman has appertains to her husband . . .; the will of a wife is subject to the will of her husband'. Those persons whom the law 'favoured', or treated as non-culpable or excused full responsibility for illegal action, were 'men out of the realm or in prison, women married, infants, mad-men, men without intelligence, strangers', and one who does things 'in the right of another person'. As late as 1845 there was little challenge to the view that 'where *baron* and *feme* commit a felony, the *feme* can neither be principal nor accessary [*sic*] because the law intends her to have no will, on account of the subjection and obedience she owes to her husband'. Examples given for the other maxims related entirely to estate, property, land covenants, purchases during marriage, indentures, and the whole panoply of civil and contract law issues, with no reference to the criminal law.[19] This uncritical understanding informed legal opinion, although it rarely prevailed in practice.

To what extent, then, did understandings of the idea of marital unity, a common law concept, have an effect on the administration of criminal justice? Some decisions in the court cases studied in this book suggest that the concept was influential, but that its effects did not operate consistently. Sometimes women benefited from decisions which saw womankind as weak, subordinate and lacking agency. Sometimes they were harmed. The discourse reflected different shades of opinion. Blackstone had expressed a Pauline, sacramental, rather than legal, understanding of marriage, with use of one-flesh and one-person language.[20] Bracton, on the other hand, had held that woman (not only a wife) was inherently inferior.[21] In treatises written in the early part of the nineteenth century, the presumed suspension of the legal existence of a woman during marriage, or at least its incorporation or consolidation into that of the husband, was seen as being for the protection of both parties: that the man should be made safe from her injuring him by disposing of his land, and that the woman should be saved from his exerting influence over her should she have land to dispose of. It was felt that great inconvenience would be experienced through departure from this code of behav-

---

18 W. Noy, *The principal grounds and maxims with an analysis of the laws of England*, ed. H. Henning, 3rd American edn from 9th London edn, Burlington, VT 1845.
19 Ibid. 29–37.
20 This view was shared by the anonymous author of *The laws respecting women*, London 1777, 23.
21 Bracton, *Laws and customs*, ii, ch. xxxi, specifies 'et differunt feminae a masculis in multis, quia earum deterior est condicio quam masculorum'.

iour.[22] Breaches of the peace would occur without adherence to such a code. Legal power had to be vested in the husband because he was the stronger:

> Give but the legal authority to the wife, and every moment would produce a revolt on the part of the husband, only to be quelled by assistance from without. . . . They who from some ill-defined notion of justice or generosity would extend to women an absolute equality, hold out to them a dangerous snare.[23]

Even this writer admitted that there had to be limits to this code, otherwise women would be reduced to a state of 'passive slavery', when in reality they stood in need of legal protection because of their 'weakness and softness'.[24] On the other hand, this dogma intended a man to have total power and control over his wife. There remained questions as to whether the unequal power relationship had been deliberately created by the law itself, as if the law had an independent existence apart from the men who made it, or whether inequality was an inevitable consequence of women's weak nature which the law was forced to recognise.[25] There is little evidence, before the twentieth century, of any understanding that the law did not create but only justified, explained and consecrated an existing system of power in which men held land and property, including their wives and children, which they would be unwilling to sacrifice.

The seemingly watertight structure of the principle of *feme covert* was breached in legal practice in a variety of situations. For instance, in relation to 'contracts, debts and injuries', Blackstone admitted that man and wife could be seen as two distinct persons (albeit the woman remaining inferior), and that in the ecclesiastical courts (which dealt with religious and moral issues, matrimonial and inheritance matters) a woman might sue and be sued without her husband:

> Yet there are some instances in which she is separately considered; as inferior to him, and acting by his compulsion. And therefore all deeds executed, and acts done, by her, during her *coverture*, are void; except it be a fine, or the like matter of record, in which case she must be solely and secretly examined, to learn if her act be voluntary.[26]

Having painted a bleak portrait of women's legal situation, the legal authorities qualified what they had written.[27] Blackstone described so many small

---

[22] R. S. D. Roper, *A treatise on the laws of property arising from the relation between husband and wife*, London 1820; J. Clancy, *A treatise on the rights, duties and liabilities of husband and wife at law and equity*, 3rd edn, London 1827.

[23] P. Bingham, *The law of infancy and coverture*, London 1816, 162.

[24] Ibid. 164.

[25] Doggett, *Marriage*, 42.

[26] Blackstone, *Commentaries*, i (5th edn), 444.

[27] M. Finn, 'Women, consumption and coverture in England, *c.* 1760–1860', *HJ* xxxix (1996), 703–22, suggests that the law of necessaries was one of the most significant of the qualifications of *coverture* within the law itself.

deviations from the dogma that it is a wonder that a system depending on the concept of marital unity did not fall apart. However, that is to suppose it was a coherent system and not a descriptive fiction or myth. In addition, a woman, as a separate person, could do a civil wrong, although her perceived position under the law and her property disabilities might mean that she was not in a position to be penalised.[28]

As more work is done by historians on the various means by which married women evaded the strictures of *coverture*, we can see that its effect was not monolithic. Despite the ideology behind the legal literature of the eighteenth century, women (mainly, but not only, elite women), found ways of using their husbands' credit, carved out for themselves a major role as consumers, manipulated marriage settlements, created independence in marriage, used the consistory courts, the small claims courts, instruments of equity and judicial separations to their advantage.[29] This indicates that the legal disabilities of married women were less sweeping and more partial and contested than legal treatise would suggest. None the less, the learned legal minds of the late eighteenth and early nineteenth centuries were influenced by legal treatises, and there can be no denying the strength of the dominant view of the subordinate position of married women. This view in turn affected how all women were seen.

'Marital coercion' and the criminal law

In Christian's 1830 edition of Blackstone's legal commentaries, it is suggested that 'In criminal prosecutions, it is true, the wife may be indicted and punished separately, for the union is only a civil union.'[30] Chitty's popular criminal law textbook of 1816 gave the advice that anyone and everyone was liable to arrest to answer an alleged or suspected crime, adding that 'The exemptions which exist in civil cases here cease to operate. Thus a married woman, when she has committed an offence . . . is liable to be apprehended.'[31] Even so, many lawyers felt that there was a lack of clarity about the situation of married women in relation to criminal law charges.[32] However, the men and women who were prosecuted through the criminal justice

---

28 Doggett, *Marriage*, 44–5, and n. 52 at p. 156.
29 Among contributions to the debate are Vickery, 'Golden age'; L. Bonfield, *Marriage settlements, 1601–1740: the adoption of the strict settlement*, Cambridge 1983; S. Staves, *Married women's separate property in England, 1660–1833*, Cambridge, Mass. 1990; A. L. Erickson, *Women and property in early modern England*, London 1993; and Finn, 'Women, consumption'.
30 Christian, *Blackstone's commentaries*, i (17th edn), 443.
31 J. Chitty, *A practical treatise on the criminal law*, London 1816, in a selection by D. S. Berkowitz and S. E. Thorne, London 1978, 12.
32 For views on the law on coercion see J. Fitzjames Stephen, *A history of the criminal law of England*, ii, London 1883, 105.

system were, for the most part, people for whom the property-orientated principle of *coverture* had little practical meaning. As a judge put it in the middle of the nineteenth century, 'The law supposes that everything is in the property of the husband and that the wife is under his control. But in point of fact, in the lower positions of life that possibly may not be the case at all.'[33] The cases considered in this book are evidence of that view. Even so, the question remains as to how far the assumptions behind the law could be ignored, even if lawyers and judges were unsure of them.

'Marital coercion' was one of a group of 'incapacities or defects', under the heading 'civil subjection', categorised in most criminal law textbooks. Such defences or excuses had the uncertain nature of legal presumptions, and a different philosophical justification from the principles of *coverture* and marital union. They could be used only in limited and particular circumstances. There were three main categories of incapacities or defects which might exempt people from legal penalties – natural, accidental and civil incapacities.[34] One – infancy – was a natural defect. Three were accidental defects – dementia, casualty or chance, and ignorance. There were four civil defects – civil subjection, compulsion, necessity and fear. In cases of crime or misdemeanour, where proceedings should lead to punishment, the law 'in some cases and under certain temperaments takes notice of these defects, and in respect of them relaxeth or abateth the severity of their punishments'.[35] Civil subjection meant the subjection of wife to husband, although lawyers appeared uncertain as to its scope.[36]

The uncertainty was summarised, and parodied, in the latter part of the nineteenth century:

As regards marital compulsion, the law is at once vague and bad as far as it goes. It is as follows: 'If a married woman commits a theft or receives stolen goods, knowing them to be stolen, in the presence of her husband, she is presumed to have acted under his coercion, and such coercion excuses her act; but this presumption may be rebutted if the circumstances of the case show that in point of fact she was not coerced. It is uncertain how far this principle applies to felonies in general . . . It does not apply to high treason and murder . . . It probably does not apply to robbery . . . It applies to uttering counterfeit coin . . . It seems to apply to misdemeanours generally . . . It is hardly necessary to point out or indeed to observe upon the defects of this rule. It admits indeed of no defence, but I think it is capable of a historical explanation.'[37]

---

[33] J. Blackburn quoted in Conley, *Unwritten law*, 69.
[34] M. Hale, *Historia placitorum coronae*, London 1800, ed. T. Dogherty, ch. ii.
[35] Ibid.
[36] Ibid. where it is stated that 'Tho' in many cases the command, or authority of the husband, either express or implied, doth not privilege the wife from capital punishment for capital offenses; yet in some cases the indulgence of the law doth privilege her from capital punishment for such offences, as are in themselves of a capital nature.'
[37] Stephen, *History of criminal law*, ii. 105. See also the confusion in anon, *Laws respecting women*, 71.

Lawyers believed that the excuse of marital coercion, seen as an example of 'modern' judicial practice, grew up because judges wished to give to married women in criminal cases some sort of rough equivalent of the benefit of clergy enjoyed by their husbands. Others, like Blackstone, explained the practice as a natural consequence of the theory of marital unity. Because of his lack of interest in criminal law, he has done historians a disservice by inaccurately summarising the situation: 'In some cases the command or authority of the husband, either expressed or implied, will privilege the wife from punishment, even for capital offences. And therefore, if a woman [commits such an offence] by the coercion of her husband or even in his company, which the law construes a coercion, she is not guilty of any crime.'[38]

This inaccurate view was repeated by other lawyers. East suggested that the general rule in cases of felony presupposes the wife to act under her husband's coercion.[39] However, in practice, rather than in theory, it can be shown that the excuse of marital coercion was possible only in very limited circumstances, far too few to provide an explanation for lenient treatment of women in criminal cases. The scope of the coercion defence was unclear, and legal commentators disagreed about it. Some of the difficulty is demonstrated in the following argument:

If the husband and wife together commit larciny [sic] or burglary ... both are guilty; and so it hath been practised by some judges ... and possible in strictness of law, unless the actual co-ercion of the husband appear, she may be guilty in such a case; for it may many times fall out, that the husband doth commit larciny by the instigation, tho' he cannot in law do it by the coercion of his wife; but the latter practice hath obtain'd, that if the husband and wife commit burglary and larciny together, the wife shall be acquitted, and the husband only convicted ... And accordingly in the modern practice, where the husband and wife, by the name of his wife, have been indicted for a larciny, or burglary jointly, and have pleaded to the indictment, and the wife convicted, and the husband acquitted; merciful judges have used to reprieve the wife before judgement, because they have thought, or at least doubted, that the indictment was void against the wife, she appearing by the indictment to be a wife, and yet charged with felony jointly with her husband. But this is not agreeable to law, for the indictment stands good against the wife.[40]

---

38 Christian admitted that this rule had its exception for crimes 'mala in se' and 'prohibited by the law of nature, as murder and the like': Blackstone's commentaries, i (17th edn), 27–8.
39 E. H. East, Pleas of the crown, London 1803. Similarly, anon., Laws respecting women, turns the presumption of coercion into a supposition, 70.
40 Hale, Historia, 44. There was similar lack of clarity in respect of cases of misdemeanour. Some lawyers believed it applied to some misdemeanours, some that it never applied to non-indictable offences, and some that it may have applied to all. See Doggett, Marriage,

In his sight – in his power

For the excuse of marital coercion to be available to a woman, she had to commit the crime in her husband's presence. She could not be presumed to have been coerced if she had only been instructed, bullied or threatened with abuse for disobedience. If she could also prove her husband's presence, coercion might be presumed. The case of John and Sarah Morris in 1814 provides an example. Sarah was charged with forging, uttering and publishing as true a forged certificate for prize money, due to be paid to her father, a naval petty officer, by the Seamen's Hospital in Greenwich. Her husband was charged that 'he did invite, move, counsel, aid, abet, charge and procure' Sarah to commit the forgery and the uttering. Sarah applied at the hospital for the prize money of £30 with her forged voucher, which was subsequently found to be false. Both Sarah and John were arrested and, when tried, got their landlord to say that he had heard John order Sarah that 'she must go for the money', and that he believed 'she went to receive it in obedience to her husband's orders'. In order to make use in the trials of the excuse of marital coercion, John had signed a paper stating that Sarah had acted entirely under his orders and directions. Counsel for the couple argued that, as Sarah had acted under the control and direction of her husband, she could not be found guilty. If she were found not guilty, then John could not be found guilty as accessory, since she was innocent as a principal. The jury found them both guilty of capital felony. The view of the twelve judges was sought and the convictions were held to be sound. Sarah was seen to be fully implicated and that, whatever her husband had suggested or ordered she did, she was not under his control when she actually went to utter the forgery.[41]

The Bank of England's cases at the Old Bailey against Jane and John Graham in 1782 provide another example of the limitations in practice of the excuse of marital coercion. The Grahams were indicted on eight capital charges of Bank note forgery, the main one involving defacing a £15 note to make it appear a £50 note. Early in the hearing, their counsel raised Jane's marital status. The newspaper report on the case reads like an inaccurate legal textbook: 'The jury could not convict the prisoners, even if they believed the evidence proved, because in all cases short of treason and murder, where it appeared that a criminal action had been performed by a man and his wife, the woman was acquitted, from a presumption that what she had done was by the influence and direction of the husband.' Without informing his readers of the facts of the case, the newspaper reporter moved quickly on:

52–3. Anon., *Laws respecting women*, excludes use of the defence in relation to treason, murder or robbery (p. 71).
41 W. O. Russell and E. Ryan, *Crown cases reserved for consideration, and decided by the twelve judges of England from 1799 to 1824*, London 1825: R. v. Sarah Morris and John Morris, Kent 1814, 270–4.

The judge summed up the evidence with great precision and clarity and in regard to the point of law, he told the jury, that in all such cases where the husband and wife acted in coercion [*sic* – presumably co-operation] then indeed the law was so tender in behalf of the woman as to presume that she acted under an influence and compulsive force from the husband. But then she had no such advantage in the present case; what she had done appeared to have been a voluntary act; her husband was not present, even though he might have commanded her to utter the note in question, yet as soon as she was out of his sight, she was out of his power, and might have claimed the power of the magistrate to defend herself.

The jury hearing the case had to ask the judge if there were in fact such a rule or presumption affecting married women. The answer was that 'a presumption is raised from the humanity of the law' if it might be presumed that she committed the offence 'under the dominion and authority of her husband'. If the woman had been 'the active person', her degree of guilt was the same; moreover, if she was not in her husband's presence then she had no 'privilege'. The facts of the case showed a long marriage, nine children, the husband freshly out of prison and the forgeries long planned between John and Jane. John had probably altered the notes, but had not 'put them off'. 'The whole of that is left to the conduct and management of the woman.' Jane had uttered the notes in Westminster and was apprehended in Southampton with more forged notes and experimental prints. There was no evidence of uttering against John, although he may have been near Jane when she did so. Both were sentenced to death.[42]

On the other hand, there were many examples where the circumstances of the crime, or the judge's attitude, or both, resulted in a simpler legal decision. James and Mary Barrett, man and wife, were indicted in 1821 at the Old Bailey for stealing 'a great quantity of articles and wearing apparel' from the house of the master for whom Mary worked as dairymaid. The stolen property was found in the Barrett's house. James had been at Mary's master's house frequently in the time leading up to discovery of the theft. In his defence, he said he knew nothing about the property. Mary affirmed his story. The judge told the jury that there was an important question, 'which was, as both could not be convicted (being man and wife) which one was the thief?' The jury decided it was James and acquitted Mary, despite the facts of the case as reported showing that Mary was fully involved in the stealing and the receiving of the goods.[43] 'Ordinary' people were aware of the excuse of marital coercion and tried to use it on the few occasions where they thought they could, whether they were entitled to or not.[44]

The effect of *coverture* and of the excuse of marital coercion continued to

42 OBSP, 11 Sept.1782; *The London Chronicle*, 14/17 Sept. 1782.
43 *The Times*, 27 Oct. 1821.
44 V. C. Edwards, 'The case of the married spinster: an alternative explanation', *AJLH* xxi (1977), 260–5.

be scrutinised throughout the nineteenth century. It was decided that the 'bare command' of the husband was insufficient to excuse the married woman.[45] Only at the end of the nineteenth century was it admitted that 'no presumption shall be made that a married woman committing an offence does so under compulsion only because she commits it in the presence of her husband'.[46] The presumption of marital coercion was not abolished from the law until 1925, when it was replaced with a statutory defence based on actual coercion by a husband.[47]

Specifically gendered judicial practices

In addition to the deeply gendered philosophy of the law, the judicial system of the eighteenth and nineteenth centuries retained a small number of specifically gendered practices. As far as women were concerned, these derived directly from their position under the common law of England. They included precedents which made it difficult for a wife to prosecute her husband. Spouses could not give evidence against each other. This applied in theory equally to men and women, although most of the discussion was about wives' testimony, and the fear that chaos could be caused in the patriarchal household if a wife gave evidence against her husband.[48] In practice, however, there were many examples of wives giving evidence against their husbands. When the Bank of England prosecuted forged note cases, a husband or a wife was frequently used as a witness for the prosecution of their spouse. The 'ordinary' criminal nature of these cases, and the plebeian class of the people involved, might explain why such a procedure was not seen as remarkable or threatening to social order.

There were other activities which might have been regarded as criminal had a marriage not existed. For instance, a wife and husband could not be found guilty of conspiring with one another. Further, it was held not to be larceny for a wife to take her husband's possessions without his consent, as it was not her business to know what he owned. Conversely, he could not steal

---

[45] 'If the *feme covert* commit theft of her own voluntary act or by the bare command of her husband, or be guilty of treason, murder or robbery in company with, or by coercion of her husband, she is punishable as much as if she were sole': Bingham, *Law of infancy*, 227.

[46] *Brown v. Attorney General of New Zealand* (J. C., 1898 AC).

[47] The Criminal Justice Act 1925 (15/16 Geo.5, c.86) s. 47, provides that, for a wife, charged in cases other than treason or murder, 'it shall be a good defence to prove that the offence was committed in the presence of, and under the coercion of the husband'. This is significantly different from the previously held legal presumption in favour of marital coercion.

[48] Christian doubted the notion of marital union/one-flesh used by Blackstone (and others) to justify the inability of a wife to give evidence against her husband. He did not believe in the propriety of the law ever ruling out crucial evidence in any kind of hearing: *Blackstone's commentaries*, i (17th edn), 443, n. 20.

from her, because she had nothing after marriage which could be stolen. A wife could protect her criminal husband without being an accessory after the fact; but a husband in a similar situation in relation to his wife was not permitted to protect her, and this again was because she was seen to be *sub potestate viri*.[49] Perhaps a more honest view of the situation was that it was 'a technical distinction for which there seems no just reason'.[50]

A further gendered practice, relating to the offence of 'petit' treason, was not abolished until 1828.[51] This offence was committed when a servant killed his or her master or mistress, when an ecclesiastic killed his or her religious superior, or when a wife killed her husband. All these relationships were held to embody obligations of duty, subordination and allegiance, similar to the feudal obligation of a man to his sovereign. Not only was husband-killing considered a more serious crime than any other class of murder, but, until the end of the eighteenth century, women guilty of 'petit' treason were punished differently from murderers in general, and from males guilty of 'petit' treason. They were sentenced to be burned alive, whilst males were to hang. In practice, many of the women were more mercifully killed before the flames burned them, but this was not always the case.[52] The offence of coining counterfeit specie came within the category of 'petit' treason (because coin bore the image of the sovereign), and the execution of a number of women at the end of the eighteenth century drew strong adverse comment.[53] For men, the punishment for 'petit' treason was 'very solemn and terrible' – drawing, hanging, disembowelling, decapitation and quartering, but

> the punishment is milder for male offenders . . . in treasons of every kind the punishment of women is the same, and different from that of men. For, as the natural modesty of the sex forbids the exposing and publicly mangling of their bodies, their sentence (which is to the full as terrible to sense as the other) is to be drawn to the gallows and there to be burned alive.[54]

However, in theory at least, from the early nineteenth century, there was no other differential in the approach specified in law for men and women, save one. A man who killed his wife, having witnessed her in the act of adultery, could be held to be guilty of manslaughter, not murder, whereas a wife acting under similar provocation would have no such defence. An explanation for

49 Hale, *Historia*, 46.
50 East, *Pleas of the crown*, 559.
51 Offences Against the Person Act 1828, s. 2 (9 Geo.4, c.31).
52 Campbell, 'Sentence of death by burning', 47–8.
53 Examples of this in this period are the burnings/executions in London of Phoebe Harris, *The Times*, 22, 23, 27 June 1786; Margaret Sullivan, *St James's Chronicle*, 24/26 June 1788; *The Times*, 24, 25, 26, 27, 30 June 1788; and Christian Bowman *alias* Catherine Murphy, *The Times*, 19 Mar.1789, *The Gentlemen's Magazine*, li/1 (1789), 272.
54 Blackstone, *Commentaries*, i (5th edn), 93.

this difference was given in the early twentieth century – the husband's right to control his wife, whereas she had no such right over him.[55]

Where a woman had been sentenced to death by a criminal court, and could show, to the satisfaction of a jury of matrons, that she was 'quick with child of a quick child',[56] she could 'plead the belly' and have her execution stayed until after the birth of the child. This had been the practice in English law since at least the twelfth century. In the late eighteenth century, the decision of this jury might be important, since such a stay of execution could be the prelude to a conditional pardon, with substitution of a secondary punishment; however, in practice this happened rarely.[57] This relatively formal practice was significantly in decline by the last two decades of the eighteenth century. Between 1780 and 1800, of 180 women sentenced to death at the Old Bailey, only four pleaded their bellies, at a time of increasing likelihood of a death sentence being carried out. Of the four, the jury of matrons found only one pregnant. By 1800 the appearance of the jury of matrons had become a rarity, and from 1820 the number of women who made this plea, and verification of it, was extremely small: Oldham finds that the jury of matrons was called once each in 1825 and in 1830.[58] Gaining time in this way was of great value, but a successful pregnancy plea was not tantamount to a pardon, certainly not if the London records are anything to go by.[59]

A further difference in the penal treatment of men and women concerned whipping. Males and females could be sentenced to be whipped for non-capital offences, as their sole punishment, or in combination with other punishments, notably imprisonment. The use of whipping was also declining, although not steadily, from the last decades of the eighteenth century into the nineteenth century, for reasons associated with the availability of other punishments and developing penal policy together with the sensitivities which changed attitudes to public flogging.[60] The public flogging of women had been largely abandoned by the 1750s. In 1817 the law specified an end to it. In 1820 private flogging of women was also proscribed, although it continued for men – publicly into the early nineteenth century, and privately well into the second half of the nineteenth century.[61] The highly gendered sentiments of the 'feeling classes' were expressed by the poet Coleridge in 1811:

---

55 R v. Greening (1913) 3 KB 846; Bray J.
56 J. Oldham in 'On pleading the belly: a history of the jury of matrons', CJH vi (1985), 1–64, refers to the 'quaint language of the jury charge', which is taken from The office of the clerk of assize, rev. edn 1660, London 1681.
57 King, Crime, justice and discretion, 282; Beattie, Crime and the courts, 431; Oldham, 'On pleading'.
58 Oldham, 'On pleading', appendix 1, pp. 34–7.
59 Ibid. 19, 21, 28.
60 King, Crime, justice and discretion, 262–6, 272–3.
61 Gatrell, Hanging tree, 336–8; King, Crime, justice and discretion, 286.

We were in hopes, that with the progressive refinement and increased tender-ness of private and domestic feelings . . . this unmanly practice of scourging females had gradually become obsolete and placed among the Inusitata of the law dictionary. It is not only the female herself, who must needs . . . be griev-ously injured in the first sources and primary impulses of female worth, – for who will deny, that the infamy which would attend a young woman from having been stripped naked under the lash of a townswoman [sic], would be incomparably greater, and have burned deeper in, than what would accrue from her having been detected in stealing half a dozen loaves? We are not shocked for the female only, but for the inflictor, at the unmanliness of the punishment itself. Good God! How is it possible that man, *born of a woman*, could go through the office . . . the woman is still woman, and however she may have debased herself, yet that we should still shew some respect, still feel some reverence, if not for her sake, yet in awe of that Being, who saw good to stamp her in his own image, and forbade it ever, in this life at least to be utterly erased.[62]

The male world of the criminal law

Suggestions that the statute law itself was gendered would have been met, by lawyers and others involved in the practice of criminal justice, with incredu-lity. 'The empire of law is masculinist, the application of legal rules have been recognised as masculinist, but the argument that the method of law itself is masculinist is not so readily conceded.'[63] Women are given far less consider-ation in written legal theory than they are in practice in the courts. 'Man' means 'woman' simply by saying so, as lawyers and others so often explain. The experiences of women are seen as otherwise irrelevant to the law, or rarely given the blessing of the law. Where women's activities are authenti-cated by the law, they appear to remain specifically feminine and without universal applicability. 'How, for example, can the partial defence of provoca-tion founded on what reasonable men do in the face of adversity truly absorb reasonable women and their reaction to adversity?'[64]

When many categories of serious crime are considered, it is apparent that the lawmakers had in mind activities that were seen to be carried out by men. The crime of stealing privily from the person is a good example. The auda-

---

[62] S. T. Coleridge, letter to *The Courier*, 13 May 1811, printed in *Essays on his own times forming a second series of 'The Friend'*, by *Samuel Taylor Coleridge*, *iii*, ed. *by his daughter*, London 1850, 762–6. It is worth noting his reference to the lash being administered by a 'townswoman'; he questions how 'man, born of a woman' could flog a woman – one of the many examples of confusion caused by the use of gender exclusive language – i.e. 'man' instead of 'human' or 'man and woman'.
[63] Edwards, *Sex and gender*, 6.
[64] Ibid. 3.

cious thieving of gangs of men in public places in the sixteenth century caused sufficient concern for it to be made a capital offence. Yet that same statute was used to prosecute more women than men, women who did not act in a way which resembled the behaviour originally feared. Another example is that of the Bank of England which, in setting up its prosecution strategy to prevent and punish the forgery of low value Bank notes, found that the statute trapped large numbers of women utterers who faced the death penalty, when male forging gangs had been the target.

From the beginning of their journey through the judicial system, women and men did not share level ground. The understanding of the place of women in English society was discriminatory and necessarily affected the operation of the criminal code. Women could, in theory, be provided with excuses and compensation for their behaviour, which reinforced their subordinate position and their perceived weak natures. It was possible for the law and the judicial system to excuse and ignore female criminal behaviour, and for the system to work to women's advantage up to a point. However, beyond that point there was no shelter. Women who threatened the hierarchical economic and social structures were unlikely to receive any advantage. Women embarked on a journey where the rules were written to control male activity. Criminal women were something of an aberration. Sometimes they could be dealt with leniently, because of their weakness and their need to be protected. Sometimes they could be mercilessly disposed of, since they undermined the reasoning behind male chivalry, paternalism and patriarchy.

However, this gendered system did not operate consistently. The men and women in trouble with the criminal law were not the sort for whom the nice distinctions, and the need to defend and conform, created by property ownership, inheritance, marriage or marriage settlements, had much meaning. The decision-makers in the justice system knew that too. Their reactions often would be coloured by the view that the people they were dealing with were people of little or no property, who would not subscribe to the same codes of practice. At the same time, the system of justice in England was built on discretion – in prosecution, in bringing in verdicts, in sentencing and, to an even greater extent, in pardoning and setting aside sentences. The penalty structure was largely devoid of any appearance of system or principle. This was the subject of debate in the early nineteenth century, between those who sought to maintain judicial discretion and those seeking to develop a system in which the punishment fitted the crime.[65] The 'rooms' of the criminal justice system were furnished with 'variations', depending on the peculiar notions of policy entertained by different individuals, or their firmness or

---

[65] D. A. Thomas, *The penal equation: derivations of the penalty structure of English criminal law*, Cambridge 1978, and *Constraints on judgement: the search for structured discretion in sentencing, 1860–1910*, Cambridge 1979.

resolution of mind.[66] Men and women faced a 'system of eking out imperfect justice by irregular mercy'.[67]

Men and women encountered this unequally applied system of law, which it is appropriate to describe as patriarchal. The most positive interpretation to be placed on this system suggests that powerful men were concerned to protect women – by means of judicial paternalism. Sometimes paternalism is interpreted as 'chivalry', suggesting a degree of respect for women. However, paternalism is contingent upon women displaying behaviour appropriate to the requirements of the decision-makers, and is about power relationships. It reflects women's social and legal inferiority to men and emphasises their putative need to be supported, guided and protected. Paternalism is little more than a particular mode or subset of patriarchal relations.[68] Judicial decisions were as much influenced by an offender's gender as by any other consideration. If the journey through the judicial system did not start on level ground for women and men, the unevenness of the starting point was not always to the advantage of women. The inherently gendered nature of the law was not the only, or perhaps even the predominant, factor which predicted the course of the journey through the judicial system. However, its influence was omnipresent.

[66] Idem, Penal equation, 20.
[67] Lord Penzance, Hansard, 20 Apr. 1870, c.1150, quoted in Thomas, Constraints on judgement, 38.
[68] K. Daly, 'Rethinking judicial paternalism: gender, work–family relations, and sentencing', Gender and Society iii (1989), 9–36; Lerner, Creation of patriarchy, 239.

3

Shoplifting

> She stooped to pick up (a half-penny) and I observed she was longer than nec-
> essary in that posture; when she arose from stooping I observed a kind of bulk
> under her cloak, that I had not observed before.[1]

London, at the end of the eighteenth and the beginning of the nineteenth
centuries, was the largest city in the world: the industrial, commercial and
political hub of a global empire. The continuous process of social and cultural
change, moving at great speed, was conspicuous in the streets of the Cities of
London and Westminster. Characters in Tobias Smollet's last novel described
its almost bewildering pace:

> London is literally new to me; new in its streets, houses . . . What I left open
> fields, producing hay and corn, I now find covered with streets, and squares,
> and palaces, and churches. I am credibly informed, that in the space of seven
> years, eleven thousand new houses have been built in one quarter of Westmin-
> ster, exclusive of what is daily added to other parts of this unwieldy metropolis
> . . . and if this infatuation continues for half a century, I suppose the whole
> county of Middlesex will be covered with brick.[2]

A German visitor to London in 1786 remarked on an obvious phenomenon
of commercial advance – the sophistication and number of well-designed
shops:

> I was struck by the excellent arrangement and system which the love of gain
> and the national good taste have combined in producing, particularly in the
> elegant dressing of large shop-windows, not merely in order to ornament the
> streets and lure purchasers, but to make known the thousands of inventions
> and ideas, and spread good taste about, for the excellent pavements made for
> pedestrians enable crowds of people to stop and inspect the new exhibits.[3]

The wonder of the developing shops of London, their architecture and
arrangement, as well as the variety of goods on sale, was indeed the talk of the
town, and far beyond. A stroll around the London shops was a standard
attraction of most tourist itineraries, male or female, in the late eighteenth
century. 'Shopping was well entrenched as a public cultural pursuit for

---

[1] Evidence in trial of Sarah Pine for shoplifting, OBSP, July 1795, 956–9.
[2] T. Smollet, *The expedition of Humphrey Clinker* (1771), quoted in R. Allen, *The moving pageant: a literary source book on London street life, 1700–1914*, London–New York 1998, 71.
[3] S. van la Roche, *Diary* (1786), quoted ibid. 77.

respectable women and men.'[4] The shops were often open until ten or eleven o'clock at night, although the busiest time was in the early afternoon. Visitors were entranced by the crowds, the excitement, the freshness of the experience of shopping and window-shopping in London, and by the artificial lighting of the streets and windows full of alluring displays.

Not surprisingly, shoplifting was rife in the face of the conspicuous consumerism which resulted from these developments. Shoplifting, 'stealing privily in a shop', was a criminal activity which provoked conflicting emotions. It attracted the sentence of death until 1823, when the punishment of transportation to New South Wales for life was substituted. Small shopkeepers pleaded desperation about 'the daily depredations' they suffered.[5] On the other hand, prosperous traders, some of whom would sit on the juries at the Old Bailey, disapproved strongly of some of the commercial methods employed in the metropolis, such as knockdown prices for bulk buying. This they regarded as unfair enticement of the ordinary person, particularly the ordinary woman. The 1819 select committee on the criminal law identified women as major shoplifting offenders; shopkeepers' goods were said to be 'flying in the face of every miserable woman who is going past'.[6]

In all the years between 1780 and 1823, more than 1,250 people were tried for the crime in London and Middlesex, a rate of about thirty cases a year. Women's involvement in shoplifting there well outstripped that of men. They constituted more than 56 per cent of those charged with the offence at the Old Bailey. In this chapter, the trials of men and women for shoplifting at the Old Bailey in selected years between 1780 and 1823 are examined to find out not only the nature of the verdicts and sentences of the court but what can be learned about the people involved, and their ways of committing the crime. Significant differences in behaviour between men and women emerge: differences in the way in which they shoplifted and in the objects they stole, differences which may have been sufficient to affect the juries' decisions. The enquiry is based on all shoplifting cases at the Old Bailey in the large sample of twenty-three of the forty-four years between 1780 and 1823.[7]

[4] Vickery, *Gentleman's daughter*, 251.
[5] This was the view of a linen draper: OBSP, Dec.1805, 7.
[6] The evidence of Thomas Shelton, clerk of the arraigns and oyer and terminer and gaol delivery at the Old Bailey, 12 Mar.1819, included the claim that women were tried for the offence 'more frequently than men a great deal': *Report from the select committee on capital punishment in felonies*, PP, 1819, viii. 25–7.
[7] For details of the twenty-three sample years see appendix. The detailed analysis includes only the cases which reached the Old Bailey petty jury. Years of war and peace are fairly equally included in the years analysed.

Defining the crime of shoplifting

Despite contemporaries' views about the prevalence of this crime, only a small proportion of cases reached a hearing before the Old Bailey petty jury. One of the main reasons for this was the precise definition of the offence. Awareness of this definition assists an understanding of why so comparatively few cases were brought in this category, and why so many defendants were found not guilty. Shoplifting had become a capital crime in 1699.[8] The new severity of the sentence was a response to public perceptions of a rapidly increasing growth of 'shoplifting' in the later years of the seventeenth century, going hand-in-hand with the development of shops in the streets of towns and cities, particularly London. A shoplifter was one who 'at any time . . . in any shop . . . privately and feloniously stole any Goods, Wares, or Merchandises, being of the Value of five Shillings or more'. The crucial feature of the crime was that it was 'private', unseen, undetected at the time. If a thief broke into a shop, or used force, say, to open a desk or drawer, or to pick a lock, this was not shoplifting.[9] If there was 'cognizance by other persons' that the offence was about to be, or was being, committed the capital charge would fall: 'the slightest glimpse of the taking, or even a suspicion of it, seemed to obviate the capital part of the charge'.[10] Such restrictions allowed juries to bring in a high proportion of outright not guilty verdicts, and an even higher proportion of 'partial verdicts', where they would find defendants guilty only of larceny, and thus not liable to a death sentence.

The major transformation in retailing in London during the seventeenth and eighteenth centuries resulted in great opportunity for theft from shops. Theft was made easier by increased display of goods in shop windows and showcases to make them more attractive, and by the way that merchandise spilled out over street space – hanging in shop doorways or displayed on the pavement – to tempt the casual shopper. However, defrauded shopkeepers had difficulty showing that a theft had been 'private'. London shopkeepers and their staff were wary and alert, suspicious of every customer they did not know. They kept their eyes open to comings and goings in the street outside their own and their neighbours' shops and, if trade allowed, watched their neighbours' shop windows. The cases at the Old Bailey show how busy London shops were, full of customers waiting to be served, and full of people, observing others.[11] London experienced a vast amount of thieving activity in its busy shopping locations – in the City, Whitechapel, Wapping, Fleet

8   10 & 11 Will.3, c. 23 (1699).
9   In such cases the crime could be burglary, a different capital offence.
10 W. Hawkins, A *treatise on the pleas of the crown*, London 1795, i. 260.
11 For description of shops in London see J. Rule, *Albion's people: English society, 1714–1815*, Harlow 1992, 76–80; Walsh, 'Shop design'; L. Weatherill, 'Consumer behaviour'; Vickery, *Gentleman's daughter*, 250–1; and J. Summerson, *Georgian London*, London 1991, 258–60.

Street, Holborn, the Strand, St Giles, Soho, St James and, later, in the early nineteenth century, in Oxford Street and the 'West End'.

Women had featured strongly in capital indictments from the end of the seventeenth century. As many as 80 per cent of those charged with shoplifting during the first twenty years after the passing of the 1699 act were women. Beattie has suggested that the common involvement of women was one of the main reasons behind the heavy-handed statutory response – a desire to bring them under control.[12] Such a perception of the behaviour of urban women suggests that female 'insubordination' was viewed in some quarters as dangerous, undermining the deference and obedience which underpinned social order. However, it is more likely that there was a more general concern that control over the labouring population, male and female, had weakened in urban communities, more than in the less anonymous and more easily supervised villages and small towns. The enduring view that women are not able, of their own volition, to be insubordinate, criminal or a danger to society, fed the nightmare of the propertied and commercial classes, that thieving women were agents of receivers, or the tools of criminal gangs.[13] This nightmare imagined not only the plunder of their goods, but also the violence of organised groups. Such a picture of shoplifting does not fit the evidence of the more opportunistic activity of the late eighteenth and early nineteenth centuries, neither for men nor for women.

'The pleasure of prosecuting a capital offence'

The average of thirty cases a year between 1780 and 1823 at the Old Bailey sessions was a modest total, considering the perceptions of shopkeepers. The difficulty involved in proving a shoplifting case was one of the reasons for such a low tally. At the start of the judicial process, the victim provided the driving force to move matters towards a formal trial. This could be an expensive, time-consuming and complex option. Other options for action were often preferred by tradesmen who were victims of theft. They might wish to avoid recourse to justice altogether by failing to pursue the theft or by instigating unofficial punishment in the community. Victims could see the thief taken before a magistrate and seek compromise, warning and discharge of the thief by the magistrate; they could attempt to pursue a summary trial before a magistrate for a lesser grade of offence where there could be no risk of a death sentence. If victims wished (or were prevailed upon) to take the matter further to the higher court at the Old Bailey, they could select indictment terms which did not permit a capital sentence, present weak cases, fail to appear to prosecute or make it clear to the court that they wanted leniency

12 Beattie, 'Crime and inequality', 128.
13 For a summary of this view of women see Walker, 'Women, theft and stolen goods', 83–5, and Crime, gender and social order, 159–60, 171.

even if the charges were proved.[14] Most stealing from shops was, therefore, dealt with by the judicial system as simple larceny – not as a capital offence. That some shopkeepers pursued a shoplifting indictment suggests they may have been particularly incensed about the unfairness of the crime. The same shopkeepers' names turn up repeatedly as prosecutors in shoplifting cases. A few might have been induced to prosecute by the reward of a certificate (or shares in a certificate) known as a 'Tyburn Ticket' granted, on conviction, to anyone who apprehended or prosecuted a shoplifter (provided they had not received any fee or other reward for doing so). The certificate permitted avoidance of undesired public office in the parish or ward in which the offence was committed.[15]

An exchange between defending counsel and a prosecution witness in a shoplifting case at the Old Bailey illustrates the strong feelings of some prosecutors. A shop assistant to a linen draper in Holborn, from whom thirteen yards of printed cotton had been stolen, thought the two women defendants had come to the shop with 'evil intent'. The shop assistant said he had seen one of the women put a piece of the material under her apron. This evidence potentially negated the case for shoplifting, as the action had not been private – it had been observed. He had intended to let her go out of the shop with the cotton. When asked why, the assistant replied, 'Because I wanted to make it a capital offence.' Defence counsel persisted: 'Your Christian charity did not prompt you to tell them you wanted them to commit a felony, that you might have the pleasure of prosecuting?', to which the witness responded, 'Exactly'. Not surprisingly, the two women were found guilty of stealing, but not privately.[16]

Overview of trials, verdicts and sentences

During the twenty-three years studied, 680 people were tried before the petty jury on indictment at the Old Bailey for shoplifting. Of these 369 (54 per cent) were female, 311 were male. Table 1 shows the total number of indictments heard by the petty jury. Shoplifting was not a crime which decreased

---

[14] See King, 'Decision-makers', and *Crime, justice and discretion*, 17–125, for full details and discussion of the options for such decisions.

[15] 10 & 11 Will.3, c. 23 provided for this certificate as an incentive to prosecutions. It had pecuniary value and could be sold on, as a whole or in parts. There does not appear to have been any other type of reward offered for agents in a successful prosecution for shoplifting, although some of the legal drafting is obscure. In 1706 (5 Annae, c.31), an amendment to the 1699 act providing for additional rewards extended only to burglary, felonious breaking and entering a house in day-time, and accessories of burglary and housebreaking: D. Pickering, *The statutes at large from the 8th year of King William III to the second year of Queen Anne*, x, Cambridge 1763, and *The statutes at large from the 2nd to the 8th year of Queen Anne*, xi, Cambridge 1764.

[16] OBSP, Apr.1805, 258.

Table 1
Shoplifting trials at Old Bailey Sessions in twenty-three sample years between 1780 and 1823

Years of war or peace	Years	Total	Average per year	Females (and average per year)	Females as % of total	Males (and average per year)	Males as % of total
War (2 years)	1780–2	63	31.5	49 (24.5)	78%	14 (7)	22%
Peace (4 years)	1789–93	93	23.25	37 (9.25)	40%	56 (14)	60%
War (3 years)	1793–5 1798–9	58	19.3	35 (11.66)	60%	23 (7.66)	40%
Peace/war (3 years)	1800–3	76	25.3	40 (13.3)	53%	36 (12)	47%
War (5 years)	1803–8	147	27	113 (22.6)	77%	34 (7)	23%
Peace (3 years)	1815–18	168	56	50 (16.6)	30%	118 (39.3)	70%
Peace (3 years)	1820–3	75	25	45 (15)	60%	30 (10)	40%
Totals	23 years	680	29.56	369 (16)	54%	311 (13.52)	46%

Sources: OBSP; HO 26/1–29.

Note: in 1821 the principal act was amended (1 Geo.4 c.117) to remove capital sentencing from shoplifting thefts between 5s.and £15.

(judged by indictment levels) during the years of war. There was an increase in indictments in some peacetime periods, in particular between 1815 and 1818, but, more generally, a slight upward trend during the earlier years of war. Immediately noticeable (in all but the last period tabulated) is the expected decline in the number of men prosecuted as wars began and continued. In the case of shoplifting, the proportion of women facing trial at the Old Bailey during the years of war increased noticeably. Nearly three times more women than men were tried for this offence during the war years. This might be expected, particularly if this sort of property crime was a response to adversity and poverty.[17] Wars resulted in increased pressure on

[17] Beattie, 'Crime and inequality', 132–4. The pattern of male indictments in London for shoplifting (and for pickpocketing: see chapter 4 below) follows that suggested by Hay, 'War, dearth and theft', 117–60. Hay did not fully consider gender in the link between theft and prices in times of war. Beattie's earlier work, 'The pattern of crime in England, 1660–1800', *P&P* lxii (1974), 47–95, also neglected the gender dimension, but pointed out the important differences in the City of London compared with Hay's analysis of Staffordshire indictments; London appears not to have been as sensitive to the combination of demobilisation and high prices as other less urban areas.

women, particularly poor urban women, to find ways to make ends meet. Shoplifting was an activity which could easily fulfil their needs and help to feed their families. The comparative scarcity of men in the indictment statistics in war years may well have been because of their absence from the streets of London, as they served in the armed forces. Their demobilisation in years of peace saw them featuring strongly again in trials at the Old Bailey. However, many men may have been allowed to escape from the corridors of the criminal justice system before trial at the Old Bailey as a result of negotiations which were the most obviously gendered manoeuvres in the whole system – through 'pre-trial enlistment'. Many of the adolescent and young males brought before magistrates for serious property offences, if they were physically fit, would have been selected for enlistment rather than being held to be charged on indictment at a higher court – if the victim was willing to agree to the arrangement and the accused was unable to resist. 'For a broad spectrum of property offenders, but more especially for those accused of indictable property crimes, there is considerable evidence that war, and the possibility of impressment, or semi-compulsory enlistment, created a parallel sanctioning system, an alternative judicial resource for both victims and magistrates.'[18] This 'broad spectrum' was, however, selected entirely on grounds of its gender.

The verdicts arrived at in the 680 cases tried at the Old Bailey in the selected years are included in table 2. Some of the features shown are those which might be expected; however, some are less so.[19] It does not seem at all surprising that juries found only a small number of cases – only 16 per cent (112 defendants) – fully proven and attracting the death sentence, in view both of the difficulty of a victim proving the capital charge in court, and also the general aversion to bringing in a capital verdict for an offence which did not involve violence. Further evidence of the reluctance of juries to make decisions which might lead to execution is the large number of verdicts in the 'partially guilty' category. Between half and two-thirds of jury verdicts lay in this area (61 per cent – 412 people). Such decisions were arrived at either through what has been termed 'pious perjury' – the jury's tendency to find ways round arriving at fully guilty verdicts: 'If they can devise means, not contrary to their conscience, and justify it to their own minds, they certainly

18 King, 'War as judicial resource', 113.
19 Comparable figures for verdicts for single specific crimes in London and Middlesex at this period, split by sex, appear to be unavailable. Beattie, Crime and the courts, used an earlier and very long period, a different area (partially urban), grouped capital and non-capital crimes, and counted both assize and quarter sessions verdicts; male offenders only were considered in some tables. See, for instance, n. 32, p. 419, and table 8.4 at p. 425. King, 'Gender, crime and justice', grouped all 'private stealing' crimes together, considered the Old Bailey and the Home Circuit together over a set of very short periods and included cases 'not found' by the grand jury, thus making his area for analysis of 'favourable' treatment for women wider. Thus it is not possible to make a satisfactory comparison with the figures I have produced from a more focused examination of cases.

Table 2
Verdicts in shoplifting cases at Old Bailey Sessions in twenty-three sample years between 1780 and 1823

	1780–2	1789–93	1793–5, 1798–9	1800–3	1803–8	1815–18	1820–3	Totals
Total verdicts	63	93	58	76	147	168	75	680
Men	14	56	23	36	34	118	30	311
Women	49	37	35	40	113	50	45	369
Fully capitally guilty								
Total and % of total verdicts	17 (29%)	18 (19%)	13 (22%)	11 (14%)	12 (8%)	35 (21%)	6 (9%)	112 (16%)
Men and % of men's verdicts	6 (43%)	8 (14%)	6 (26%)	8 (22%)	0 –	19 (16%)	3 (11%)	50 (16%)
Women and % of women's verdicts	11 (22%)	10 (27%)	7 (20%)	3 (8%)	12 (11%)	16 (32%)	3 (7%)	62 (17%)
Partially guilty verdicts								
Total and % of total verdicts	21 (31%)	64 (69%)	27 (47%)	46 (61%)	92 (63%)	106 (63%)	56 (75%)	412 (61%)
Men and % of men's verdicts	5 (36%)	45 (80%)	14 (61%)	19 (53%)	24 (71%)	81 (69%)	22 (73%)	210 (68%)
Women and % of women's verdicts	16 (33%)	19 (51%)	13 (37%)	27 (68%)	68 (60%)	25 (50%)	34 (77%)	202 (55%)
Not guilty/ acquitted								
Total and % of total verdicts	25 (42%)	11 (12%)	18 (31%)	19 (25%)	43 (29%)	27 (16%)	13 (18%)	156 (23%)
Men and % of men's verdicts	3 (21%)	3 (5%)	3 (13%)	9 (25%)	10 (29%)	18 (15%)	5 (17%)	51 (16%)
Women and % of women's verdicts	22 (49%)	8 (22%)	15 (43%)	10 (25%)	33 (29%)	9 (18%)	8 (18%)	105 (29%)

Sources: OBSP; HO 26/1–29.

will take every means they can to excuse the party charged of the capital part of the charge.'[20] They would decide that the value of the articles stolen was below 5s. and therefore not subject to the shoplifting statute,[21] or they might find themselves able to say that the facts of the case did not amount to private stealing in a shop – for instance, that the act of stealing had been

[20] Shelton's evidence in report of *Select committee on capital punishment in felonies*, PP, 1819, viii. 23.
[21] In 1821 the statute was amended to remove capital sentencing from shoplifting thefts between 5s. and £15.

observed. Finally, a large percentage of cases (23 per cent – 156 people) resulted in a not guilty verdict. This proportion of acquittals is not surprising for a property crime and entirely predictable when the offence was so difficult to prove.

In the 'not guilty' group, the distribution of verdicts between men and women is particularly marked. Twenty-nine per cent of females were found not guilty, 16 per cent of males. However, the proportion of men and women sentenced to death following a fully guilty verdict was almost equal (at between 16 and 17 per cent). The 'partial verdict' group contained a large proportion of males – 68 per cent, compared with 55 per cent of females. It is not immediately apparent, from evidence available in the trial reports, why the juries' partial decisions appear to have worked like this, more in favour of women than of men. Juries exercised a large measure of discretion, but their decisions were not systematic. The option of deciding that goods stolen were worth less than the minimum specified in the statute exposed partial verdict decisions for what they were – open attempts to avoid a death penalty. The other, more frequently used partial verdict option, of finding the defendant guilty of stealing but not privately, was more subtle, but achieved the same result – a sentence which could be either transportation, or imprisonment, a fine, hard labour or other options. Decisions based on this apparent respect for the facts adduced in court might have been attempts at leniency, but might have resulted from consideration of the defendants' specific behaviour when they committed the alleged crime. The jury might also have heard facts that suggested that shoplifting, as defined by law, had not been committed – that the defendant had been suspected before the stealing took place, or had been watched, observed, followed, heard, had used force, had not realised the articles were on his or her person and so on. There was a tendency to be lenient towards the theft of articles positioned temptingly outside shop door-ways, or thefts from shops which asked for trouble, attracting crowds by the offers of sales discounts.[22]

Sometimes the judge, the defendant's counsel or a remorseful prosecutor, would encourage the jury to arrive at a partial verdict. When an eighteen-year-old man, 'troubled with fits and often delirious, very seldom having the right use of his understanding', married and with a young child, stole a printed cotton gown and a pair of muslin ruffles from a second-hand clothes shop in Oxford Street, their combined value was set at 15s. by the prosecutor. When the sad story was told in court, the prosecutor himself asked the jury to under value the items. The jury obliged, stating their worth to be 4s. 10d. The young man was sentenced to two years' hard labour on the Thames navi-

[22] See Walsh, 'Shop design', for descriptions of marketing strategies relying on display and enticement, particularly in the more 'down-market' types of shops in London where the less well-off were customers.

gation.[23] (This case also exemplified a tendency for defendants perceived to have mental health problems to be treated leniently by the court.)[24]

In order to destroy a case for private stealing, cross-examination of prosecution witnesses by defendants' counsel was often aggressive, for instance in trying to show that the theft had been observed. A linen draper's wife fell into the trap when giving evidence against two women for stealing fifteen yards of calico. She said she had suspected them 'by the bulk they seemed to have under their gowns'. She watched them and 'saw them secreting something'. In case the jury might not have heard this or might have missed the meaning, the judge immediately interpolated, 'Gentlemen, the capital part is taken off, it is stealing only.' The jury obliged with 'stealing but not privily' verdicts.[25] Another woman benefited from both types of partial verdict. In the first case against her, for stealing twenty yards of printed cotton valued at 50s., the jury found her guilty of stealing but not privately. In the immediately subsequent case against her, although the eight pairs of worsted stockings she stole from another shop were valued at 12s. by the prosecutor, the jury valued them at 4s. and she was sentenced to be branded on the hand and to spend three months in prison.[26] These two different pictures of partial verdict cases were reproduced endlessly in Old Bailey shoplifting cases, at times in favour of men, at times, women.

Where the jury reached a partial verdict, the judge had a choice of sentence. He could opt, for most of this period, for seven years' transportation or a range of lesser punishments. The sentences for those judged partially guilty at the Old Bailey are given in table 3. Sentences handed down in partial verdicts were fairly equally divided between transportation and some form of custodial sentence, with or without fining or whipping. However, the proportion of women and men in these two categories differed somewhat. The proportion of men sentenced to transportation was 49 per cent and of women, 43 per cent. The type of punishment allocated to women found guilty on a partial verdict was mainly imprisonment. Fifty-two per cent of them were sentenced to prison terms of varying lengths, many to pay a fine as well. Prison sentences were much more likely for women than for men: 41 per cent of men were sentenced in this way. This type of sentencing for women follows patterns observed elsewhere, although the actual figures are different.[27]

23 OBSP, Feb.1781, 108.
24 J. P. Eigen, *Witnessing insanity: madness and mad-doctors in the English court*, New Haven, Conn.–London 1995.
25 OBSP, Oct.1806, 510.
26 OBSP, Apr.1781, 205–6. The record subsequently notes that the sentences in both cases were to be respited.
27 Close comparisons with other studies (for example Beattie, *Crime and the courts*, and King, 'Gender, crime and justice', and *Crime, justice and discretion*) cannot be made. It is apparent in any case that figures for London frequently differ widely from those for non-metropolitan circuits.

Table 3
Sentences in partial verdict shoplifting cases at Old Bailey Sessions in twenty-three sample years between 1780 and 1823

		1780–2	1789–93	1793–5, 1798–9	1800–3	1803–8	1815–18	1820–3	Totals	% of partial verdicts
Partial verdicts	Total	21	64	27	46	92	106	56	412	100%
	Men	5	45	14	19	24	81	22	210	51%
	Women	16	19	13	27	68	25	34	202	49%
Transport-ation	Total	–	39	14	31	45	34	25	188	46%
	Men	–	29	10	14	12	27	10	102	49%
	Women	–	10	4	17	33	7	15	86	43%
Prison*	Total	14	16	12	13	43	66	26	190	46%
	Men	1	9	3	4	10	50	9	86	41%
	Women	13	7	9	9	33	16	17	104	52%
Whip only	Total	2	0	0	0	3	2	1	8	2%
	Men	1	0	0	0	1	2	1	5	2%
	Women	1	0	0	0	2	0	0	3	1%
Other**	Total	4	1	1	1	1	0	3	11	2%
	Men	3	1	1	0	1	0	1	7	3%
	Women	1	0	0	1	0	0	2	4	2%
No record found	Total	1	8	2	1	0	4	0	16	4%
	Men	0	6	2	1	0	2	0	11	5%
	Women	1	2	0	0	0	2	0	5	2%

Sources: OBSP; HO 26/1–29.

* Sentences varied from 1 month to 2 years. Many prison sentences were combined with imposition of a fine (nearly always of 1s). This was the case for 55 of the women given custodial sentences, and for 36 of the men; the imposition of a fine along with a prison sentence became the norm from 1803 onwards. Some prison sentences were combined with a whipping: 8 women and 14 men.

** Punishments recorded as 'other' were, for men, 3 navigation, 1 army, 2 of 1s fine, and 1 free discharge; for women, 1 branding plus 3 months prison, 3 of 1s. fine only.

The study of individual capital crimes – the starting point for the discussion in this book – contributes to understanding the differences in treatment of men and women at all stages of the criminal justice system better than the use of more generalised statistics. This is a particularly useful approach in the case of crime committed in a metropolitan location in which women were highly active. The statistics of crime have a good deal to tell, but it is important to link qualitative details to the bare figures and to look at the behaviour, character and history of the women and men involved, and at the nature of the commission of crime itself. In so doing, clues emerge which can explain the high acquittal rate for women and the greater likelihood of their being given a custodial sentence rather than initially being sentenced to transportation. Without such explanation, it may be necessary to fall back on the somewhat unsatisfactory suggestion that the difference depends only on some expression of paternalistic leniency.[28]

Shoplifting and the death sentence

Since such a large proportion of women seem to have been leniently treated by the court and acquitted of the alleged crime, the equal balance of men and women in the fully guilty category, where the sentence was death, is surprising. It is worth considering possible reasons. Two people only, both men, were, in the end, hanged for shoplifting in this period – exceptions which proved the general rule that, despite death sentences passed by judges, people did not hang for this offence. The unusual end for these two men was probably because they were members of a gang believed to be dangerous and violent, previously implicated in the death of a jeweller. They were therefore not hanged for shoplifting, but for their well-known violence.[29] In many cases in which juries found the facts fully proved they were swayed by issues other than the story told in court – such as previous history, behaviour, age, appearance and demeanour.[30] An experienced jury probably knew that those it found fully guilty, and whom the judge sentenced to death, would not be executed. The dynamics of jury decision-making are difficult to assess. Their decisions had to be unanimous, and were often reached quickly after brief discussion in the courtroom. The need for unanimity and speed worked in favour of the defendant, since it was likely to be more difficult for jurymen who wanted a full guilty verdict to over-ride the determination of those who held out for an acquittal or partial verdict. There is also evidence in the Old Bailey cases of scrupulousness about technical issues, such as the wordings of indictments, which would work in favour of a prisoner.

Another crucial nexus was the one that lay between a sentence of transportation and some other outcome. A full guilty verdict might have been a way for the jury to secure transportation, rather than a custodial or other

---

28 For a particularly useful presentation of the importance of the use of focused quantitative and qualitative evidence in uncovering women's crimes see Walker, *Crime, gender and social order*, passim, esp. pp. 159–89 on theft.

29 John Rabbitts and William Brown were hanged on 5 Feb.1794 (OBSP, Dec.1793, 51–7; HO 26/3). They were part of the gang 'vulgarly known as the Floorers' implicated in an earlier killing. Other official statistics show that the last execution for shoplifting was in 1763 (*Select committee on capital punishment in felonies*, PP, 1819, viii. 25).

30 Such factors are similar to those that influenced decisions in the later process of considering petitions and appeals for pardon or remission of sentence. See King, 'Decision-makers', 40–7, and the development of his arguments in chapter 7 below.

sentence, banking on a later conditional pardon to that effect.[31] The reasoning of judges and juries, as they returned verdicts and passed sentence which they knew would not be carried out, has been seen by some historians as a means to enhance the terror of the law at the same time as underlining the monarch's justice and humanity towards his subjects.[32] However, when their decisions are matched with the circumstances of cases and the personalities involved, their reasons appear a good deal less political and more idiosyncratic.

Some of the motives for the juries' decisions can be deduced from the stories which were told in the cases in which sentence of death was passed. Table 4 suggests factors which may have influenced juries in cases where they reached capital verdicts. One of the factors which strongly affected their decisions was the youth of the offender. This may partly have been a response to growing public concern about youth crime. The jury could be certain that none of these young people would hang, but that there was a strong chance that they would be separated from bad influences, restarting their lives in a new country, or, at worst, spending some time in prison, with the hope of reformation.[33] Some of this group were very young. Amongst the boys, one was nine, one was ten, two were eleven and three were twelve years of age. One of the girls was ten, but there were no others under the age of sixteen. This tends to confirm a gender-based concern about the danger of young male criminals.[34] The jury, in some cases joined by the victim prosecutor, recommended eight of these twenty-six juvenile offenders to mercy because of their 'tender' age. Since a partial verdict could have been returned in any of the cases, had the jury been so minded, the recommendation to mercy seems a deliberate attempt to instil terror,[35] as well as an artifice to send the young person on a stage on the journey through the judicial system which would, in the end, secure their transportation.

Where the jury or prosecutor made a recommendation to mercy, to meet due legal process, they had to give their reasons to the judge. Unfortunately, the reasons were not usually specified in the court reports. Only in one shoplifting case was the reason formally stated. Thomas Hopkins was a young man

---

[31] See chapter 6 below. Although the majority of those sentenced to death for shoplifting received conditional pardons to life or lesser periods of transportation, it was not a standard substitution. Many sentenced to death in the end received short custodial sentences, service in the army or navy and free pardons after a few years in prison or on the hulks.

[32] J. M. Beattie, 'The royal pardon and criminal procedure in early modern England', *Canadian Historical Papers* (1987), 9–22; Hay, 'Property, authority and the criminal law'.

[33] H. Shore, *Artful dodgers: youth and crime in early nineteenth-century London*, Woodbridge 1999, 115–21; P. King and J. Noel, 'The origins of "the problem of juvenile delinquency": the growth of juvenile prosecutions in London in the late eighteenth and early nineteenth centuries', *CJH* xiv (1993), 17–41; King, *Crime, justice and discretion*, 288–96.

[34] H. Shore, 'The trouble with boys: gender and the "invention" of the juvenile offender in early nineteenth-century Britain', in Arnot and Usborne, *Gender and crime*, 75–92.

[35] See Shore, *Artful dodgers*, 119–20, for reports of the lack of success at instilling terror in young offenders under sentence of death.

Table 4
Death sentences for shoplifting at Old Bailey Sessions in twenty-three sample years between 1780 and 1823: possible factors influencing decisions to find fully guilty

Factors	Males	Females
Particularly high value of goods stolen	9 (18%)	2 (3%)
Previous or persistent offences	7 (14%)	7 (11%)
Running away from arrest	0	4 (6%)
Unemployed, very poor, indigent and hopeless cases	6 (12%)	0
Age – young (17 years old or under)	17 (34%)	9 (15%)
Age – 'old' (50 years and over)	4 (8%)	6 (10%)
Behaviour or appearance – suspicious	4 (8%)	7 (11%)
Drunkenness	1 (2%)	3 (5%)
Troublesome, difficult, haggling	0	6 (10%)
Physical violence, swearing	0	2 (3%)
Dubious sexual morals perceived or confirmed	0	4 (6%)
Laughed in victim's face, joked	0	3 (5%)
No factor able to be drawn from account	2 (4%)	9 (15%)
Total	50 (100%)	62 (100%)

Source: OBSP.

(no age given), son of the head butler to the archdeacon of London, unemployed (although he had previously had a job as shopman to an oilman) and living in poor lodgings. He was charged at his trial with high value shoplifting: £18-worth of jewellery. He was robustly represented by counsel, but was sentenced to death. He was given 'an exceeding good character' by several witnesses, and the jury recommended mercy. The Recorder (the Old Bailey judge) required 'the ground of the recommendation'. The foreman replied 'Only as we have not heard of any other offence and as he is so extremely young, and has a reputable father.'[36] Mercy was recommended in court in twenty-six of the total 112 cases where a death sentence was pronounced. In twenty-one cases where reasons can be deduced – apart from the eight on grounds of youth mentioned earlier – two gave reasons of old age, three good character, two a reputable family, five a first offence and one allowed a young man to go to sea as he had, apparently, long desired.

There were some interesting gendered differences in the factors behind the harsh initial sentences passed on these men and women. For men, apart from the significance of youth, those who were unemployed, poor and indigent appear also to have been targets for initial death sentences, and those who had stolen particularly high value goods. For women, the choice of those to stand (for a while) under sentence of death, and thereby to be more likely

36 OBSP, May 1790, 494–8.

to be transported later, was made quite differently. They were mainly women who were seen as troublesome, swearing, drunk, of lax sexual morals – in other words 'unfeminine' women.

Troublesome, difficult, drunk, violent, swearing and provocatively attired and jocular women often offended the jury's sense of propriety. The court shorthand writer also found them of interest. He did not record the same particulars of the men sentenced to death. Elizabeth Hill and Sarah Dancer had behaved in a manner which did not impress the jury. They were charged with stealing eight yards of dimity, a yard and a half of cambric, a yard of muslin, a linen handkerchief and a lace-edged linen cap, to a total value of £2 16s., from a haberdasher's shop in the City Road, kept by a widow. Elizabeth, referred to as Mrs Hill, was a nineteen-year-old 'out of place' servant, and Sarah Dancer was an eighteen-year-old children's pump maker. The shop-keeper did not know she had been robbed until a neighbouring shopkeeper brought the women back to her with some of the stolen property. He told how he and another man had chased them, and how the women had scaled high palings to escape. When they were caught, Hill had sworn 'dreadfully', and 'made a blow' at him, whereas Dancer 'I thought behaved in a very becoming manner; she cried'. Hill was described as 'pretty violent'. The two women were represented by counsel, but Hill provided many interventions of her own – about the shopkeeper's unhelpful service, how seven or eight men had come after them to catch them and how poorly the magistrate and constable had treated her. Both were found fully guilty, and there were no recommendations to mercy.[37]

Another 'troublesome' woman was Mary Palmer, eighteen years old and with a baby. She was charged with stealing two shirts, valued at 20s. The opinionated fourteen-year-old shop assistant was suspicious of her: 'I did not much like her appearance, she looked like a girl of the town.'[38] Perhaps lax sexual behaviour landed Frances Elliott, aged twenty-three, with a death sentence and no recommendation to mercy. She was spotted by a shopowner as she solicited clients in Covent Garden, wearing a fur tippet that she had stolen from his shop the day before. He recognised the hat, not the woman, since his sister had been looking after the shop when it went missing. He expressed interest in her services, made her dismiss the other 'girls' standing around with her and asked her to go with him. This she did happily, until they arrived at the Bow Street police office where she was charged with shop-lifting.[39]

Women with drink problems may have been seen as suitable for the warning of a harsh sentence. Catherine Burn, aged twenty, charged with stealing ten yards of printed cotton, valued at 20s., had been 'troublesome and difficult to suit', demanding from the shopman a running bill total which

37 OBSP, Sept.1795, 1011–18.
38 OBSP, Feb.1799, 182.
39 OBSP, Jan.1802, 105.

he refused, talked a lot and was found with the cotton hanging from under her cloak. She defended herself: 'I was much in liquor, perhaps cotton sticks to flannel, I have been only three weeks in this country.'[40] Another woman sentenced to death, Catherine Forrester, was known as a woman who liked her drink. She came to a chandler's shop for ½d.-worth of beer to drink in the shop. When she left, the chandler's wife missed a cheese valued at 10s., which was soon found under Forrester's long cloak. She excused herself: 'I had a drop in my head – I knew nothing till next morning, when the officer told me of it.'[41]

The large proportion of women sentenced to death is perhaps related to the significant proportion of females on trial at the Old Bailey. Juries may have taken them more seriously as they were well-represented in this crime. The view that female offenders can be seen as less of a threat, and therefore less deserving of harsh punishment, depends on few of them reaching the courts and not having acted with violence or in a threatening way.[42] If those conditions are not fulfilled, it is less likely that their criminal activities will be seen as trivial, unimportant, unthreatening and unpremeditated. Judicial paternalism may not operate to the same extent when women are no longer a minority in court.

Marriage and social status

It was rare for married couples to be charged with shoplifting. There were only two in this period. So the concept of the *feme covert* had virtually no effect in practice. In only one case was reference made to marital status, and consequently to marital coercion by way of defence or excuse. Women were now and then cited as 'wife of', but there was no subsequent interest in this status. William and Mary Kelly had actively considered the effect of their marriage on the outcome of their trial. They were charged with stealing thirty-six cotton handkerchiefs, and three pairs of cotton stockings, together valued at 27s., from a linen draper in St Giles's High Street. The shopman's evidence showed both, 'especially the prisoner's wife', to be engaged in 'tumbling' the goods around and pulling them off the counter. Mary Kelly left the shop first. She was seized by the shopman a few doors down the street, and voluntarily handed over stolen items from under her cloak. William Kelly had been seen lifting the items from the counter and passing them to Mary. Throughout the case, it was taken for granted by witnesses that the two were married. But William Kelly said that he had arrived in London the night before and had met a male friend he had known in Dublin. The next day, as

40 OBSP, Apr.1802, 294.
41 OBSP, Sept.1807, 388.
42 For an expansion of this view see King, *Crime, justice and discretion*, 278–84, and Beattie, *Crime and the courts*, 439.

his friend was showing him the city, 'I saw the prisoner (Mary) at the bar whom I knew in Ireland standing at the door opposite me'. His friend had wanted to buy some handkerchiefs. Mary and William followed him into the shop. He was amazed, he said, to be charged with having something that was not his, since the stolen goods were found on 'the woman'. Mary supported William's story in an oblique way: 'I never asked him to buy me a halfpenny worth of linen, nor handled any thing of his since I was born', but finally agreed that 'He desired me to say I was not his wife to get himself clear of this.' The facts did not support a verdict of private stealing against either of them, for the theft had been seen. The jury convicted William of larceny. He was sentenced to seven years' transportation. Mary they found not guilty. The jury may have accepted that they were married, applied the strict principle of marital coercion and decided that Mary's activity, committed completely in the presence and at the requirement of her husband, amounted to marital coercion. They may have disapproved of William inducing her to lie about their relationship, or perhaps had sympathy for her voluntarily giving up the stolen goods. It may be that Mary Kelly's married status saved her, but the facts of the case do not help us to conclude that any legal principle was in play.[43]

The other case involving a married couple was that of John and Elizabeth O'Neal, and their twenty-six-year-old servant, Eleanor Ray. The O'Neals were found not guilty, Ray was found guilty of stealing, but not privately. Defence counsel was engaged to make sure nothing was brought home to the couple, that the servant took the blame, but that her punishment was lenient. It was not difficult to succeed in this since the shopman said he had seen Ray 'fumbling about her pockets as if she had taken something'. She admitted to taking three yards of muslin, and denied that her mistress had any part in this. It might be thought strange that the O'Neals had been committed by the magistrate for trial at the Old Bailey. The arresting constable said that only Ray had been delivered into his keeping, but 'I did not like to take her into custody without I took the other two likewise.' There were features of the O'Neal's behaviour which suggested that they, particularly Elizabeth, were not innocent. Elizabeth had been 'difficult', rejecting calicos as too coarse, sending the shopowner to the back of the shop to get more to show her, attempting to pay under value for the calico, and leaving the shop when the shopowner declined her offer. John O'Neal attempted to block the shopowner's view of Eleanor Ray's exit from the shop, and, when she was accused of stealing, he went down on his knees to beg that his wife should be let go.[44] The case may be more an example of the importance of relative social status, another factor which may have been in the minds of juries.

---

43 OBSP, Dec.1794, 50–2.
44 OBSP, Apr.1794, 711–12.

The case of Elizabeth Brown shows the court's response to a distressed genteel, elderly female. She was charged with stealing nine lawn handkerchiefs, valued at 18s., from a linen draper in Oxford Street. She was not seen stealing, but the shop assistant thought he saw the lawn under her cloak. She was followed and brought back to the shop. She was recognised as someone who had been 'troublesome in the shop before'. It was unlikely that a full guilty verdict could have been reached, but the sentence could well have been transportation. In fact, she was sentenced only to twelve months in the house of correction with a fine of 1s. She evinced the court's sympathy, telling them she was

> a gentlewoman of Hamburg, and was very much distressed to pay my lodgings; I acknowledge taking the handkerchiefs; I have a very good family, and though I have been in confinement ten weeks, I have not let my friends know all the time.[45] I have been twenty-eight years in England, I kept a house at Mary-le-bone; I am now a widow, have had many friends within that time, but they are dead mostly; since I have been a widow I have been twice abroad with a lady, and since then I have maintained myself by my industry, by sewing.[46]

The social or financial status of defendants had another effect on the outcome of trials. Some were able to pay for defence counsel. This period saw an increasing use of defence counsel, especially in London.[47] A sample of cases between 1789 and 1795 in which defence counsel was engaged, shows that in these six years, 36 per cent of shoplifting cases (forty-six cases) were heard with defence counsel, with women shoplifters twice as likely as the men to resort to this assistance.[48] Twenty-nine women (48 per cent) and seventeen men (24 per cent) had defence counsel.[49] This may suggest that shoplifters, or their friends, were sufficiently well off to be able to afford the lawyers' fees. However, in these early days of the use of defence counsel, many barristers, desperate for work, charged surprisingly low fees for defence repre-

---

[45] See chapter 7 below for female shame at offending, resulting in lack of 'character' in court.

[46] OBSP, July 1794, 860–1.

[47] Beattie, 'Garrow', and 'Scales of justice'; Landsman, 'Contentious spirit'; Langbein, 'Shaping the eighteenth-century criminal trial'. None of the research so far has analysed success rates of counsel. Useful on legal detail and use of defence counsel is Bentley, *English criminal justice*, 97–124.

[48] Cases identified as involving defence counsel are regarded as the minimum potential number. It is difficult to be sure from the printed record that counsel was present: Beattie, 'Scales of justice'. I include only trials where defence counsel was named. I believe this caution is correct, since many trials where there was an exchange of questioning do not bear the hallmark of defence counsel cross-examination. This analysis relates only to shoplifting. See chapter 4 below for defence counsel for pickpocketing.

[49] Bentley, *English criminal justice*, 108, suggests that about a quarter of defendants at the Old Bailey had defence counsel, although he bases this on scrutiny of one month (July 1800) when 25 of the 104 trials involved defence counsel (24%). This accords with Beattie, 'Scales of justice'. On costs of counsel see May, *The Bar and the Old Bailey*, 95–6.

sentation – between one and two guineas, and often much less. Those at the Old Bailey went in for a good deal of touting for business, flouting the usual understandings between barristers, such as the custom that a lawyer should not appear for less than a guinea. If a defendant had suitable and sufficient friends, it might not have been difficult to cover a barrister's fees. They might also appear without fee if they believed a poor person was in danger of facing a capital verdict unrepresented. There were also other means of obtaining charitable assistance with fees.[50]

The use of defence counsel was a reasonably successful strategy, particularly for men. With defence counsel, 41 per cent of women and 23 per cent of men secured not guilty verdicts; whereas the overall not guilty rate (with or without defence counsel) was 29 per cent for women and 9 per cent for men. Where defence counsel was used, the chance of a partial verdict was greatly reduced for both men and women. On the other hand, the chance of the women being found fully guilty of shoplifting with defence counsel (31 per cent) was higher than without (23 per cent). For men, the chance was about the same. It is likely that counsel was engaged in some cases when the situation was already desperate for the defendant. However, the aggressive questioning and behaviour of some counsel may have adversely affected the verdict by offending the jury and the judge. William Garrow, at the start of this period, was a favourite defending counsel. His rudeness and sarcasm towards prosecuting shopowners may have offended their peers on the jury. However, other counsel, notably Knowlys and Knapp, could sometimes outdo Garrow in devastating cross-examination.[51]

Information about the status, social and financial, of those who hired defence counsel is sparse. Most were young, in their late teens and twenties, and the cost was born by parents. Sometimes friends put up money. Amongst those with defence counsel were some who seem unlikely customers for lawyers: a deaf young man; a poor insane old man who frothed at the mouth; and a woman who drank a lot and was described by her counsel as a 'poor woman'. However, the record of events in court shows that shoplifting defendants were often well dressed. It may be that shoplifters were a little above the bread line; a few were regarded as being 'in a respectable sphere of life', particularly some of the women, but this was not generally so.[52]

Table 5 gives information on the ages of those involved in shoplifting offences. In the youngest category – those under the age of twenty-one –

50 Bentley, English criminal justice, 97–124.
51 Note especially OBSP, Dec.1794, 68–72, where, during long, aggressive cross-examination by defence counsel, the shop assistant witness fainted under the strain. Bentley, English criminal justice, 100–1, states that the Old Bailey bar 'had a foul reputation' for the bullying of prosecution witnesses and rudeness to the jury and the Bench. May, The Bar and the Old Bailey, 138, refers to a particularly vituperative encounter in 1816 between counsel, Alley, and Adolphus, law reporter at the Old Bailey, which led to the two men fighting a duel on the beach at Calais.
52 Evidence to Select committee on capital punishment in felonies, PP, 1819, viii. 26–7.

Table 5
Age groups (where known) of men and women convicted of shoplifting at Old Bailey Sessions, in nineteen sample years between 1791 and 1823*

Age	% males	% females	Total % males and females
Up to and including 20 years	51%	32%	43%
21 to 30 years	28%	35%	31%
31 to 40 years	11%	20%	15%
41 to 50 years	5%	5%	5%
51 to 60 years	4%	6%	5%
Over 60 years	1%	1%	1%

Source: HO 26/1–33.
* Information recorded only since 1791.

males predominated (51 per cent of males prosecuted for shoplifting were in this age group). However, in the age groups twenty-one to thirty years and thirty-one to forty years, the proportion of women well exceeded that of men. This provides an indication of the link between female property crime and poverty in the lives of women which has been noted elsewhere. It indicates the varying needs of the female life-cycle – with family responsibilities combined with the difficulty of obtaining and maintaining paid employment, with their urgent need to make ends meet extending to a later stage in their lives than for men. Women, whether single or married, experienced the greatest economic stresses in trying to provide for their dependants in their thirties and early forties.[53]

Gendered shoplifting behaviour

The stories told in court showed significant differences in male and female shoplifting behaviour. Juries and judges were not comparing like with like when they listened to the stories, although the charge was the same. The difference in behaviour was not as distinctive as in pickpocketing cases, considered in the next chapter; nevertheless, it was considerable.

Examination of what was stolen and where it was stolen shows that women were well placed to steal from shops. The preponderance of stolen items were textile materials in their unmade-up state (cotton, calico, silk and lace) or small made-up items for sale in the same type of shop, such as gloves and stockings. They were stolen from mercers, linen drapers, haberdashers,

[53] King, 'Female offenders'.

hosiers and milliners, where most of the customers were female, and were expected to be female.[54] However, there were no hard and fast boundaries between male and female choices of goods. Men sometimes stole textile materials, and small items of clothing. Women occasionally chose other items – pencils, leather, a looking glass, a parasol. Now and then both chose cheeses and hams, although some of these items were large and heavy, a deterrent to women. More frequently both stole shoes, coats, cloaks and shirts, although in the years following the end of the Napoleonic wars, this was predominantly a male area of activity, with the theft of shoes reaching a peak. Where men's shoplifting of higher value items differed significantly from women's was in their choice of jewellery, watches and clocks, a variety of hardware, with a slight interest in larger items such as carpets.

The motivation behind the thefts was likely to have been varied. Where the information was given, we know that a substantial amount ended up in the hands of pawnbrokers, who were both the credit system and the wearing apparel 'middlemen' for a great part of the population.[55] One woman on two occasions stole to add to the stock in her own shop.[56] In some cases, thieves were seen somewhat brazenly wearing stolen clothing and headgear about town close to the scene of the crime. There is evidence that the theft of textiles was not generally indulged in to gratify a universal longing to dress-make, nor even to obtain raw material for paid work in the clothing or accessory trades. In one unusual case, however, twenty-one yards of cotton were traced to a woman's lodgings and were found converted into a dozen or so little girls' frocks, some completely sewn up and some cut out ready to sew.[57]

Table 6 shows the types of items stolen. The information given bears out the view that the world of stolen clothes and textiles was a woman's world, in which the type of goods taken were those of which they had knowledge and a means of disposal. Their thefts of un-made-up textiles and of small made-up textile items were far in excess of men's thefts in these categories – as much as 86 per cent of women's shoplifting theft took this form, against 49 per cent of men's thefts. Historians of crime have suggested that such theft bore the hallmark of 'less terrifying' petty crime, which led to more lenient treatment.[58]

---

[54] The figures here are similar to Walker, 'Women, theft and stolen goods', 87–97, and *Crime, gender and social order*, 162–5. Her study is earlier (alternate years in the 1590s, 1620s, 1650s and 1660s) in Cheshire, but her figures together with mine confirm a predictable continuity. In cases between 1780 and 1823 not included in the sample which has been analysed in detail in this study, the same pattern of theft holds true.

[55] B. Lemire, 'Peddling fashion: salesmen, pawnbrokers, taylors, thieves and the second-hand clothes trade in England c. 1700–1800', *Textile History* xxii (1991), 67–82, and *Dress, culture and commerce: the English clothing trade before the factory, 1660–1800*, London 1997; Ginsberg, 'Rags to riches'.

[56] OBSP, Oct.1795, 1338–41, 1343–5.

[57] OBSP, May 1822, 359.

[58] See, for instance, Walker, 'Women, theft and stolen goods ', 88–9.

Table 6
Items stolen: shoplifting cases tried at Old Bailey Sessions in twenty-three sample years between 1780 and 1823

Type of item stolen	Females	% all females	Males	% all males
Unmade up textiles: lawn, linen, cotton, silk, calico, printed cotton, gingham, baize, net, lace, satin ribbon, muslin, tiffany: in any amount from 1 yard to a maximum of 180 yards.	237	64%	95	31%
Made-up haberdashery and millinery: bonnets, tippets, cap, hats, stockings, gloves, handkerchiefs, shawls, ruffles	78	22%	56	18%
Clothing (new and second hand): including shoes, jackets, waistcoats, shirts and boots, coats and cloaks	29	8%	71	22%
Jewellery and precious objects: rings, brooches, pins, watches, clocks, silver-plated objects	8	2%	27	9%
Food: cheese, ham, bacon, raisins, beef	5	1%	21	7%
Other items: pencils, leather soles, looking glasses, umbrellas, ink bottles, hardware items, carpets, cases, shop till, tobacco, starch, milk jugs, cutlery, books, etc.	12	3%	41	13%
Totals	369	100%	311	100%

Source: OBSP.

However, it was an important crime. These goods had a high market value, and, after food, were the main items of household expenditure,[59] and, if stolen privately, could have serious consequences for the offender. If the courts viewed the theft of textile materials as a 'less terrifying' crime, and, because of this, treated women more leniently, then here is an example of gendered decision-making in practice. Criminal activities were being seen through the filter of male perceptions of what mattered, what was important, what threatened society and commerce. Such perceptions would go a long way towards explaining the different trial outcomes for men and women at this stage of the criminal justice system.

A further factor which might have affected the sentencing of men and women was the value of the goods they stole. This is shown in table 7. It will be seen that the values are not polarised between men and women. Most thefts were valued in indictments between 10s.1d. and £2. Men featured

[59] Weatherill, 'Consumer behaviour', 298.

Table 7
Value (specified in indictment) of items stolen in shoplifting cases at Old Bailey Sessions in twenty-three sample years between 1780 and 1823

	Totals	10s. and under		10s.1d to £2		£2 0s.1d. to £5		Over £5	
		M	F	M	F	M	F	M	F
1780–2	Male 14	1 7%	9 18%	7 50%	24 49%	1 7%	15 31%	5 36%	1 2%
	Female 49								
1789–93	Male 56	15 27%	12 32%	23 41%	17 46%	14 25%	6 16%	4 7%	2 5%
	Female 37								
1793–5, 1798–9	Male 23	3 13%	7 20%	10 43%	20 57%	4 17%	5 14%	6 26%	3 9%
	Female 35								
1800–3	Male 36	11 31%	6 15%	21 58%	25 62%	4 11%	9 23%	0 –	0 –
	Female 40								
1803–8	Male 34	10 29%	18 16%	17 50%	69 61%	5 15%	23 20%	2 6%	3 3%
	Female 113								
1815–18	Male 118	41 35%	9 18%	60 51%	36 72%	14 12%	3 6%	3 2%	2 4%
	Female 50								
1820–3	Male 30	10 33%	18 40%	17 57%	22 49%	1 3%	4 9%	2 7%	1 2%
	Female 45								
Totals 680	Male 311	91 29% all men	79 21% all women	155 50% all men	213 58% all women	43 14% all men	65 18% all women	22 7% all men	12 3% all women
	Female 369								

Source: OBSP.

proportionately more at either extreme of the value spectrum, whilst women featured proportionately strongly in the theft of goods in the more average value range.[60] This emphasises that there is no reason to assume that women generally stole goods of less value. In shoplifting indictments, prosecutors had little reason to undervalue goods: they often stressed how valuable they were as a way of showing how much this crime hurt them.[61]

Among the men who stole in the most valuable range, half stole jewellery and watches valued at between £13 and £67. The remainder stole carpets, shawls and large amounts of textiles valued between seven guineas and £20. Of the twelve women stealing in the highest value category, ten stole textiles, large amounts, valued between £6 and £20. One stole sixty pairs of shoes (over a long and undetected period), and one stole a ring worth £30. Most of the men stealing in the highest value category were initially sentenced to death, but few of the women. This suggests that theft of high value articles, especially of jewellery, was seen as a 'threatening', serious crime. It may have been seen as serious because men did it, and this behaviour needed to be controlled. When women stole in the same high value category, this may have been seen merely as an aberration, causing little concern, and perhaps some compassion.

The evidence presented at the trials highlighted another area of difference between the activities of males and females, which is at least as significant as the types and value of the items they stole. This was the way in which they concealed the activity of stealing, an important part of their *modus operandi*. This had much to do with the way males and females dressed when about town, and bore relation to what they stole, or were able to steal. Female clothing played a crucial role. Witnesses for the prosecution gave details of how this was done in 192 female cases, and in 145 of men's cases. Table 8 gives details of methods of concealment of stolen goods in these cases. Women's clothing provided a useful means of effecting a specific type of theft, whereas men operated in a more *ad hoc* manner, and none too discreetly in some cases. The use of the cloak in female shoplifting was an outstanding feature. Shopowners and their assistants were highly aware and suspicious of women in cloaks. Questions from counsel and judges often sought to establish whether a woman was wearing a cloak. Asked what sort of cloak a woman was wearing, whether it was long or short, a linen draper's brother described it as grey, 'such as women commonly wear'.[62] Confronted by two women in long red cloaks, a hosier immediately thought them 'strange'.[63]

---

[60] This correlates with Walker, 'Women, theft and stolen goods', 86, table 4.2, and *Crime, gender and social order*, 161, table 5.1, where men and women are distributed in the same proportions in the scales of value of goods stolen.

[61] See Beattie, *Crime and the courts*, 181–4, for reasons for undervaluing goods in various types of larceny cases.

[62] OBSP, Dec.1798, 47.

[63] OBSP, Jan.1799, 82.

Table 8
Methods of concealing movement of stolen items in shoplifting cases
tried at Old Bailey Sessions in twenty-three sample years
between 1780 and 1823

Method	Females	% female cases described	Males	% male cases described
In clothing: Cloaks	60	31%	0	–
Petticoats, skirts, gowns, shawl	58	30%	1*	0.5%
Under coat, waistcoat, shirt	4	2%	31	21%
In or under apron	22	12%	14	10%
In loose or fitted pocket	13	7%	12	8%
In muff or glove, up cuff	6	3%	2	1%
Down bosom, up stays	7	4%	0	–
In hat	0	–	8	5%
In breeches	0	–	5	4%
Otherwise: In hand	7	4%	9	6%
Under or in arm	12	6%	33	23%
Under sack or wrapper	0	–	3	2%
In bag, basket, pillow case	2	1%	5	4%
Worn on body	0	–	5	4%
Carried on shoulder, over arm	0	–	14	10%
Drawn on a string, on stick	0	–	2	1%
Taken as delivery agent	1	0.5%	1	0.5%
Total	192	100%	145	100%

* This man wore a long country smock.
Source: OBSP.

Red cloaks were particularly suspicious.[64] In 1808 Maria Smith was charged with stealing eleven shawls from a linen draper in Ludgate Hill. The jury was antagonistic towards the shopkeeper. His was 'the shop to which so many people are thronging to purchase goods', needing nine shop assistants to deal with the fifty or sixty people in the shop, 600 in the course of a day. How

[64] Red cloaks were seen as an old-fashioned mark of poverty by Pastor Moritz in *Travels in England*, quoted in R. Bayne-Powell, *Travellers in eighteenth-century England*, 1st edn, London 1951, 84. J. Tozer and S. Levitt, *Fabric of society: a century of people and their clothes, 1770–1870: essays inspired by the collections at Platt Hall, the Gallery of English Costume, Manchester*, Manchester 1983, show red cloaks as country women's dress, out of fashion in town by the second decade of the nineteenth century, worn only by the elderly. There is no suggestion that a red cloak marked out a prostitute, although the link between poverty, life-cycle distress and prostitution might indicate such a link.

could he suspect any particular person of shoplifting? The shopkeeper knew how he could – she wore a red cloak and a straw hat. The jury asked if he thought people in red cloaks excited suspicion. He said red cloaks and straw hats were fashionable,[65] and they certainly excited his suspicion. The jury dismissed his prejudices. He should have more reason to suspect a woman in a genteel dress, they said, rather than this flamboyant woman. She was found not guilty.[66] A poor, old woman indicted for stealing twenty-one yards of printed calico, wore two cloaks:

> She stooped to pick up (a half-penny) and I observed she was longer than nec-
> essary in that posture; when she arose from stooping I observed a kind of bulk
> under her cloak, that I had not observed before; she had two cloaks on, and
> she appeared very much in liquor . . . I told her that I thought she had taken
> away with her more than her own; she threw back her cloak immediately . . .
> she seemed very ready to be searched; she had got two cloaks on, a black one
> and a red one.[67]

Witnesses recalled items being put under cloaks, cloaks being lifted or flung aside to reveal stolen goods, cloaks rustling suspiciously, bulging shapes under cloaks, cloaks of women tangling together, and a cloak which a woman kept passing over her face ostensibly to smother her cough. A picture is presented of a female world of flowing clothes, rustling skirts and a confused dance of concealing movements, adjustments of dress, shufflings, waddlings and materialisation of swathes of textiles from secret places under women's clothing, some warm from where they had been hidden. The case against Catherine Drew and Catherine Carney gives a vivid example of this sort of scene. The two women were charged with shoplifting as much as fifty-four yards of printed calico from a linen draper in Holborn. They had come to the shop on two consecutive days to buy calico. On neither occasion did they have sufficient money to pay for the piece which had been cut for them. On the second day, the shopman had observed Drew

> stoop down in pretence of tying up her stockings. I perceived her making a
> great bustle in tying up her stockings, which excited my notice, when she
> arose up, she took both her hands, pretending to draw up her petticoat . . . I
> perceived the sides of her waist to have increased very much, nearly double to
> what it was before, which induced me to go round the counter immediately;
> her eyes were fixed on me; her sides decreased and I picked up that piece from
> beneath her petticoats near the counter; I accused her of having taken it, and
> she denied it.

While this bustle was going on, the other woman was moving out of the shop door with the large amount of printed calico under her arm.[68]

---

65 A contrary view of fashion: see previous note.
66 OBSP, Feb.1808, 182.
67 OBSP, July 1795, 956–9.
68 OBSP, Sept.1804, 416.

Women's dress was of interest in other ways. Jane Norton, indicted for stealing thirteen yards of black silk lace from a haberdasher at Holborn Bridge, was described by prosecution witnesses as not being short of money, and 'dressed in a very decent manner; and being an old woman, one could not suspect her'.[69] A decently dressed woman was certainly not above suspicion, perhaps to the contrary. Charlotte Power, a fine dresser, was indicted for stealing a pair of silk stockings from an Oxford Street hosier. Her long-tailed white muslin gown and her smart parasol were her undoing, raising the shopman's suspicions. The court, on the other hand, was impressed with her, calling her a 'lady', an unusual form of address for a female prisoner. They sympathised with her difficulties in handling her 'train' in which she was accused of secreting the stockings. When the stockings were found in her dress, she had seemed confused. 'I should think so too', responded the jurymen. Power explained that she wore the same gown to court – to show them that 'it is a nice dress, I held it up a great deal'. The stockings she had desired, she said, 'I wanted them as good as I could get them and as rich.' Finally, dissatisfied with what she had been offered, she had swept her train off the counter, taken her parasol and bade the shopman good-day. Her astonishment at being accused of shoplifting seemed sincere to the jury, who found her not guilty.[70] In the trial of Frances Nowland, her counsel made a feature of finding out how she was dressed at the time of her shoplifting offence. 'Not as she is now', was the reply. She had turned up to court less well dressed. Her co-defendant, Ann McDougal, turned out in the good clothes Nowland had worn on the day she went to the shop.[71] Dress, as well as appearance was important for the female shoplifter and to the court.

Men and women working together

Most men and most women shoplifted on their own, or were charged with the offence as individuals. When thieving was carried out in a group, women were more likely to work with other women than to work with men. During the years in the sample period, 150 women (40 per cent of all female shoplifting defendants) and 73 men, (24 per cent of all male shoplifting defendants) were charged in same sex groups.[72] The more common tendency of women to shoplift in twos and threes might have contributed to their lower

---

[69] OBSP, Sept.1790, 719–21.

[70] OBSP, Sept.1805, 543.

[71] OBSP, Dec.1816, 22.

[72] The tendency of women to associate in crime has sometimes been seen as reflecting female dependency on male agency. For instance, Beattie, 'Criminality of women', 92, suggests this, without statistical evidence. The evidence in this chapter shows that female association is with other females. See also Walker, 'Women, theft and stolen goods', 83–6 and fig. 4.1, and *Crime, gender and social order*, 170–6.

overall conviction rate. A jury might have been content to apportion blame to one of the pair or three whom they could regard as the ringleader, finding the others not guilty. This happened in twelve of the sixty-seven female groups. One (or more) of the group was found not guilty, the other(s) fully or partially guilty. This split occurred in only four of the thirty-three male groups accounting for a much smaller overall number of male acquittals. The numbers are small, but they indicate the need to look in detail at small differences in order to explain larger differences in the judicial treatment of men and women. Over the whole of the sample period, there were only twenty-two instances of indictments of mixed-sex groups or pairs. Where verdicts were split – not guilty and guilty – the decision could go either way, in favour of male or female.

Gendered behaviour, gendered leniency

This examination of the details, both quantitative and qualitative, of shop-lifting trials at the Old Bailey, provides clear pointers to reasons behind judi-cial decision-making, and strong clues as to why men and women might have been treated differently by the justice system. These pointers and clues are developed and refined in the following two chapters which deal with other categories of property crime. Women were highly visible in the shoplifting category, constituting over 50 per cent of those charged with this crime at the Old Bailey between 1780 and 1823. This fact in itself is important, since women are so often believed to be little implicated in felonies.

Juries and judges did not have a uniform response to the men and women appearing before them. Women, as a category, were not the recipients of lenient judgements. Some women were; indeed, many more women than men. Men and women were equally found fully guilty of this offence and, at this stage, equally sentenced to death. Where partial verdicts were reached, women were, at the conclusion of their trials, more likely to receive custodial sentences, while men were more likely to be sentenced to seven years' trans-portation. However, the most obvious manifestation of judicial leniency towards women lies in the much greater proportion of women found not guilty and acquitted – 29 per cent of females compared with 16 per cent of men. It is not by any means easy to discover why juries exercised this discre-tion in favour of females. The evidence presented in this chapter does not bear out stereotypical views about 'feminine' behaviour – for instance, the suggestions that women are less brave, more dependent, less criminally inclined, or behave less threateningly are not supported. To the contrary, many of the women tried for shoplifting were seen by the jury to be auda-cious, independent, serial thieves, stealing items of high value.

Where fully guilty verdicts were returned, where no leniency was exer-cised towards females, examination of the stories told in court suggests that decisions were prompted by reactions which differed according to the gender of the offender. The men who faced the death penalty at this stage were likely to be young (sometimes very young), unemployed, poor and indigent, suggesting that the middling and trading sort who made up the Old Bailey juries feared this sector of the plebeian, urban population. The other significant group of males sentenced to death were those who stole particularly high value goods, especially jewellery, and whose behaviour was seen as a particular danger. The selection of women found fully guilty was of a different order. The stories drawn out in court show them to have been 'troublesome', loud, swearing, fighting, drunk, resisting arrest, of lax sexual morals. They too were part of the poor, urban, rabble, 'unfeminine' in behaviour and needing to be treated severely, or at least given an effectively stern warning. Decisions at the Old Bailey were strongly affected by the gendered understandings and expectations of the jury.

Acquaintance with these shoplifting cases shows that women's and men's experiences of shoplifting activities were significantly gendered – in their method of working, and in the type and value of goods stolen. Women mainly stole textiles and clothing, which may have been seen by the court as crimes of necessity, and a minor threat to the security of society, despite the fact that, after food, clothing was the most important staple of daily life, of considerable value. Women did not steal mainly in the least valuable category; that was the arena for poor men's opportunistic thefts. They did not, however, steal in the most valuable category. Most men stole different items from women. They also stole textiles and clothing, but often hardware items, money and jewellery. High value money and jewellery thefts were seen as serious. Expected, and feared, male behaviour defined the criminal norm, and the seriousness with which the crime was viewed.

The details of shoplifting activity provide evidence of a significant diversity in the way men and women operated. We see the subtle use of female clothing for secreting stolen items, the crucial role of the cloak and the frequent location of the offence in shops in which women were 'at home', the expected customers, often working in small groups. Men could be subtle too, but their more open, sometimes brazen, methods of stealing, a more 'snatch and grab' approach, is distinctive and different from female shoplifting. These distinctions, put together with similar and contrasting evidence from the crimes observed in the next two chapters, show that a highly gendered environment existed for judicial decision-making, created by the very behaviour of the men and women charged with crime.

4

Pickpocketing

I opened my door: there is no lock: and there I saw this man lying asleep on the bed; I waked him, and asked what brought him there; he said eh! eh! who brought me here! a woman in the dark.[1]

This chapter deals with the crime known as pickpocketing or the act of 'stealing privily from the person', and the men and women charged with this offence at the Old Bailey Sessions between 1780 and 1808. Until 1808 pickpocketing was a capital crime. Its tight legal definition, and its specialised and intricate nature, made successful prosecution even more difficult than in shoplifting cases. The cases which reached trial at the Old Bailey in the period examined were a mere fourteen a year. These trials, in seventeen sample years between 1780 and 1808, have received detailed examination, together with the results of the prosecutions and the sentences passed. (See appendix for the selected years). Close attention has been paid to evidence about the ways in which the accused men and women stole – where and when they did so, and who they were – in order to establish whether differences in life-style and *modus operandi* affected the verdicts and sentences.

During the whole of the period 1780 to 1808, the proportion of women indicted for this offence in London and Middlesex significantly exceeded that of men. Of a total of 400 people appearing before the petty jury charged with stealing privily from the person, 53 per cent were females. However, it was a very different crime from shoplifting, both in its history and in the wide variation of situations in which it was committed. In particular, the divide between the sexes in their ways of committing the crime was deep. Offences which appeared superficially the same before the law were in fact markedly different, and the difference was based on profoundly gendered behaviour. This division can be clearly seen in the following two accounts offered to the Old Bailey court which are typical of the ways in which men and women operated to carry out this particular crime.

Mary Hughes, a forty-year-old Londoner, appeared at the Old Bailey in October 1791 charged with stealing privily a silver watch valued at 40s., a steel chain and a seal, said to be worth 1s., a half-crown piece and 6d., from the person of a labourer, James Mann. On the night of Saturday 20 September, between 9 and 10 o'clock, Mann said he was walking from

---

1 Part of the defence of Charlotte Walker, charged with pickpocketing at the Old Bailey: OBSP, Sept.1790, 748–9.

Dartmouth Street a short distance to St James's Park. In the park, he met four or five women, one of whom was Hughes, loitering in the company of a soldier. According to Mann, she asked him to 'go along with her', an offer he said he steadfastly refused – since he was a married man. Undeterred, Hughes proceeded to unbutton his breeches, saying she wanted him 'to be connected with her'. Mann, sounding like a defenceless victim, stated that 'During this time she took my property; she was with me about ten minutes. She had hold of me, I tried to get away, I gave her civil words and said I was married. I am sure she is the woman, I saw her the next morning. I was very sober, it was star light.' Hughes had little to say in her defence after two other prosecution witnesses explained how they had retrieved and returned the watch which was in the possession of her women friends. She merely stated, 'I never saw the gentleman till that morning, he said I will not hurt you.' The jury decided that Hughes was indeed guilty of stealing a valuable object from Mann, but that she had not stolen 'privily from his person'. The judge sentenced her to be transported for seven years to New South Wales.[2] Not all cases against women as pickpockets fitted this pattern, but it was a scenario so frequently presented as to provide ample reason for the apparently lenient decisions and gender divergent attitudes towards these women on the part of Old Bailey juries.

By way of contrast, when George Wakeman was tried in March 1790 for stealing privily from the person of Allen Wall a silver watch worth 40s., and two stone seals set in gold, also worth 40s., the details of the case show the distinctive features which often marked pickpocketing by men. The theft occurred at four o'clock in the afternoon on 18 January 1790 in a very crowded St James's Street, where people had gathered to watch Queen Charlotte's birthday procession. Allen Wall was on his way to meet fellow tradesmen for dinner at the Thatched House tavern in St James's Street. Here in the crowd, he felt his watch being taken from his pocket and saw Wakeman beside him, passing the watch to other men nearby. Wakeman, a hairdresser, explained that his sole purpose for being in the crowd that day was to study 'the present fashions' in hairstyle, a usual and necessary thing for a hairdresser to do. He was amazed to be accused of pickpocketing. It was, he said, a case of mistaken identity. The jury found him not guilty of stealing privily, but guilty of theft for which he also was sentenced to seven years' transportation to New South Wales.[3] The pattern of this story fits well with the salient features of cases involving male pickpockets – incidents in broad daylight, and in crowded and public places.

2 OBSP, Oct.1791, 576–7.
3 OBSP, Mar.1790, 390–2.

The capital crime of pickpocketing

Pickpocketing – larceny 'clam et secrete' from the person – became a capital offence in 1565.[4] It was the act of 'feloniously taking any money, goods or chattels, from the person of any other, privily, without his knowledge, in any place whatsoever'. From early practice, the stolen item had to be worth more than 12*d.* in order for the accused to be deprived of benefit of clergy (that is, liable to a death sentence). Lesser amounts stolen 'clam et secrete' were categorised as petty larceny. The preamble to the 1565 act clarified the activity which the law drafters wanted to deter and to punish by death. The language used is that of a section of society outraged by the audacity and impropriety of 'cut-purses or pick-purses'. Thus

> certain kind of evil-disposed person . . . do confeder together, making among themselves as it were a brotherhood or fraternity of an art or mystery, to live idly by the secret spoil of the good and true subjects of this realm. (This they did) at time of service or common prayer, in churches, chapels, closets and oratories . . . also in the Prince's palace, house, yea and presence, and at the places and courts of justice . . . and in fairs and markets, and other assemblies of the people, and . . . at . . . (the) execution of such as been attainted of any murder, felony or other criminal cause, ordained chiefly for the terror and example of evildoers . . . without respect or regard of any time, place or person, or any fear or dread of God . . . under the cloak of honesty of their outward appearance, countenance and behaviour, subtilly, privily, craftily . . . to the utter undoing and impoverishing of many.[5]

Whether this hyperbole was justified by reality, either in the sixteenth or in the eighteenth centuries, is uncertain. However, the image which provoked horror and shock was of gangs of thieves, one man stealing and handing the stolen item on to accomplices in places where the public gathered, much like the case involving George Wakeman. The statute provided the death penalty only for the individual whose hand took the item, not for those who aided and abetted. Eighteenth-century case law built on this distinction; for example: 'it depends almost generally upon a nice species of dexterity which does not require the assistance of a second person to perform'.[6] (This meant that, if two people were indicted together, and there was not clear proof as to which one made the final act of taking, neither should be found guilty.) The apparent mismatch between the intention and words of the statute was a cause of some of the technical difficulties which judges and juries experienced in dealing with this crime. Its intention was directed at activities

---

4 8 Eliz. c.4, s.2 (1565).
5 8 Eliz. c.4, preamble: D. Pickering, *The statutes at large from the 2nd to 31st year of Elizabeth*, vi, Cambridge 1764.
6 See, for instance, R *v* Murphy 1783 quoted in L. Radzinowicz, *A history of English criminal law and its administration from 1750*, I: *The movement for reform*, London 1948, appendix 1 at p. 661; Hawkins, *Treatise*, i. 253–4.

almost entirely, but not exclusively, carried out by men, not women. In practice, women in London and Middlesex were more often caught by it than men, and for activities which did not seem to have been in the minds of the lawmakers.

The statute also stipulated that the theft must be effected without the victim's knowledge. This was hard to demonstrate. Failure to do so led to many unsuccessful prosecutions, when the victim had to admit that he had some idea of what was going on in an encounter in which he was deprived of possessions. Gradually, through practice and precedent, by the last quarter of the eighteenth century, criteria were established requiring that there should be no knowledge on the victim's part that a theft was happening. The statute was 'intended to suppress a certain species of dexterity, against the success of which the common vigilance of mankind was found not to be an adequate safeguard and protection, and therefore if the larceny is in the slightest degree detected at the time it is committing, the offender is not within the penalty of the act'.[7]

The circumscriptions went further. An Old Bailey case of 1782 established precedent on the words 'without his knowledge', extending it to cover situations where the victim was intoxicated. The judge said that 'the statute was made to protect that property which persons awake can secure'.[8] This simple statement was elaborated in case-law:

> The act was intended to protect the property which persons by proper vigilance and caution should not be able to secure; but that it did not extend to persons who by intoxication had exposed themselves to the dangers of depredation, by destroying those faculties of the mind by the exertion of which the larceny might probably be prevented.[9]

This principle explains why judgements went so frequently in favour of female defendants and against their male victims. If the victim of a pickpocket had removed or opened items of his clothing, an offence of private stealing would be difficult to sustain. If the victim was drunk, the restrictions about 'proper vigilance and caution' made the case equally difficult to prove. There were many instances where pickpocketing law was used to penalise plebeian men's behaviour, their drunkenness and, hypocritically perhaps, their resort to prostitutes. There might even be a sense in which men as victims were in 'double-jeopardy', while the behaviour of female pickpockets was seen as unthreatening.

Another constraint related to the place in which the crime occurred. Two women had emptied the pockets of a coachman asleep in his carriage as he waited for a fare at the door of a brothel. Their action did not wake him. The court ruled that it was not the intention of the statute to find this sort of act

---

[7] Hawkins, *Treatise*, i. 255; East, *Pleas*, ii. 706.
[8] OBSP, Feb.1782, 230–1.
[9] Radzinowicz, *History of English criminal law*, i, appendix 2 at p. 663

worthy of capital punishment since it was 'evident from the preamble of the statute, that it was intended only for the protection of persons in public meetings, and places of proper resort'.[10] The statute did indeed have such an intention, but if the principle had been followed, few cases would ever have been proved against a woman. Margaret Kennedy's trial in 1797 established that the privily stealing law was not infringed where a drunken prosecutor, picked up by a woman of the town, having fallen asleep in the house they had gone to, was relieved without his knowledge of two guineas. 'There having been no fraud used by the prisoner in making the prosecutor drunk, but he having fallen into that state by his own default; and that it was all to be taken as one transaction.'[11] This established a precedent that could influence judgements about thefts which took place in women's rooms and lodgings. Sometimes it did and sometimes it did not.

It is even more difficult than in shoplifting cases to understand why victims prosecuted these thefts under a capital statute, rather than as petty larceny. However, meticulous consideration of pre-trial procedures for property offences in the eighteenth and early nineteenth century provides copious information about why victims failed to pursue the crime and its perpetrator to court.[12] The reasons for such failure are many and apparent. In the case of theft privily from the person, the reasons might include personal embarrassment arising from the situation in which the victim had found himself at the time of the theft, or he might have considered it a trivial event. Frequently there was reluctance to afford the time, travel and loss of work and money that would be required to follow through prosecution on indictment. Further, the specific offence was difficult to prove in court. The victim might have felt sufficiently satisfied if the thief had been held in the watch-house or prison for a while awaiting a hearing before the magistrates, or if customary informal 'justice' had been wrought on the wrongdoer.

However, the reasons for preferring a capital charge are elusive. The various safeguards in the pre-trial process should have reduced the likelihood of such charges being made and sustained up to the trial before a petty jury. Prosecutors could be consulted at an advanced stage in the process when indictments were being drawn up by the court clerks for presentation to the grand jury. They could decide whether to prefer a capital charge of pickpocketing or a non-capital charge of petty larceny and indicate this by the way they described the event, and the value they placed on the stolen goods. It was generally held that, at this time, victims of minor property offences took advantage of ways of avoiding a route that could lead to capital punishment.[13] Mistakes and misunderstandings about the wordings of an

---

10 Ibid. i, appendix 2, n. a) at p. 663.
11 Case decided before the twelve judges (1797), quoted in East, *Pleas*, ii. 706.
12 Beattie, *Crime and the courts*, 35–50, 268–81, 283–8, 333–5; King, *Crime, justice and discretion*, 11–46, 82–117.
13 Beattie, *Crime and the courts*, 333–5.

indictment might occur, but it seems likely that those who insisted on bringing a capital charge intended to do so, and that their reasons were personal and reflected their views on society, law and order. Peter King notes that 'with pre-trial processes there is more darkness than light; more silences than explanations; more anecdotal evidence than systematic data'.[14]

Even anecdotal evidence is thin. In only one of the pickpocketing cases in this period was there a recorded exchange between parties in the courtroom about the reason a capital charge was brought. The shock and outrage of a victim, John Marshall, a surgeon from Bloomsbury, mirrored the sentiments of the preamble to the pickpocketing statute. John Scape, a twenty-one year-old, picked the surgeon's pocket of a silk handkerchief as he walked down Chancery Lane at six o'clock on a sunny July evening. Marshall said that he had been 'wholly unconscious' of the theft until told by other people in the street. Although Scape had knelt before him to beg forgiveness, he 'could not think of doing that, in consequence of his robbing me at that time of day'. Another witness heard Marshall say, 'it was such a daring thing that he could not think of (forgiving) it'. The jury appeared to share the victim's sense of outrage and found Scape fully guilty. When he was sentenced to death, no recommendation to mercy was made.[15]

Pickpocketing trials, verdicts and sentences

It is reasonable to suppose that pickpocketing was a common crime, far more common than prosecutions suggest. Newspaper articles reported such thefts at public gatherings, fairs, playhouses and processions. The *Gentleman's Magazine* warned of 'expert genteelly-dressed men and women' who went to such public occasions to plunder watches, purses and pocket books.[16] Rarely did one of those 'genteelly dressed' women reach court, and few of the men either. During the seventeen years analysed, an annual average of only about thirteen cases of pickpocketing were brought before the petty jury at the Old Bailey Sessions, less than half the annual average number of shoplifting cases. No doubt the difficulty of proving the facts of the charges because of the circumstances, often embarrassing, in which many of the thefts had occurred, was deterrent enough to the victim. This, combined with the nature of the law, and the generally low value of goods stolen, was a further deterrent. A charge of simple larceny could bring punishment enough.[17] Small as the

---

14 King, *Crime, justice and discretion*, 46.
15 OBSP, Feb.1805, 491.
16 *The Gentleman's Magazine and Historical Chronicle* lxv/ii (1795), 657.
17 Simple larceny (whether grand larceny, where the item stolen was worth more than 1*s.*, or petty larceny for goods of lesser value) encompassed a group of 'clergyable', i.e. non-capital, offences, and these were by far the greatest majority of property offences tried on indictment, certainly in the London metropolitan area: Beattie, *Crime and the courts*, 181–5 and tables 4.1,4.7.

Table 9
Pickpocketing trials at Old Bailey Sessions in seventeen sample years between 1780 and 1808

Years of war or peace	Years	Total	Average/ year	Females (average/ year)	Females as % of total	Males (average/ year)	Males as % of total
War (2 years)	1780–2	37	18.5	28 (14.00)	76%	9 (4.5)	24%
Peace (4 years)	1789–93	51	12.75	27 (6.75)	53%	24 (6.00)	47%
War (3 years)	1793–5 1798–9	37	12.33	26 (8.66)	70%	11 (3.66)	30%
Peace/war (3 years)	1800–3	46	15.33	10 (3.33)	22%	36 (12.00)	78%
War (5 years)	1803–8	51	10.2	32 (6.4)	63%	19 (3.8)	37%
Totals	17 years	222	13.05	123 (7.23)	55%	99 (5.82)	45%

Source: OBSP.

London and Middlesex totals for pickpocketing indictments are for this period, they are in excess of figures for Surrey,[18] emphasising that this was an urban crime, perpetrated in places where crowds gathered and where prostitution flourished.

As shown in table 9, female pickpocketing defendants constituted, in the sample years, as much as 55 per cent of the total – 123 individuals. There were ninety-nine male defendants.[19] There is little doubt that pickpocketing was a crime committed largely from economic need.[20] The year on year figures suggest that pickpocketing, like shoplifting, was not a crime where indictments decreased in years of war. Indictments against women were at a high level in wartime but the pattern is not simple. The peak time for male indictments (1800–3) coincides with some years of exceptionally high

[18] Ibid. 180, and 'Criminality of women', 91. In Surrey only 112 people were indicted for pickpocketing during 61 years between 1663 and 1802.

[19] The proportion of women pickpocketing defendants was found by Beattie, *Crime and the courts*, 180, to be higher in Surrey than I have found in London and Middlesex in nearly all the years between 1780 and 1808. In Surrey, there were around two women charged to every man. However, in Beattie, 'Criminality of women', 91, sample years in Surrey during 1663–1802 give different proportions, with men at 53.3% and women 46.7%, but in a total of only 30 cases.

[20] Pickpocketing may fit the crime category, 'serious and more skilled', proposed by Hay, as far as some of the men's activities were concerned. However, the exercise of skill does not mean that the theft was not motivated by need: Hay, 'War, dearth and theft', 145.

Table 10
Verdicts in pickpocketing cases at Old Bailey Sessions in seventeen
sample years between 1780 and 1808

	1780–2	1789–93	1793–5, 1798–9	1800–3	1803–8	Totals
Total verdicts	37	51	37	46	51	222
Men	9	24	11	36	19	99
Women	28	27	26	10	32	123
Fully capitally guilty						
Total and % of total verdicts	3 (8%)	3 (6%)	0 –	6 (13%)	2 (4%)	14 (6%)
Men and % of men's verdicts	1 (11%)	2 (8%)	0 –	5 (14%)	1 (5%)	9 (9%)
Women and % of women's verdicts	2 (7%)	1 (3%)	0 –	1 (10%)	1 (3%)	5 (4%)
Partially guilty verdicts						
Total and % of total verdicts	15 (41%)	37 (73%)	14 (38%)	28 (61%)	23 (45%)	117 (53%)
Men and % of men's verdicts	4 (44%)	16 (67%)	5 (45%)	24 (67%)	11 (58%)	60 (61%)
Women and % women's verdicts	11 (39%)	21 (78%)	9 (35%)	4 (40%)	12 (38%)	57 (46%)
Not guilty/ acquitted						
Total and % of total verdicts	19 (51%)	11 (22%)	23 (62%)	12 (29%)	26 (51%)	91 (41%)
Men and % of men's verdicts	4 (44%)	6 (25%)	6 (55%)	7 (22%)	7 (37%)	30 (30%)
Women and % of women's verdicts	15 (54%)	5 (19%)	17 (65%)	5 (50%)	19 (59%)	61 (50%)

Source: OBSP; HO 26/1–14.

consumer goods prices.[21] Like shoplifting, some planning of the thieving was needed, but it seems to have been mainly opportunistic. Where male victims of women were concerned, there was a strong presumption in court that the victims' unwary and foolish behaviour had resulted in an outcome which was only to be expected as a hazard of such an encounter.

Study of cases at the Old Bailey in the sample period makes the general lack of success in proving a charge of private stealing from the person immediately noticeable (*see* table 10). The number of men and women found fully guilty and liable to a death sentence was very small. Considering the growing aversion of juries towards the death penalty, the question arises as to why these few were found fully guilty, rather than why so many were not. Of the 222 people tried for pickpocketing, only fourteen (6 per cent) were found fully guilty and were sentenced to be hanged – nine men (9 per cent of all the men tried) and five women (4 per cent of all the women tried).

The large proportion of defendants found not guilty or otherwise acquitted is striking – ninety-one of the 222 prosecuted (41 per cent). The difference between men and women in this 'acquitted' group is particularly important, with half of all the women charged being acquitted, compared with less than a third of the men. Men more frequently fell into the partially guilty category (61 per cent) than women did (46 per cent). Compared with shoplifting verdicts, there were far fewer fully guilty verdicts (6 per cent compared with 17 per cent for shoplifting) and many more not guilty verdicts (41 per cent compared with 23 per cent for shoplifting). Smaller proportions of pickpockets than shoplifters received partial verdicts, although there is more similarity here (53 per cent for pickpockets and 60 per cent for shoplifters). The reasons for the widely varying decisions between males and females, discussed later in this chapter, appear to be almost entirely a factor of diverse gendered behaviour and the highly gendered nature of the statute itself.

This set of verdicts is remarkable. When the jury found a case of 'privily stealing from the person' fully proved, the judge would pass a sentence of death. If there was a partial verdict – when either the theft had not been proved to be 'privily' carried out, or the jury had decided to value the stolen objects at less than 12*d.* – the judge could hand out a variety of sentences, from upwards of seven years' transportation, to various lengths and types of imprisonment, corporal punishment, fines, or maybe a sentence of service in the armed forces. The allocation of sentences for those receiving a partial guilty verdict is shown in table 11. This demonstrates a continuing divergence between men and women. Overall, transportation to New South Wales for seven years was the favoured sentence for this group of 117 people. Eighty-one of them were to be initially dealt with in this way – 69 per cent of all those found partially guilty. There is significant difference here from the

21 B. R. Mitchell and P. Deane, *Abstract of British historical statistics*, Cambridge 1962, 468, table 1.

Table 11
Sentences in partial verdict pickpocketing cases at Old Bailey Sessions in seventeen sample years between 1780 and 1808

		1780–2	1789–93	1793–5, 1798–9	1800–3	1803–8	Totals	% of partial verdicts
Partial verdicts	Total	15	37	14	28	23	117	100%
	Men	4	16	5	24	11	60	51%
	Women	11	21	9	4	12	57	49%
Punish-ment								
Trans-portation	Total	1	26	12	27	15	81	69%
	Men	0	12	5	22	9	48	80%
	Women	1	14	7	5	6	33	58%
Prison*	Total	10	8	2	2	7	29	25%
	Men	2	1	0	2	2	7	12%
	Women	8	7	2	0	5	22	39%
Other**	Total	1	1	0	0	0	2	2%
	Men	1	1	0	0	0	2	3%
	Women	0	0	0	0	0	0	–
No record found	Total	3	2	0	0	0	5	4%
	Men	1	2	0	0	0	3	5%
	Women	2	0	0	0	0	2	4%

Sources: HO 26/1–14.

* Sentences varied from 2 years (2 females, 1 male) down to a week. Most prison sentences were combined with imposition of a fine (1s.) or with a whipping. Ten of the female custodial sentences incorporated fines, and two of the males. Three female sentences incorporated whippings, and three of the males.
** Two men were sent to serve in the navy.

comparable figures for shoplifting cases where only 46 per cent of the defendants found partially guilty were to be transported.

It is striking how many male pickpocketing thieves received sentence of transportation – 80 per cent of all the men found partially guilty, compared with 58 per cent of women found partially guilty. This suggests that the life-style profile of these men and boys made them, in the eyes of the judiciary, ideal candidates for the new penal colony in New South Wales; moreover, the streets of the capital would be well rid of their deplorable activities. Although the proportion of females sentenced to transportation was significantly lower than that of the men, it was nevertheless a substantial number, and well in excess of the proportion of female shoplifters similarly sentenced. The court may have seen women pickpockets as a different category of woman from female shoplifters. Sometimes shoplifters were seen as practised criminals, and sentenced to death, or they were seen as unfortunate and were treated more leniently through imprisonment. The activities of female pickpockets on the other hand may not have been seen as seriously criminal. However, transportation might have been considered a useful way of dealing with the undesirable presence of 'their sort' on the streets of the capital. The high male transportation rate left few men to receive a prison sentence (12 per cent), most of them sentences of six months or less. A much larger proportion of women (39 per cent) received custodial sentences, the majority for six months or less.

As in shoplifting cases, pickpocketing defendants were sometimes able to acquire the help of defence counsel, even to an extent that might surprise us. The use of defence counsel in pickpocketing cases did not have a major impact on verdicts and sentencing. Cases in sample years 1789–95 showed that a much lower proportion of pickpocketing defendants used counsel and, unlike the shoplifting cases, a smaller proportion of the women used counsel than the men. In fact, the proportions were reversed, with male pickpockets being twice as likely to acquire this help as the women. This may suggest that female pickpockets were poorer than female shoplifters, although fees for criminal counsel could be as low as one guinea and could have been within the reach of some pickpocketing defendants or their friends.[22] Between 1789 and 1795 twenty-one per cent of pickpocketing defendants used counsel (36 per cent of the men, and 15 per cent of the women). None of this small number was found fully guilty. Although the numbers were small, use of counsel was a worthwhile strategy for the five men found not guilty (a higher than normal proportion of men found not guilty). It made little difference to the women.

Little information is available about the personal situations of those defendants who were able to afford the services of counsel. One of the men was the notorious George Barrington, who led a colourful, gentleman's life as a result

22 Bentley, English criminal justice, 97–9.

of his criminal activities and fitted the prevailing public perception of the genteel and well-dressed pickpocket.[23] Another was the ladies' hairdresser, George Wakeman. The other six men remain shadowy characters although they all produced copious character witnesses at their trials. Two of the seven women with counsel were sisters, described as 'so genteelly well-dressed' by the prosecutor. However, the other five women included an out-of-work housemaid and a thirty-five-year-old widow with two young children; the three others were women who attempted to earn money from sex, one of whom may have secured the court's sympathy (a sentence of one week in Newgate with a 1s. fine) with her description of how her client victim refused to pay her what he had agreed for her sexual services, giving her a black eye instead.

The ages of those prosecuted capitally for pickpocketing are shown in table 12. A similar pattern emerges as for those involved in shoplifting. Again, males were highly represented in the youngest (under twenty-one) age group, although not to the same significant extent as shoplifters, with females much less apparent in this group. Women's participation extends into the thirty-one to forty-year-old age group to a much greater extent than men's, suggesting the same link between female needs and poverty at this later stage in their life-cycle.[24]

Pickpockets and the sentence of death

As shown in table 10, a very small number of pickpockets received sentence of death at the end of their Old Bailey trials – fourteen in all, five women and nine men, the sentences spread thinly and evenly over the seventeen years. It has been suggested that the reason juries would return a fully guilty verdict, when everyone involved with the process knew that a death sentence would not be carried out, was to ensure that any reduction of sentence achieved later in the criminal justice system would lead to transportation.[25] Since so few cases resulted in a decision requiring the judge to pass sentence of death, it is worth considering who were the few who heard this sentence passed on them.

There was Elizabeth Hylett, who stole a canvas bag containing 4½ guineas from a soldier. She was described as 'a girl that came from America', was well known to the watch and, in her trial, used forthright language, accusing the

---

[23] See S. Rickard (ed.), *George Barrington's voyage to Botany Bay: retelling a convict's travel narrative of the 1790s*, London–New York 2001, for an account of the life and works of this extraordinary character.

[24] King, 'Female offenders'.

[25] *Select committee on capital punishment in felonies*, PP, 1819, viii.137, appendix 2, shows no executions for stealing privately from the person in London and Middlesex since 1767. I have found no evidence to the contrary.

Table 12
Age groups (where known) of men and women convicted of pickpocketing at Old Bailey Sessions in thirteen sample years between 1791–1808*

Age	% males	% females	Total
Up to and including 20 years	36%	18%	29%
21–30 years	36%	36%	36%
31–40 years	18%	36%	25%
41–50 years	–	9%	4%
51–60 years	9%	–	5%
Over 60 years	–	–	–

Source: HO 26/1–14.

* Records of age kept only since 1791.

soldier of 'compulsion' in the sexual act.[26] Hannah Carryl, another 'woman of the streets', told a complex tale in her defence against the charge of stealing a silk purse containing 5 guineas and 8s., which involved her in an encounter in a playhouse passage, where she held her victim's coat while he joined a street fight.[27] Mary Smith robbed a drunken Chelsea College pensioner of 7½ guineas and 4s. with which he had gone out to buy clothes. There was evidence that she was violent towards the old man when they met up in a public house.[28] Ann Watson stole 8s. from a hotel porter in a private room in a gin house;[29] and Eliza Kelly stole a pencil, 2 guineas and a few shillings from a man in a dark yard.[30] Kelly was the last pickpocket to be sentenced to death, a few months before the crime was made non-capital, and the only one so sentenced in the whole of that sessions' year. Her story told in court varied so little from that told by so many females charged with pickpocketing that it is difficult to explain the jury's motives. In general, apart from the suggestion of strong language and rough behaviour in two of these cases, there is little to explain why these five women should have been selected for a fully guilty verdict, since their stories are typical of the cases of nearly every female 'pickpocket'.

In the cases of the nine men found fully guilty, it is possible to suggest reasons for some of the decisions. Lucius Hughes stole a gold watch, worth £30, together with a gold chain worth £5, and two gold seals from his Excellency Baron Kutzleben, a German nobleman attending the opera house. Hughes paid for upsetting nobility – but may also have been known as a thief, as he was before the court again in the same session on another charge of

26 OBSP, Dec.1780, 15–16.
27 OBSP, Sept. 1781, 413.
28 OBSP, May 1792, 230.
29 OBSP, Feb.1802, 149–50.
30 OBSP, July 1807, 410.

theft.[31] William Jones, a 'poor boy', aged eighteen, stole £16 and bought himself a coat. His victim was asleep, having drunk half a pint of mulled raspberry. The verdict here was harsh in the circumstances – a drunken victim, asleep and the theft seen by others. Perhaps this was the jury's way of putting new opportunity in the way of a young man who seemed to have little chance in life in London.[32] Lawrence Keen, from America, feigned lameness and stole a handkerchief, worth only 5s., from a clergyman. The clergy often appear to have been strong upholders of the law. Keen had chosen a victim who believed in deterrence and retribution.[33] Thomas Houghton stole a watch worth £3 at Hendon fair.[34] Thomas Wynch, who stole £1 and a pocket book from a wool sorter in town from Northampton, at eleven o'clock in the morning, was twenty-three years old, and a good candidate for life at the other side of the world.[35] John Scape, who stole from the surgeon, Marshall, a case referred to earlier, chose his victim unwisely.[36] The remaining three cases involved thefts in crowded streets of pocket books containing substantial sums of money (from £6 to £172).[37]

In the men's cases the verdicts may have been appropriate responses to appease the outrage of a German baron, a clergyman and a surgeon, or to make a gesture to show that crime at public fairs was intolerable, and that visiting traders should not be molested. However, the reasoning in the women's cases is difficult to tease out. The stories which emerged in court and resulted in the passing of a death sentence were not much different from the stories where the jury decided to return a partial verdict. It may be that some women came across as more troublesome than others, acting with more agency, less 'troubled' and less unfortunate. However, this is a subjective reading of the stories and we can become involved in a whole series of 'perhaps' and 'maybe'. There is some possibility that juries showed a sense of fair play towards women providing sexual services, or thought that male victims received their just deserts for seeking out women on the city streets at night. In general, juries did not seem to find the behaviour of most female pickpockets as threatening. They may even have sought to penalise male victims for stupidity, drunkenness and lewdness. When Priscilla Hodder stole a half-guinea, two half-crowns and 3s. from a cooper, while 'stroking him down' at midnight behind a public house, she was found partially guilty. The jury may have taken against her prosecutor since he appeared to have been mean in his payment for her services, offering her only 6d.[38] These brief stories rehearsed in court may provide glimpses of justification for the deci-

31 OBSP, Mar.1782, 191
32 OBSP, Apr.1791, 270.
33 OBSP, May 1792, 259.
34 OBSP, July 1801, 389.
35 OBSP, Oct.1802, 508.
36 OBSP, Feb.1805, 491.
37 HO 26/8.
38 OBSP, Dec.1790, 139.

sions arrived at by juries and judges, but just as much they still keep hidden the motives for those responses. Each response was still prompted by the personal histories and social perceptions of those charged with judicial decision-making, together with the reaction of the moment of one human being to another in the setting of the court room.

Gendered diversity in pickpocketing

The Old Bailey records provide ample evidence of difference of treatment of men and women. The diverse decisions could have resulted from jury reactions to the diverse nature of the stories told in court. Apparently the same crime was being committed, but in varying environments, and demonstrating different behaviours between men and women. This difference is evident in what was stolen and from whom; in what is known about the defendants and how they operated – and, most significantly, where they operated. With respect to items stolen, the differences between men and women do not appear to be significant, emphasising the opportunistic nature of much of the crime. However, in the method and location of the crime, the differences are most striking.

The range of items stolen by pickpockets was limited – watches and accompanying items – keys and seals, money, handkerchiefs and occasionally other items, some of which must have been a surprise to the thief – such as the haul of a steel elastic truss. Table 13 gives an account of the items stolen. Men were more likely to steal handkerchiefs, and women watches and money, which meant that the overall value of women's thefts was greater than men's. This small difference relates entirely to gendered ways of operating, women having easy access to their victims' more valued possessions, whereas men were more often operating in crowded areas where dexterity and rapidity of movement was required to pull an object, like a handkerchief, from a pocket; dexterity in such environments was held by young male pickpockets to be a specifically male skill.[39]

Victims of indicted pickpockets in the sample years analysed numbered 194, of whom 175 were male, nineteen female.[40] The nineteen female victims were evenly targeted by male and female thieves. They were a varied group of married and unmarried women, servants, a lodging-house keeper and a few genteel ladies on outings to shops and houses in various parts of London. Amongst the male victims no particular group or class was predominant. This is especially true of the male victims of female pickpockets. The

[39] Shore, *Artful dodgers*, 59. In all the years in the period 1780–1808, the range and distribution by gender of items stolen was very much the same, with an overall higher percentage of money over watches for the women.

[40] In the years between 1780 and 1810 not included in the full analysis, it was rare for there to be a private theft from a woman.

Table 13
Items stolen: pickpocketing cases tried at Old Bailey Sessions
in seventeen sample years between 1780 and 1808

Items stolen (most valuable item in one 'haul')	By females	By males
Watches (with keys, seals etc.)	43 (35%)	20 (20%)
Money (plus purses, pocket books, sometimes empty)	77 (63%) maximum £154	38 (38%) maximum £172
Handkerchiefs	0	31 (31%)
Other items	3 (2%) opera glasses, spectacles, manicure set	10 (10%) e.g. spectacles, steel elastic truss, inkstand, shirt, breeches, cord binding, garnet studs, pencil case
Totals	123 (100%)	99 (100%)

Source: OBSP.

men who tangled with prostitutes, and who were prepared to indict them for a capital offence, were a fairly wide cross-section of the less financially flourishing members of male society, mainly tradesmen, artisans, labourers, shopkeepers, clerks, servants, a farmer, surprisingly few soldiers and sailors (only six were so identified), an attorney and a handful who said they had no trade or who lived on inherited money (three only). The group most vulnerable to the women's attentions, and presumably the most threatened by such criminal activities, were porters and similar types of servants – from grocers' shops, hotels, restaurants, coffee houses, the post office, livery stables, East India and West India company offices – presumably men who had to earn their living by being able to move around the city at all hours, and to demonstrate reliability and honesty with money and other goods entrusted to them.

Male victims of male pickpockets came from nearly as wide a cross-section of society as the females' victims, although with a higher representation of the slightly better-off merchant and gentry group. The cases brought against pickpockets were not often brought by victims in a higher station in life. The gentry and the successful middling sort were presumably wise enough not to find themselves in the areas of London where such misfortune could befall them. If they should be so unwise, then they would avoid becoming involved in prosecutions which could easily damage their reputations and family standing. Their losses would not be sufficiently significant to them. The stage was left to ordinary tradesmen, artisans and other working men.

There is little evidence available as to who exactly were the male pick-

pockets. There were men designated as 'labourers' and others in a wide selection of urban occupations – coachmen, servants, errand boys, shop assistants,
an earring seller and a debt collector; a hairdresser, a chimney sweep and a
harness maker; small artisans too – weavers, jewellers, printers, watchmakers,
chairmakers, shoemakers. There were soldiers and sailors, a 'man from
America' and the notorious 'gentleman thief', George Barrington.

It is always impossible to state with any certainty the status and background of women appearing as defendants in criminal cases. Their occupations are rarely mentioned in court or other official records. It would be an
over-simplification to say that the vast majority of women indicted for
pickpocketing were prostitutes. Nevertheless, the evidence of both victims
and accused showed that private stealing from the person happened as an
adjunct to sexual activity or 'treats', in encounters on the streets of London in
the dark hours, alone or in 'parcels of girls'. The views held by judges and
juries about the life-styles of poor women who found themselves on trial
made a link with prostitution almost inevitable.[41] It is not surprising that the
court records suggest that 76 per cent of female pickpocketing defendants
were, or were seen as, prostitutes, streetwalkers, whorehouse owners or young
women out for a 'good', preferably lucrative, time in male company. In a few
other cases, alternative means of earning a living were mentioned – fruit
seller, watercress seller, market traders, pot-scourers, a washerwoman, out-of
work housemaids, a woman who ran a greengrocer's shop. All were typical of
the marginal, insecure world inhabited by urban woman, where boundaries
were blurred between servanthood – whether in domestic or in casual trades
– and the service of male sexual appetites. Prostitution, characterised by its
transitory, seasonal and part-time nature, may have been on the increase on
the London streets in the late eighteenth century as other employment
opportunities for women declined.[42] Relieving 'clients' of their personal
belongings was an extra benefit to be derived from a package of treats and
sex, and was a better way of earning a living than relying solely on the small
amounts of money negotiated with them for sex. The number of women who
found themselves at the Old Bailey for so doing significantly exceeded their
proportion in any other property crime in London.

Women operated in pairs more often than men, but their joint indictments did not have the same effect on the jury's decisions as they did in shoplifting cases. Twenty-eight of the women were indicted in pairs, and six in
two groups of three. Verdicts were generally identical for the pair or group;
only in two pairs were different verdicts returned on the individuals. Just
eight men were indicted in pairs, and verdicts and punishments were equal. It

41 Shore, quoting John Fielding, in 'The trouble with boys', 78.
42 King, 'Female offenders', 191–216. In 1791 and 1793 about a fifth of all women tried at
the Old Bailey (two-fifths of those where a work context was established) 'involved alleged
sexual transactions for money'. See also Hill, *Women, work and sexual politics*, and
Henderson, *Disorderly women*.

was unusual for men and women to be indicted together. There were only three such indictments – two involving one man and one woman, and one involving two men and one woman, and in all three the decisions involved harsher verdicts and sentences against the women. The irrelevance of issues related to marriage or 'marital coercion' is even more marked in this crime than in shoplifting cases.

The most striking difference which emerges between the ways in which men and women went about their pickpocketing activities lies in the 'where' and 'when' of the commission of the crime. Table 14 summarises the place, the time and the environment of the alleged crime as the victim and defendant presented the facts in court. The differences in 'where' and 'when' between the men and the women are so great that they beg the question as to whether the same crime was being committed. The evidence in table 14 runs downwards from the most private, enclosed and dark, to the most public, open and light. The division is subjective, but reasonable. The halfway-point between dark and light, private and public, comes after the grouping 'in the street in the hours of darkness'. By this point 78 per cent of the women's activities had happened, and only 12 per cent of the men's. Then, as the table continues into the more public areas of shops, public house tap rooms and supper houses – and thence out onto the streets and other very public gatherings, 80 per cent of the men's activities happened, and only 12 per cent of the women's. The inversion of the method, place and time of operating between men and women is virtually complete.

Darkness and light concerned the Old Bailey Court, as it concerned all who were anxious about street crime and effective policing. Street lighting, the watch and criminals were intimately joined in the public mind.[43] In court proceedings it was essential for a victim to be able to identify the perpetrator of the offence, and questions about candles and lamps formed part of the ritual of the courtroom evidential catechism. Sarah Strickland's apartment was candle-lit;[44] Mary Ann Deochean ran off with the candle from her room leaving her victim stranded in the dark;[45] Henrietta Spencer's victim held a candle to see her face in a dark alley;[46] Sara Smith's victim said there was a very bad light in her room and there was no candle;[47] Mary Partridge's victim, picked up whilst he made water at a cab stand, said that all the time he was with her it was so dark, he could not see her face.[48] The watchman had to call the lamplighter to assist in searching the ground for the watch that Mary Ann Fisher was accused of stealing.[49] St James's Park gateway thefts were said to have taken place by starlight.

43 Beattie, *Crime and the courts*, 67–72.
44 OBSP, Feb.1781, 114–15
45 OBSP, Sept.1806, 385–6.
46 OBSP, Oct.1781, 494–5.
47 OBSP, Feb.1791, 205–11.
48 OBSP, Feb.1791, 215–18.
49 OBSP, Sept.1802, 460.

Table 14
Place, time, environment of pickpocketing cases tried at
Old Bailey Sessions in seventeen sample years between 1780 and 1808

	Females	Males
Private lodgings, rooms, apartments and whorehouses, at night	38 (31%)	2 (2%)
Private rooms in public houses, drinking clubs, boxes in public houses, any time	9 (7%)	0 –
In coaches, any time; in the watch-house cage, night	1 (1%)	6 (6%)
In yards, alleys, dead ends of streets, park gates, public house lobbies, at night	26 (21%)	0 –
In the street, in the hours of darkness	22 (18%)	4 (4%)
In supper-houses, wine vaults, in a shop, in the open in public house, by the fire, in the tap room	3 (2%)	11 (11%)
Openly in the street by daylight, people around, no large crowds	5 (4%)	39 (39%)
In public places with crowds, fairs, theatres, opera house, processions, watching events and people, Custom House, Tyburn etc.	7 (6%)	30 (30%)
Unknown – details not given	12 (10%)	7 (7%)
Totals	123 (100%)	99 (100%)

Source: OBSP.

Table 14 shows that there were cases of women operating in public, brightly lit space, and men in private dark spaces. The few cases of women or girls operating in public open space include some operating with male companions – one in a public house tap room,[50] one in Oxford Street on a summer afternoon[51] and one in the crowds on Lord Mayor's Day.[52] Another picked a pocket in the Royal Theatre where her client had fallen asleep with his head in her lap,[53] and another stole from a country girl newly arrived in London, persuading her to join a group of drinking friends in an Oxford Street public house.[54] A group of young girls was involved in tricking two different women in the street, informing them that their petticoats were trailing and offering

50 OBSP, May 1792, 230.
51 OBSP, June 1789, 385.
52 OBSP, Dec.1802, 8.
53 OBSP, Dec.1805, 14.
54 OBSP, June 1799, 422.

help to pull them up, on each occasion stealing purses and money.[55] Another group of girls had fun jostling an old woman as she watched children going to St Paul's School.[56] Conspicuous for their unusual female behaviour were Hannah and Mary Wheeler, accused of stealing a purse and money from a woman in a large crowd at Charing Cross in the afternoon, looking at a building which had burned down the night before.[57] Particularly unusual was Hannah Findale, who, showing unusual skill for a female pickpocket, stole a pocket book containing a well-fitted-out manicure set from a woman waiting in the Bow Street entrance to the Covent Garden Theatre as a small crowd waited for the doors to open for a matinée performance. She cut the woman's petticoat down the length of its pocket, turned the pocket inside out, removed the pocket book and manicure set and was apprehended as she went in a second time, attempting to remove a watch she had detected there.[58]

As a rule, men and boys did their private stealing amongst crowds watching processions, at public hangings, at fights, in crowds watching 'the quality' pass by, at horse fairs and theatre foyers, and were pulling handkerchiefs from pockets in the streets in broad daylight. Women, on the other hand, were taking fair advantage of inebriated, importunate and unwise men in dark alleys, public house yards, dead ends, up against walls, at park gateways and during sexual activity in more private places. They took men to their lodgings, through dark alleys and lanes, and in total darkness or by candlelight, relieving them of money and watches, breeches on or off, having ensured that the men had been plied with alcoholic beverages and made sure that they had a girlfriend near at hand to receive the items removed from the men's persons or clothes.

The differences in the place, time and manner of committing the crime of pickpocketing are so great, that it is clear that like is not being compared with like. The diversity cannot have been lost on juries and judges and, even if their decisions were not deliberately and systematically based on these gendered differences, it is inconceivable that they were not subconsciously affected. Such differences might contribute a further dimension to the public/private distinction which has become an important concept for historians of gender, yet which is a distinction which seems to have little explanatory power for the lives of the urban poor. The paths of women and men crossed and collided as these plebeian folk, labourers, servants, women of the town, moved about, making ends meet, acquiring as good a living as they could, doing what they could, when they could and, not surprisingly, doing it differently, at different times and different places. It is not only that 'spaces, places and our senses of them (and such related things as our degree of

---

[55] OBSP, July 1805, 424.
[56] OBSP, July 1807, 332–3.
[57] OBSP, July 1785, 1010–11.
[58] OBSP, May 1793, 663–4.

mobility) are gendered through and through'[59] but that public and private space is interchangeable depending on who is defining the public and private, on what is done there, who does it and when it is done.

The 'wrong' crime and the 'wrong' gender

The analysis presented in this chapter shows how a law made to address largely male activities was used more often to judge the activities of urban women. These women stole 'privately' and secretly, but not in the way envisaged by the statute-makers. The crime was extremely difficult to prosecute successfully, particularly because of the need for the victim to have been sober, vigilant and acting with propriety. It was therefore particularly difficult to prove in respect of nearly all the women defendants who had carried out their thieving as an adjunct to providing sexual services. The overall acquittal rate was high, especially high for the women (at 50 per cent compared with 30 per cent for men). Very few indeed were found fully guilty and there was a significant difference in punishment allocated to men and women found partially guilty. The men were much more likely to be transported (80 per cent of men found partially guilty, only 58 per cent of the women). The women were much more likely to be given a custodial sentence.

These differences reflect the sometimes extreme divergence in life-style and behaviour of male and female pickpockets. Most of the women earned all or some of their money on the streets of the capital, offering sexual intercourse or other sexual 'treats' to men; some were also, or alternatively, engaged in earning some money in some of the most marginal and insecure urban occupations, as washerwomen, pot-scourers, watercress sellers, in menial domestic service or as sewing women. Male pickpockets were not in secure occupations, but a little more so than the females – sometimes in skilled and semi-skilled artisanal trades, as servants, in the armed services and other service occupations. Difference in occupation and, perhaps, in needs, meant a hugely varying way of going about the task of secret stealing, in method, in place, in environment and in time of day. At this stage of the judicial system, gender – and the divergent gendered behaviour and life-style of men and women pickpockets on the streets of London – was likely to have been the strongest influence on decision-making and judicial discretion.

Perhaps the most important result of this examination of pickpocketing trials is to demonstrate the necessity of getting behind the statistics of indictments, trials, verdicts and sentences to see if it is possible to learn why decisions were made as they were. It is necessary to try to hear the stories that the

---

[59] D. Massey, *Space, place and gender*, Cambridge 1994, 186; R. B. Shoemaker, 'Public spaces, private disputes? Fights and insults on London's streets, 1600–1800', in Hitchcock and Shore, *Streets of London*, 54–68.

juries and judges heard. This closer attention is vital if there is to be any chance of finding out why women were treated differently by the judicial system, if not always more leniently than men. It is possible to see in the property crimes of shoplifting, and particularly of pickpocketing, that many of the hypotheses based on use of more global figures, do not help to answer the question. Here there is no evidence that women were seen as less of a threat and thus less deserving of heavy punishment. They were present in majority numbers in court, sufficient to permit them to be taken as seriously as the men. Their thefts were not less serious, less premeditated, more trivial. There is little evidence that they were less 'troublesome' than men, although it is certain that their economic vulnerability and their poverty was greater than the men's. However, since the stories told about them and by them were totally different from the stories about men, it is not surprising that the juries made different decisions on a gendered basis.

5

False Money

A crime which . . . can never afford even a hope for the royal mercy in this commercial country.[1]

The production of forged Bank notes and the ways of getting them into circulation – uttering – are activities rarely examined by historians.[2] These crimes provide a useful contrast to shoplifting and pickpocketing. In this chapter consideration is given to these activities, mainly in London and Middlesex between 1804 and 1834. They involved a very slightly better off strata of society and, although women were significantly involved, their proportion was much lower. The general perception of forged currency crime was entirely different. The likelihood of fatal outcomes to trials was much higher, reflecting public fears but at the same time provoking much horror and distaste. Further, the institutional nature of the victim-prosecutor – the Bank of England – the effectiveness of its prosecution machine and the unusual way in which indictments were drawn up all provide an interesting view of the justice system in the early stages of the judicial process. A focused analysis of these crimes, those involved and the conduct of their trials shows the pragmatic way in which the dynamics of gender, paternalism and politics were affected by these activities at a specific period in history. It provides a useful contrast to the study of crimes of private stealing.

The analysis has been carried out for the years during and just after the period, from 1797 to 1821, when the convertibility of cash payments was suspended by the Bank of England.[3] During this time the Bank produced low value paper money, of poor quality, easy to forge. The huge and sudden surge of forged paper money in circulation created public and institutional panic, and a costly but highly successful prosecution exercise against more than

---

1   S. Foote, *Memoirs of Samuel Foote*, i, London 1810, 195.
2   This is with the notable exception of R. McGowen, 'Forgery discovered or the perils of circulation in eighteenth-century England', *Angelaki* i (1994), 113–29; 'From pillory to gallows: the punishment of forgery in the age of financial revolution', *P&P* clxv (1999), 107–40; 'Making the "bloody code" '; 'The Bank of England and the policing of forgery, 1797–1821', *P&P* clxxxvi (2005), 81–116; and 'The Bank of England and the death penalty' (forthcoming).
3   For discussion of the period of suspension and some of the complex political, economic and monetary reasons for it see W. M. Acres, *The Bank of England from within*, i, London 1931, 275–90, 299–348; J. Clapham, *The Bank of England*, Cambridge 1944, i. 253–72; ii. 1–16; B. J. Hilton, *Corn, cash, commerce: the economic policies of the Tory governments, 1815–30*, London 1977; and D. Byatt, *Promises to pay*, London 1994.

2,000 people nationally.[4] This chapter explains some of the unusual aspects of the legal processes connected with Bank note forgery. It is difficult in respect of the felonies of pickpocketing and shoplifting in London to trace in a systematic way the 'pre-trial' processes in the records of the lower courts before they were referred to the Old Bailey for prosecution on indictment. The nature of the Bank of England's records, however, means that it is possible to probe, to a modest extent at least, the prosecutor's reasons for preferring indictments, or not, on the cases it considered from all over the nation. In this process it is possible to examine whether the decisions were affected by the gender of the prisoner.

After consideration of the pre-trial processes, the results of the London and Middlesex cases which reached the Old Bailey have been examined. Since, unusually for the period, the Bank of England offered a plea bargain deal to so many of those it prosecuted, the judicial process was rather different from that in shoplifting and pickpocketing cases. There were few 'not guilty' pleas and therefore few stories told in court from which details of the activities of men and women can be analysed. Nevertheless, a number of valuable observations on the role of gender can be made which provide a contrast to, or restraint upon, the kinds of distinctions observed with the other two crimes.

Processing crimes against the national currency

In 1802 the Bank found it necessary to set up a committee to deal specifically with the criminal law business in which it was involved – its Committee for Law Suits. Most of this business was to do with the capital crimes of Bank note forgery and uttering, and the possession of forged notes.[5] The committee

---

[4]   The compilation of accurate figures for cases is, as usual, not easy. The best source is the BECLS minutes, M5/307–33, for July 1802–Dec.1834; BEFP, F2/108, Nos of convictions, 1791–1829; F2/120, Names committed for trial, 1809–29. See also draft of 'Return of prosecution for forgery on bankers for ten years commencing with the year 1818', CLRO, MISC.MSS.368.14. Figures in McGowen, 'Policing', come close to those I have counted. V. Gatrell, 'The decline of theft and violence in Victorian and Edwardian England', in Gatrell, Lenman and Parker, *Crime and the law*, 268, may have misunderstood the due process in these crimes; the figures he used do not recognise the alternative indictment system of plea bargaining, which allowed conviction for possession rather than for forgery or uttering and the consequent dropping of the alternative case, nor that an indictment could cite a number of notes rather than there being one indictment/conviction for each forged note presented.

[5]   Bank of England note forgery or fraudulent alteration had been made a capital offence in 1697 (8 & 9 Will. 3, c.20). In 1725 the offering, disposing or putting away of a forged note (uttering) was also made a capital offence (12 Geo.1, c.32). The death sentences were removed in 1832. In 1801 further offences, including possession of instruments for making Bank note paper, or of making the paper, or of possessing forged notes knowing them to be

was made up of the governor, or deputy-governor, of the Bank and five other directors. The committee secretaries kept meticulous records of high quality. These records provide evidence of the size and success of the Bank's prosecuting enterprise, its high rate of apprehension of criminals and its efficient and effective system of communication up and down the nation, as well as the enormous cost of the prosecution process. A complex network of police and other public officers, together with Bank-appointed and paid investigators, did the Bank's will – some tempted by large rewards – together with informers and a well-informed constituency of traders and shopkeepers who knew what to do if 'bad' notes were passed off on them. The Bank's resources provided for a smooth bureaucracy, with effective record keeping, the finest legal advice and a system of influence that was irresistible, inscrutable and self-righteous.[6]

The Bank guarded jealously its right to make its own decisions about whom to prosecute and about the nature of the charge. It saw interference from juries, judges, petitioners, magistrates and members of parliament, as irritating obstacles to curbing and curing the evil of forgery. The Secretary of State at the Home Office and the Lord Advocate of Scotland rebuked the Bank for usurping the prerogative of the courts when it went so far as to promise defendants sentences of life transportation rather than death if they pleaded guilty to a capital charge. Their rebukes were recorded by the Bank committee without comment.[7] The Bank's system of handling criminal prosecutions was discretionary, directed to ensuring success in the public legal confrontation with the prisoner. The outcome of the case in court was all-important and decisions to prosecute were made with only that outcome in mind.

The directors of the Bank were taken by surprise by the amount of criminal legal business forced upon them by the issue of low denomination notes after 1797. The Committee for Law Suits managed the prosecutions, gave direction as to the retention of counsel and preferred indictments 'as they may judge expedient'.[8] Use of the word 'expedient' might suggest a lack of underlying proactive policy, more a reaction to events and situations, or a

forged, were added to the statute book, largely at the Bank of England's instigation; these offences were punishable by 14 years' transportation: 41 Geo.3, c. 39.
6 Costs for the Bank of England's criminal business were recorded each half-year. These varied from approximately £114 to £150 per person prosecuted at times of high activity (1811–20), to £380 per person in times of low activity (1822). During 1820 the 411 prosecutions cost an average of £149 15s.3d. per person (BECLS, M5/311–24). At the Old Bailey, fees paid by the Bank to counsel were £44 1s. per case, and for drawing a brief another £51. At county assizes, four counsel might be appointed, in addition to one standing counsel, who took what the committee regarded as 'exhorbitant' fees: M5/325, 21 Mar. 1821. Rewards paid in addition to these costs varied from around £200 each half-year to £2,800, recorded in May 1818 after the prosecution of 132 cases: M5/320.
7 BECLS, M5/320, 2 July 1818; M5/321, 5, 9 Feb. 1819; BEFP, F2/94, R v MacKay.
8 BECLS, M5/307, 7 July 1802.

response to a short term need. However, the Bank had a policy to which it adhered tenaciously – a policy driven at all points by the need to detect and punish those believed to be putting the nation, and the Bank, in danger. Successful capital prosecutions of forgers, dealers and utterers were necessary as warning examples to others. Rather than fail in a capital prosecution, the Bank used an extensive policy of plea bargaining. It preferred alternative indictments and, in theory with the courts' agreement, accepted a guilty plea to the lesser, non-capital charge of possession. One way or another, the Bank was determined that it and the country should be rid of people engaged in the evil of forgery. Rather than lose a case, the Bank would not prosecute and required magistrates to discharge suspects they had examined. Frequently, a discharged prisoner would be carefully watched and would appear later on a charge for which the Bank felt there was safer evidence. Discretion was largely, if not exclusively, exercised to the benefit of the Bank.

Between 1802 and 1834, the Bank Committee for Law Suits considered over 3,000 cases of criminal currency activity from all parts of the kingdom.[9] It read depositions made before magistrates, and letters and statements from police, informers and witnesses from all parts of the nation. It discussed the evidence and decided whether to prefer an indictment against a prisoner. Arrangements were made to send police or solicitors to expedite the next stages of the process. Of 3,054 cases (some involving the same person more than once), 2,298 were males (75 per cent) and 756 females. Table 15 shows the numbers of cases considered nationally between 1802 and 1834.[10] It can be seen that between 1811 and 1822 the number of cases increased hugely, and that the involvement of women increased from around 16 per cent to around 28 per cent of the total.[11]

Evidence against women rarely related to the activity of producing forged notes. Most note forging was carried out by male artisans in and around

---

[9]   Between 1805 and 1819 these included counterfeiting of silver coin temporarily in circulation and for which the Bank of England was responsible. This coin included dollars, valued at between about 4s. 6d. and 5s. 6d. and tokens for 5s. 6d., 3s. and 1s.6d. The dollars were reused Spanish dollars captured from Spanish vessels and over-stamped at the Mint with an impression of the head of George III in a small oval on the neck of the Spanish king; several millions were issued from 1797 to provide the public with coin for making small payments: 44 Geo.3, c.71. From about 1811 to 1819, silver tokens were minted from melted-down French crowns and ingots; an even larger number was circulated: 51 Geo.3, c.110, 52 Geo.3, c.139. For details see Acres, *Bank of England*, 278–80, 299–310; E. M. Kelly, *Spanish dollars and silver tokens*, London 1976; and BEFP, F2/118, F24/3–51. Cases involving counterfeit dollars and tokens constituted about one tenth of cases considered between 1805 and 1819: tables 15 and 16 include them.

[10]   It should be noted that the Bank of England Committee for Law Suits did not consider cases where good evidence was significantly lacking. McGowen suggests that this meant that a large number of cases up and down the country were just not considered for prosecution: 'Policing', 7 n. 14.

[11]   A connection between the number of notes in circulation and the level of prosecution is suggested ibid. 7 table 1.

Table 15
Bank of England currency prosecutions: cases considered by the Bank's Committee for Law Suits, 1802–34*

Years	Total	Females	Females as % of total	Males	Males as % of total
1802–4	66	9	14%	57	86%
1805–7	102	20	20%	82	80%
1808–10	157	22	14%	135	86%
1811–13	361	100	28%	261	72%
1814–16	488	145	30%	343	70%
1817–19	918	244	27%	674	73%
1820–2	768	195	25%	573	75%
1823–5	33	5	15%	28	85%
1826–8	103	8	8%	95	92%
1829–31	30	1	3%	29	97%
1832–4	28	7	25%	21	75%
Totals	3,054	756	25%	2,298	75%

Source: BECLS, M5/307–33.

* All cases in Great Britain and Ireland including counterfeit dollar and token cases.

Birmingham and Liverpool. Few London men were forgers. The vast majority of men and women were involved in getting notes into circulation. Some did so in a major way, in gangs and groups of note sellers, using others to utter them in shops and public houses, and at markets and fairs. This was an activity in which women might be less obtrusive and more useful than men. They were just as likely to work for organised gangs as to be working casually. In London and Middlesex most of the charges against men and women cited the uttering of only a few notes, but often this was likely to have been the tip of an iceberg. Large caches of notes were found in their lodgings when the police or Bank investigators carried out a search. The activities of London men and women in this crime differed little from one another.

Responses to 'trivial' offences

The Bank records allow an unusual insight into the pre-trial deliberations of the prosecutor, and give some idea why decisions were taken to prosecute for forged note offences on indictment, or not, in the higher courts. This kind of evidence is almost entirely lacking for other felonies in the period. Most of those arrested for Bank note forgery offences had been taken before magistrates, who did not make further decisions on what should happen next without referring each case to the Bank. The great majority of the deliberations by the Bank on the cases forwarded by magistrates resulted in decisions to prosecute on indictment. A further decision was made as to whether a forgery charge was to be capital only (for uttering), or whether a lesser charge (for possession) would be put, or a plea bargain alternative should be offered to the prisoner. If a prisoner pleaded guilty to possessing forged notes, with its sentence of fourteen years' transportation, the Bank would withdraw the capital charge.[12]

In the 3,054 cases considered on a national basis, a decision not to prosecute was recorded in 505 cases (16.5 per cent of the total). These decisions favoured 324 men (14 per cent of all men referred to the Bank for decision on prosecution) and 181 women (24 per cent). The proportion of decisions in women's favour suggests that there may have been significant gender-based discretion. It is, therefore, useful to look more closely to see what factors may have led to such a significant proportion of women escaping prosecution on indictment. Table 16 shows that in 434 (86 per cent) of the 505 cases in which there was a decision not to prosecute, it may be possible to understand the reasons behind that decision.

Two reasons predominated. Most significant was the category where the Bank decided that the offence was too slight or too trivial to warrant prosecution, its fear being that a grand jury might throw the case out on these grounds before it reached trial before the petty jury. Such an outcome might suggest to forgers that they could get away with a certain low level of criminal activity. There were cases where prosecution was not recommended when evidence to prove the charge was regarded as insufficient or defective; this was also connected with the over-riding need not to lose cases. In most of the cases rejected for prosecution on grounds of 'triviality', the offence for which proof was available was indeed trivial.[13] Defective or insufficient evidence included uncertainty that the forged note or notes could be traced from hand to hand through the essential narrative of the crime, doubts about the technical specification of the note, suspicion that the person uttering it was innocent of its nature, or that the Bank was unable to prove it was put into circulation knowingly.

Table 16 shows a high proportion of women in the 'trivial' category. It is almost impossible, from the records, to detect any obvious differences between the activities of the men and women in these 'trivial' cases. Women uttered notes extensively as part of their apparently legitimate business – at

[12] For cases involving Bank of England dollars and tokens, the act of counterfeiting was a felony with punishment of 7 years' transportation; first and second uttering offences were misdemeanours, punishable respectively with 6 months' imprisonment with sureties for a further 6 months, and imprisonment for 2 years and sureties for 2 years. A third uttering was a felony punishable with 14 years' transportation. All Bank cases were prosecuted as misdemeanours: BEFP, F24/39.

[13] The degree of triviality was defined by the political atmosphere. Towards the end of the period of suspension, 'trivial' might mean the uttering of a note of £5 or £10, whereas in earlier years, it related to one or two £1 or £2 notes.

Table 16
Reasons for not prosecuting in Bank of England
currency cases, 1802–34*

Reasons for not prosecuting	Total	Women	% of women not prosecuted	Men	% of men not prosecuted
Offence too slight, too trivial	266	106	59%	160	49%
Evidence insufficient or defective	79	27	15%	52	16%
Legal or procedural problem	19	5	3%	14	4.5%
Other charges pending take precedence	17	7	4%	10	3%
Prisoner coerced/induced/ or instrument of others	18	11	6%	7	2%
Wish to use as a witness against others	17	4	2%	13	4%
Age: too old, too young	7	3	1.5%	4	1%
Good character	9	1	0.5%	8	2.5%
Unfit to plead (mental illness)	1	0	–	1	0.5%
Arrest was malicious	1	0	–	1	0.5%
No reason deduced	71	17	9%	54	17%
Totals	505	181	100%	324	100%

Source: BECLS, M5/307–33; BEFP, F24/3–51.

* All cases in Great Britain and Ireland including counterfeit dollar and token cases.

fairs, in shops and public houses. This resulted, proportionately more often than in the case of men's activities (where often the passing of notes was in bulk at secret meetings in public houses), in the Bank being able only to prove a one-off attempt to pass a note, or maybe two. Although some women were involved in major selling networks, it was less common for a woman to utter more than one note in one place at one time. In the majority of cases, however, women did what men did and were prosecuted in the same fashion, although the more frequent likelihood that they would be disposing of single notes meant that they were slightly more often favoured with a decision not to prosecute. The degree, rather than the nature, of their involvement was the essential factor in the decisions. Therefore 'gender' worked indirectly in this selection for prosecution, allowing many women to escape trial on indictment. Although some of those who fell into the Bank's hands were members of well-organised networks, and sometimes financially well-off, most of the men and women apprehended for note offences were poor folk, who had found a useful way of meeting their material needs. Women may have formed a significant proportion of those involved in note circulation to this end and it is not surprising that their activities were more trivial and that they were thus favoured in the decision-making process at this stage.

Other reasons for not prosecuting were less likely to be gendered – such as a prisoner's old age or youth, mental illness, or good character. There were also reasons connected with the Bank's meticulous prosecuting enterprise; it would not prosecute if another serious charge were pending against the prisoner. There were cases where it would rather use some prisoners to give evidence against more serious offenders. A category worth attention is the one dealing with 'coercion' in its various forms. Few people avoided prosecution because of this. This is significant, in view of the theories about married women being able to avoid prosecution. The excuse of coercion was more likely to be used in favour of women than of men, although it can be seen how very small are the numbers. The seven men in this category were said to have been coerced by, or to have been instruments of, other men. The eleven women were said to have been induced or coerced by, or the instruments of, a more varied group of people. In four of those eleven cases, coercion was said to have been by a husband or by a man with whom they cohabited; in another, by a casual male acquaintance; in three more cases, by an agent of the Bank; in one case by a servant; and in the two remaining cases, by the women's mothers. A woman's civil status was of no interest to the Bank as prosecutor. Its legal advisers knew how limited were the circumstances permitting use of the excuse of marital coercion. At the very least in order for this to be a viable excuse, a woman would have had to be in the immediate presence of her husband, and acting under his instruction.[14]

The Bank's legal advisers worked only with reasonably watertight cases. They were not prepared to lose cases on trivial or ill-founded evidence. It is interesting to see how successful they were in this as far as grand jury hearings were concerned.[15] The number of rejected bills in Bank cases was extremely small.[16] This could have been because Bank cases were well prepared. On the other hand, the members of the grand jury may have been ill-equipped to

---

[14] See, for instance, BEFP, F24/15. Bank lawyers advised (20 Oct. 1812) on the drawing up of an indictment as follows: 'as we should not suppose the Prisoner would be advised to plead in abatement, you may describe her in the Indictment as a Spinster'. In F24/39, advising similarly (20 Apr. 1816), they wrote: 'We seldom indict a woman as a married woman.'

[15] For grand juries at the end of the eighteenth and beginning of the nineteenth centuries, and changes taking place, see Beattie, *Crime and the courts*, 318–35, 400, and 'London juries of the 1690s', in J. S. Cockburn and T. A. Green (eds), *Twelve good men and true: the criminal trial jury in England, 1200–1800*, Princeton 1998, 214–53.

[16] Idem, *Crime and the courts*, 401–3, found that grand juries threw out 'significant numbers' of bills (for all crimes) at Surrey Assizes (1660–1800) but attached 'little significance' to the fact that 92% of forgery accusations were 'found' by the Surrey grand juries between 1600 and 1800. If it is insignificant that 8% of bills were rejected, it makes the Bank of England's level of success extraordinary. 15% of bills were marked 'ignoramus' for property offences in Surrey (1660–1800), and 25% for minor personal offences. The grand jury was less likely to reject bills where a capital offence was alleged. King, *Crime, justice and discretion*, 231, found a minimum of about one-seventh of bills brought before the grand jurors of Essex between 1740 and 1805 'not found'.

Table 17
Bills of indictment 'not found' by grand juries in Bank of England forged Bank note cases*

	Total bills heard by grand jury	Bills not found (% bills not found)	Bills against men	Bills against men not found (% not found)	Bills against women	Bills against women not found (% not found)
Assize hearings (i.e. outside London)	564	7 (1.24%)	425	5 (1.17%)	139	2 (1.43%)
Old Bailey Sessions	511	18 (3.52%)	393	10 (2.54%)	118	8 (6.77%)
In all courts	1,075	25 (2.32%)	818	15 (1.83%)	257	10 (3.89%)

Source: BECLS, M5/307–33.

* Hearings in England and Wales between April 1818 and September 1821 (the only period in which bills were recorded as 'not found').

challenge the technical complexity of the charges, or they may have thought that currency forgery was so heinous an activity that the cases must go to the petty jury. It was only during the period of maximum activity in Bank note forgery cases, from April 1818 to September 1821, that any record was made of a bill 'not found' in Bank cases.[17] For these years of high activity table 17 shows details of bills of indictment in Bank of England cases which were 'not found' by grand juries, divided between London and Middlesex, and the rest of the country. It can be seen that the proportion of 'not found' bills was very small: for the whole country only twenty-five out of 1,075 cases. Amongst this small number, women feature proportionately more than men, at 3.89 per cent compared with 1.83 per cent for men. The records do not reveal a reason for this. The grand jury for the Old Bailey threw out more bills for forgery crimes than their counterparts in other areas of the country – 3.52 per cent of cases compared with 1.24 per cent in other regions. They also did so more in favour of women – in 6.77 per cent of bills against London women (compared with 2.54 per cent of London men and 1.43 per cent of women elsewhere in the country).[18] It is possible that the Old Bailey rejection rate

17 This is not to say that outside this period there were no 'not found' bills. However, the Bank records (BECLS) give results for all cases taken and appear, when matched against other evidence, to be reliable.

18 Beattie, *Crime and the courts*, 403–4, shows that grand juries in Surrey (1660–1800) were also more likely to send men rather than women to trial. See his table 8.2 at p. 404. This was noticeable in cases involving murder, fraud and certain property offences, but not forgery.

was higher because the grand jurors here were more used to dealing with forged note cases than juries in the rest of the country, and could spot a defect in a case. Perhaps the high number of cases brought by the Bank for offences in London and Middlesex in these years meant that its bill drafting was less meticulous.

Men and women often operated together in activities involving forged Bank notes. This was unlike their behaviour in many other property crimes and provides a rare opportunity for comparing decisions made about men and women when they were operating as co-perpetrators of crime, as married couples, cohabiting couples, as members of gangs, or otherwise joined in the legal process through the combined reading of depositions against them, or facing joint indictments. The Bank records show that 218 men and 203 women were grouped or coupled in this way. Taking into consideration the ratio of men and women coming within the clutches of the judicial system for forged note crimes, this is obviously a much higher proportion of the women than of the men. This unusual feature is particularly important in Bank note crime. Surprisingly, the Bank's decisions about whether to prosecute usually resulted in similar treatment of these men and women at this stage of the system. In the very few cases where dissimilar decisions were made on prosecuting members of mixed sex groups, women were more favoured. Twenty-two of them (11 per cent of the women operating in mixed sex groups) were ordered to be discharged, compared with ten men (5 per cent of men operating in mixed sex groups).

Although the numbers are very small indeed, it is possible to consider whether, within these mixed sex groups, the marital status of those involved had an effect on the Bank's decisions. In the mixed-sex groups, there were seventy-three pairs who shared a surname because of 'marriage' and not for any other reason. Sharing a surname is not taken to mean the existence of a legal marriage.[19] In forty-five (62 per cent) of the seventy-three relationships, the decision on prosecution was the same for both partners. In the other twenty-eight of the seventy-three relationships, one of the couple was more leniently treated by the Bank – not always the female.[20] In seventeen of these cases (23 per cent of the total relationships), the decision went in favour of the women, and in eleven (15 per cent) the men were favoured. Discretion leading to leniency was not exercised in one direction only. The proportion of married women benefiting from more lenient decisions was greater than

[19] In only 21 of the 73 relationships do the records show that legal marriage was proved. In the other 52 relationships marriage was assumed, and the couple was at least known to go about as husband and wife.

[20] 'Leniently' here means that one of the couple was discharged (13 women, 7 men) while the other was charged; or one was charged with the lesser offence while the other was capitally charged or charged on alternative indictments (2 women, 4 men); or the name of one of them disappears from the whole process (1 woman).

that of men, but to a surprisingly small extent. The suspicion must be that leniency was shown to the spouse or partner who could be of most help to the Bank in ensuring a watertight case against his or her partner. Most married/cohabiting couples were treated equally at this stage of the judicial process. Married women were rarely protected by the effect of marriage itself.

Overall, at this stage of the judicial process, the Bank used its discretionary powers entirely to safeguard its own interests. Decisions not to prosecute related to the chances of a successful outcome, and not significantly to other possible choices. The Bank was defensive about the views of government, the judiciary and the public on the role discretion played in its prosecuting system. Its papers contain several written justifications of its actions.[21] Its policy was directed to successful prosecution and the preferring of indictments which had a reasonable chance of victory in the courts. It also sought to control the expense of the exercise, and to distinguish petty offenders from the major fabricators and dealers in bad currency.

Plea bargaining

Coupled with the decision to prosecute was the consideration of an offer of a plea bargaining deal. The prisoner who was believed to have uttered forged notes could choose to plead guilty to a lesser charge of possession of the notes, with the almost certain sentence of fourteen years' transportation to New South Wales, or could take a chance with a not guilty plea to the capital charge of uttering. If the former choice were made, the Bank would not prefer the capital charge.[22] Criticism of the Bank for this method of handling forgery crimes came from many quarters, but was never strong enough to deter it from a policy which was successful and held capital sentencing at a 'tolerable' level. [23] The Bank's legal advisers were forced on several occasions to justify this 'manipulation' of the judicial system. If all offences were prosecuted capitally, they said, the majority would be recommended to pardon on condition of transportation. 'This will be mischievous . . . remission of sentence always tends to the encouragement of crime which . . . will inevi-

---

[21] For instance, BEFP, F2/84, in which the Bank set out its defence of the way cases were taken.

[22] Plea bargaining was a rare strategy in felony trials at the time. It receives no attention in Landsman, 'Contentious spirit'. See P. King, 'Punishing assault: the transformation of attitudes in the English courts', *Journal of Interdisciplinary History* xxvii (1996), 43–74 at pp. 50–1, for the tendency in the late eighteenth century for cases to be over before they got to court because of defendants' confessions. However, this is a different legal process. Since the Bank of England used the procedure with little comment as early as 1804, it would be surprising if it had not been used in other felony trials during the eighteenth century. Ignorance of the use of this procedure in such a dramatic way by the Bank of England may be because of lack of interest by researchers in the action of the Bank in its criminal cases.

[23] See, for instance, the entries in BECLS, M5/320, Jan., July 1818.

tably destroy the present salutary impression that convictions for forgery are almost always fatal.'[24] On the other hand, there was growing support for the benefit of transportation of people involved in this sort of crime, since it 'removed them from the scene of offence and temptation, cut them off by a great gulf of space from all their former connexions, and gave them the opportunity of redeeming past crimes by becoming useful members of society'.[25] Throughout the first three decades of the nineteenth century, the Bank, through its lawyers, felt it had control of the judicial procedure, rarely coming off second best, whatever the pressure of criticism.

The Bank was at its most arrogant in prosecution strategies in 1817. Thomas Edwards, to be capitally charged at the Old Bailey with extensive selling of forged notes, petitioned the Bank to negotiate a charge for possession in return for information on other offenders. The Bank responded that, if he pleaded guilty to the capital charge, it (not the court) would see that he was granted life transportation.[26] The Bank continued with such a strategy throughout 1817 and 1818. Objections were raised by the Secretary of State following the capital conviction at the Old Bailey of Elizabeth Wingfield and Hannah Polley. The Bank 'allowed' them to plead guilty to the capital offence on condition of their being transported for life, and was rebuked by the Secretary of State, who noted that this was 'extremely unusual and as he [Lord Sidmouth] believes unprecedented and that he is satisfied that HRH the Prince Regent will not approve of the prisoners having been induced to plead Guilty, by an assurance which compromises the Royal Prerogative, and is likely if drawn into precedent, to be attended with serious inconveniences, not only to the public but to the Bank of England itself'.[27] From this point, this strategy ceased.

Reviewing its annual prosecution figures and costs in 1820, the Bank commented that, of 411 people taken to court nationwide that year, 251 (61 per cent) had accepted the plea bargain offer, 111 in 'the country' and 140 at the Old Bailey.[28] The tendency of London and Middlesex defendants to accept the plea bargain is marked. In the main prosecuting years in London (1812–21), the plea bargain offer was made by the Bank in 86 per cent of cases (574 cases). The offer was made to 88 per cent of the London women (144) and 85 per cent of the men (430). The overall acceptance rate of the offer was 88 per cent (503 cases), men and women accepting in equal proportions. It is difficult to comprehend the calculations these men and women made at this stage of the risky journey to the next stage of the criminal justice

---

24 These are the observations of Serjeant Bosanquet on the manner of conducting Bank prosecutions: BEFP, F2/84. The papers are undated. From incidents described in them they are likely to be from 1821 when consideration was being given to changing the punishment for forgery.

25 H. Merrivale, *Lectures on colonization and colonies*, ii, London 1841, 17–18.

26 BECLS, M5/319, 26 June, 3 July 1817.

27 OBSP, June 1818, 293; BECLS, M5/320, 15 June, 2 July 1818.

28 BECLS, M5/325, 21 Mar.1821.

system. Their responses and the pressures they faced in their gamble on the best outcome appear to have been similar for both sexes. The idea that women might get a better deal from the court if they pleaded not guilty and told their stories was conspicuously absent from the calculation, perhaps an acknowledgement that their criminal actions were unlikely to be viewed with compassion.

The plea bargaining system exemplified the Bank of England's determination to win this legal battle against utterers. With this weight on its mind, it is not surprising that the discretion exercised does not easily fit a gendered explanation. The evidence about the Bank's prosecution decisions suggests that women were slightly more leniently treated. However, evidence about the degree of women's involvement in criminal transactions was crucial, and may have weighted decisions slightly in their favour. The small differences warn against simple views of gender-biased discretion at this stage in the judicial process. The crimes around the circulation of forged low value Bank notes certainly seem to be sharply distinguished from the overwhelming majority of property offences. To consider them at this juncture in this study emphasises why it is important not to treat all capital property crimes as if they were homogenous. Information about the involvement of women and the perceived leniency shown to them does not emerge unless the enquiry is more focused. In the case of these forgery crimes, there are many factors which make it a special and unusual crime, one which was so often described in alarming terms, and more likely to lead to offenders being executed than other offences. The Bank's careful, efficient, planned and highly financed performance as prosecutor appears at many points to run contrary to the assumptions frequently made about the discretionary nature of the system of justice at this time. Its purposeful endeavours, its single-minded pursuit of its specific aim of ridding the nation and itself of the evil of forgery, and the mastery of the technicalities of cases by its lawyers, against the background of the perceived national importance of the crime, injects distinctive features into any analysis of this episode in criminal justice history. Moreover, the Bank was able, give or take a few annoying disagreements with the government and would-be reformers of the judicial system, to proceed on its way with acquiescence of judges, juries and the Secretary of State, a way which differed significantly from the usual characterisation of English criminal justice.

Public attitudes to forgery trials

It is important to set the forged Bank note prosecutions in the context of wider attitudes to Bank note forgery, and the death sentence it attracted. These varied from year to year during the period of suspension, depending on the numbers of prosecutions instigated by the Bank of England up and down the country. In the earlier years, Bank note forgery crime was regarded most seriously by many in English society. It was believed to threaten the nation's commercial well-being and carried with it a strong aura of treason. Insidious in nature, difficult to observe and apprehend, it was particularly detested by upholders of English freedoms. However, as the years went by, and the numbers prosecuted, hanged and transported for this crime rose, public unease was expressed. The attention it provoked contributed significantly to the debate on capital punishment and penal policy in the early decades of the nineteenth century. The Bank was never troubled by more than transient opposition from the law and judiciary. However, adverse responses to high levels of prosecutions and executions around 1818 were printed in news-papers, private publications and in parliament, and local traders were constantly anxious about low value notes, greatly fearing having a forgery passed off on them, since they would not be reimbursed by the Bank and would become involved in further loss of money and time in assisting the Bank in its prosecutions.[29] At times, it was said that unless forgers and their associates were punished with utmost severity, their activities would prolif-erate until all trade and activity ceased as the circulation of money and infor-mation halted. This type of fraud concerned not property itself, but the instruments that facilitated the movement of property. The offence seemed to many to be less a form of theft, more a life threatening assault on the forms that sustained a commercial people.[30]

After 1818 a different attitude prevailed.[31] The period of 'suspension' was seen to have 'diffused depravity' and 'an effusion of human blood' had resulted.[32] 'It could not be denied that in the course of the last ten years, no capital punishment had excited so much odium, and rendered the adminis-tration of public justice so unpopular as that in cases of forgery'.[33] The government equivocated during the first three decades of the century, unable to decide on the appropriate response to the crime.[34] Public opinion also wavered. The executions of men for dealing in higher value notes in 1821 were welcomed by the correspondent of The Times.[35] In wider debates about Bank note forgery and the death penalty, the Bank of England was the conve-nient target for all shades of antagonistic opinion. Yet, day to day, in the courts, as the numerous cases were heard, few men and women were

[29] BEFP, F2/84.
[30] See McGowen, 'Forgery discovered', 114–15, 121–2, 126.
[31] This is encapsulated in the famous cartoon by George Cruickshank: 'Bank restriction note: a protest against the severity of the penalty for forgery', in W. Horne, The Bank restric-tion barometer, London 1818.
[32] The Sun, 25 Feb. 1818, reporting Sir James MacIntosh in debate in the House of Commons.
[33] J. Mackintosh, speech in the House of Commons, Debates of the House of Commons, n.s. ix, 1823, 412.
[34] For details of the incompatibility of suggested government strategies see J. Miller, An enquiry into the present state of the statute and criminal law of England, London 1822, 126–35.
[35] The Times, 22 Nov. 1821.

acquitted, scores of death sentences were passed and carried into effect, and automatic sentences of transportation resulted from use of the 'liberty' to plead to the lesser offence of possession. The lack of room for discretionary manoeuvre by juries and judges was infrequently lamented.

Forged Bank note cases at the Old Bailey

Although forged note uttering took place in London in the same shops, public houses, coaches, alleys and lodgings where pickpockets and shoplifters operated, and the names of constables, watchmen, counsel and some shopowners involved are similarly familiar, the stories told in court were not. The prosecution process worked, for the most part, like a well-oiled machine and, with the extensive use of the plea bargaining system, there was infrequent need for juries to deliberate and little need for judges to use discretion in sentencing. The personal relationship between victim and defendant, which could affect decisions, was also lacking in the courtroom. The Bank of England presented a professional, bureaucratic face as victim, and, having decided to prosecute, was not likely to ask for discretion from the court for prisoners. This changed the dynamics of court procedure and decision-making and may have made capital sentencing easier.

The Bank of England prosecuted 737 people at the Old Bailey between 1804 and 1834 – 551 men (75 per cent) and 186 women (25 per cent).[36] Prosecutions in London took longer to reach the substantial proportions attained in other parts of the country since, in the early years of the 'suspension' period, London was not a centre of currency crime. Birmingham, Liverpool and Manchester dominated. Detection increased slowly in London as the policing endeavours of the Bank developed. The years from 1812 to 1821 saw a huge increase in prosecution both in the metropolis and in other parts of the country. The plea bargaining system, although it had been used as early as 1804, was manipulated extensively in these years to push scores of people quickly through the judicial system. In 1821 the period of 'suspension' ended. There was no longer need for significant use of low denomination paper money. In London, prosecution virtually came to a standstill, although not in the major cities of the rest of Britain.[37]

---

[36] Numbers of trials have been counted from the OBSP. Three cases in BECLS records do not appear in the OBSP (3 men, all of whom, according to BECLS, were found guilty of possession and sentenced to 14 years' transportation). These have not been included in the numbers in this study. One woman was not recorded in BECLS records, but her case was reported in the OBSP (Sept. 1821, 411–12). Her case has been included. The majority (669) faced trial between 1812 and 1821. In London, the proportion of men prosecuted was slightly lower, and of women slightly higher, than in other parts of the country. The out-of-London proportions were 78% men: 22% women.

[37] See BECLS, M5/325–33, Jan. 1822–Dec. 1834. During this time, the committee considered 190 cases from towns outside London, and 26 from London and Middlesex.

Table 18 (a)
Pleas and verdicts in Bank of England forged note cases:
Old Bailey Sessions, 1804–21

Plea	Women (% of all women's pleas)	Women found not guilty	Men (% of all men's pleas)	Men found not guilty
Not guilty to capital charge	17 (9%)	4	51 (9.5%)	9
Guilty to capital charge	3 (2%)	0	10 (2%)	0
Plea bargain accepted	136 (74%)	0	392 (73%)	0
Plea bargain refused	19 (10%)	6	53 (10%)	16
Not guilty to lesser charge	7 (4%)	3	26 (5%)	5
Guilty to lesser charge	1 (1%)	0	3 (0.5%)	0
Totals	183 (100%)	13 (7% of women's pleas)	535 (100%)	30 (6% of men's pleas)

Sources: OBSP; BECLS, M5/307–25; HO 26/8–28.

As prosecutor and defendant entered the trial arena, there were six options for proceeding. The Bank, if certain of proving the guilt of a serial forger, or a seller or utterer of bad notes, preferred an indictment for a capital charge only. The normal response of the defendant would be a plea of not guilty. Being found guilty in such a case meant that the judge had to pass sentence of death. The second option was the unusual plea of guilty to the capital charge, a response disliked by the court which exhorted defendants not to plead guilty, since it wished to hear all the evidence so it could make its own decision.[38] The reasons for such an apparently fatalistic response to a capital charge are hard to understand, and may have come about through misunderstanding on the defendant's part about what exactly the Bank's legal officers had been offering.

The third option was the popular one – the plea bargain. If defendants were willing to plead guilty to the lesser charge of possession of forged notes and face an automatic sentence of fourteen years' transportation, the Bank would not put the capital charge. This had a huge effect on trial outcomes and, later, on the future of the convicted men and women as they sought to mitigate their sentences. Most cases were pursued on this basis, preventing discussion in court. The fourth option was for defendants who were offered this 'bargain' to decline the Bank's 'clemency', refuse to plead to the lesser charge and stand their ground with a not guilty plea to the capital charge. Of

[38] This occurred in 2% of cases between 1812 and 1821.

Table 18 (b)
Pleas and verdicts in Bank of England forged note cases:
Old Bailey Sessions, 1821–34*

Plea	Women	Women not guilty	Men	Men not guilty
Not guilty (death penalty still in place)	2	1	10	2
Not guilty (when maximum sentence life transportation)	1	0	4	1
Guilty (death sentence still in place)	0	0	2	0
Totals	3	1	16	3

Sources: OBSP; BECLS, M5/325–33; HO 26/27–40

* Table 18 (b) kept separate from 18 (a) since the period of the suspension ended in 1821, and in 1832 the death penalty was removed from the crime of uttering Bank notes. Prosecutions were usually only instigated when large value notes were uttered, providing a different environment from the earlier years.

the 600 Londoners offered the plea bargain option between 1804 and 1821, seventy-two refused it. Of these refusers, twenty-two were winners and were found not guilty by the jury and discharged (*see* table 18a). Many of the other fifty who refused and who were found guilty of the capital offence, found that the Bank became their implacable enemy when they later petitioned for commutation of sentence or other favours. It is a mark of the Bank's determination that many of those who refused the offer, and were found not guilty, were later charged with further offences. The second time around they were unlikely to be offered another chance of a plea bargain. There remained two further options for pleading in court – a plea of not guilty, or a plea of guilty to a charge of possession of forged notes, presumably because this was all the Bank stood a chance of proving.

Pleas, verdicts and sentences at the Old Bailey

The pleas made in response to the various charge options have been analysed (*see* tables 18a and 18b). Where a plea of 'not guilty' was entered, the tables show whether that plea was successful. The analysis confirms how dominant were the effects of the plea bargaining system. Perhaps the most remarkable, and terrifying, feature is how few defendants were found not guilty, of either the capital or the transportable offence. In all twenty-nine years, only fourteen London women were found not guilty (7.5 per cent of women on trial) and only thirty-two London men (5.8 per cent of all men on trial). It is also evident how, between 1804 and 1821, there was virtually no difference between the pleading strategies of men and women – equal percentages taking the decision to plead guilty or not guilty, or to accept or reject the plea bargain offer. In addition, there was no real difference between men and women in the results of the cases where they had decided to plead not guilty. A considerable difference between men and women arose after 1821 when the Bank changed its prosecution policy after the ending of 'suspension' (table 18b), but the numbers involved at this point were very small. The Bank was, at that stage, prosecuting in London only for uttering of larger value notes, £5 or £10, and these tended to be in men's possession. Apart from these final twelve years of sparse prosecution activity in London, the parity in the outcome of cases in court between men and women was particularly remarkable. There is little doubt that this was indeed a special and different set of offences, not only in the perceived severity of the offence, but in the conduct of the prosecution and the technical legal procedures used.

In spite of the parity exposed by examination of pleas and verdicts over the whole of this period, there was still a common presumption that the court was lenient towards women, and that female defendants were more likely to avail themselves of the 'clemency' of the plea bargain procedure. A newspaper report of two trials involving Eliza Burnham, in 1820, told how, on her first appearance in the Old Bailey, after refusing a plea bargain offer, she was found not guilty. She told the court that she had been 'seduced to a bad house by a gentleman named Smith', and had been given three notes. She spent them with no idea they were forged. The jury at first returned a verdict of 'guilty of uttering but not with a felonious intent'. The judge advised that such a verdict amounted to an acquittal since the law required criminal intent. When the foreman repeated that they were certain that she was without knowledge of the offence, the jury were instructed to find her not guilty. Ever determined, the Bank had her back in court a month later for a similar offence. Unusually, it offered her another plea bargain, which she had indicated to the court that she would again refuse. As the case commenced, she called out, 'My Lord, my Lord, I wish to withdraw the plea and plead guilty.'

> Mr Serjeant Bosanquet [for the Bank] said he had not the slightest objects [sic] and begged to add that all the prisoners charged at the Session with the same offence had been allowed the Bank's privilege (if they chose to avail themselves of the indulgence) of pleading guilty to the minor offence; but they had chosen at first to adopt a different course, under the idea perhaps that as they were females the severity of the law would not be exercised upon them. This however was a fallacious notion because the public security required that the law in these cases should be carried into full *execution*.[39]

When it came to handing down sentences, the judges were left with no scope for discretion in their decision-making. If a capital charge was proved, there

---

[39] *London Packet and the Lloyds Evening Post*, 18/20 Sept., 27/30 Oct.1820; BECLS, M5/324, 23 Aug., 11 Oct.1820; M5/325, 2 June 1821; OBSP, Aug.1820, 527–8; Oct.1820, 624, with 19 others.

Table 19
Results of forged Bank note trials: Old Bailey Sessions, 1804–34

Result	Total	Women	Men
Death sentence	126 (17%)	30 (16%)	96 (17%)
Transportation	565 (77%)	142 (76%)	423 (77%)
Not guilty/acquitted	46 (6%)	14 (8%)	32 (6%)
Totals	737 (100%)	186 (100%)	551 (100%)

Sources: OBSP; BECLS, M5/307–33; HO 26/10–40.

had to be a death sentence (until 1832). If a lesser charge was proved, there had to be a sentence of fourteen years' transportation. Table 19 shows the results of forged Bank note cases at the Old Bailey. The particular way of proceeding in these cases resulted in an unusual situation between men and women in relation to death sentences and sentences of transportation. Out of the total of 126 death sentences, thirty affected women (16 per cent of all the women's sentences). Ninety-six affected men (17 per cent of all the men's sentences). Of the 565 transportation sentences, 142 were for women (76 per cent of all women's sentences) and 423 for men (77 per cent of all men's sentences). This shows an unusually equal situation in stark contrast to that for shoplifting and pickpocketing. This is a reminder that there are drawbacks in combining statistics for property crimes, treating them as if they were the same and as if attitudes to them were the same.

Puzzling decisions

Because of the way in which the court cases were handled, a good deal of quantitative evidence is available, but little qualitative evidence since the vast majority of prisoners accepted a plea bargain and therefore did not tell their stories in court. The few stories which were told suggest that, unlike shoplifting and pickpocketing, there was little difference between the activities of men and women in London in their handling of forged Bank notes. This further explains the parity of trial outcomes. In other parts of the country, a higher proportion of men was indicted for forgery of notes, and for having plates, instruments and paper. This was not so in London. A handful of cases for actual forging activities was heard at the Old Bailey, but generally prosecutions related to the various means of getting into circulation notes obtained elsewhere. London men and women did not display behaviour that was noticeably dissimilar from each other as they went about this business. There is some evidence that women were more likely to be apprehended for uttering notes and men for possessing the stocks of notes. Women were less obvious in the work of uttering since they were more likely to be buying small items in shops. Tea, sugar, as well as ham, candles and small items of clothing, were frequently the triggers for passing off forged notes. It was also usual for men and women to work together in the false note trade, and male/female co-operation continued after conviction as they waited in prison for the transport ships, men and women using their visitors of the opposite sex to supply notes which could be traded in confinement.

The court reports of the limited number of cases which led to not guilty verdicts (forty-six) have been scoured to see if it is possible to deduce reasons for the decisions in these cases. These records must be used with caution. Information gleaned from them comes from a reading of a report which, although likely to be accurate about the facts given in court, can only record what was admitted before the jury. Some of the verdicts could be called 'technical' – in a few cases the defendant's identity was not proved satisfactorily, or the complex chain of evidence was found to be faulty, or the prosecution did not prove that the defendant had knowledge that the notes in question were false. These technical reasons accounted for not guilty verdicts in the cases of four women and fifteen men who pleaded not guilty. In a few other cases the Bank decided at the last moment that the full case would not be put as evidence emerged which suggested that the prisoner in the dock would be better used giving evidence against other suspected utterers (three men and three women). In the cases of another three men, the jury took exception to the way the Bank had used sophisticated entrapment procedures and discharged the prisoners. Readings of other evidence given in court strongly suggest that five women and four men were acquitted as the jury felt that they had been used or tricked by someone else, for instance by a client, a spouse or another known offender.

The relatively 'gender-balanced' outcomes of the cases may suggest an equivocal role for gender in these crimes and in the judicial process. Sometimes the relationships between men and women did not protect women in the way that might have been anticipated. Mary Jenkinson, found capitally guilty of uttering in 1805, was, at the time of her arrest, living with Cornelius Holt, well known to the Bank as a major trader in forged notes. She was apprehended for proffering a forged £2 note in a pawnbroker's shop. She was plied with brandy in public houses by the constables on the way to Bow Street public office. Their aim was to get her talking about Holt. She would only say she had got him off forgery charges when he came before the magistrates earlier, and had told him 'he would bring her to the gallows'. She accused the constables of getting her drunk and 'behaving ill' to her, threatening her with death because Holt had given her the money. Although the jury recommended her to mercy, since they felt she was under Holt's influence, his involvement did not protect her since he had not been in her company when she passed the note.[40]

A married couple, Susannah and Michael Gerain, met differing fates.

[40] OBSP, Feb.1805, 185–9.

Susannah, an 'old woman' of seventy-seven, was capitally charged with uttering notes in a shop. She said she had picked up the notes in the street. Her husband, Michael, aged sixty, said he found the notes on his round as night watchman. While she was saying that he knew nothing about them, he was saying, 'My wife is very wrong, she is telling you stories, I gave them to her.' A quantity of forged notes was found in their lodgings. At the trial, Susannah changed her story, claiming innocence, saying that her husband had found the notes and brought them home. Her case was heard before that of her husband (the Bank charged him only with possession) and she was capitally convicted; he was found guilty of possession and sentenced to fourteen years' transportation. Susannah died in prison awaiting execution. There must be a strong suspicion that Michael was instrumental in his wife's conviction. It is probable that Susannah was known to the Bank for this sort of activity. The Bank, by varying the nature of the charges against man and woman, precluded the use of the excuse of marital coercion.[41]

When Thomas and Elizabeth Leach were apprehended for uttering notes, the Bank offered them the opportunity of a plea bargain. Thomas took the offer and was sentenced to transportation. Elizabeth took her chance, pleading not guilty to the capital charge of uttering. Her unsuccessful defence strategy relied on the involvement of her husband in what she did, even his presence with her. The details provide an interesting view of a rare occasion when marriage emerged as a major issue in a criminal case. Elizabeth Leach had gone to a pawnbroker's shop to buy some stays with a £1 note. The pawnbroker recognised that the note was forged, took her name and address, wrote it on the note, and continued with the usual procedure of enquiring where she had obtained it. There was a good deal of argument between them about this, with Elizabeth changing her account frequently, finally saying that 'her husband would make a fine piece of work with her if he knew it to be a bad one, that he had taken it for two shirts that had been sold in [their clothes] shop'. A small supply of forged notes was found in the Leach's premises. Under examination by the magistrate at Bow Street, Elizabeth had been anxious to protect her husband. She said she had taken the money in their shop and had hidden it, not telling her husband. The jury wanted to know if she was trying to prevent suspicion falling on her husband and what the relationship was between them. Bank counsel said, 'She is indicted as a single woman. The husband, as he is called, was apprehended for a different offence than the woman at the bar now is indicted for.' Elizabeth's counsel established that Thomas and Elizabeth were 'man and wife'. Elizabeth made her own submission:

> Them notes that were in my work bag, my husband gave me the day before, to purchase some articles I wanted in the house – he said he'd come with me to buy them, I thought that would be good, so left them there till he was able.

41 OBSP, Jan.1810, 64–5; BECLS, M5/309, 28 Dec.1809, 24 Jan., 12 May, 3 Aug.1810.

The reason that I denied these notes being in the work bag, I did not know what to say, being in the hands of officers, I imagined my husband might know something of them, I knew I was in the hands of officers, I said I knew nothing about it; my husband was at the door when I went in for the stays and when I came out he was gone.

This attempt to seek protection through the excuse of marital coercion failed and a death sentence followed.[42] The Bank thwarted any possibility of Elizabeth's success in the use of this legal excuse by separating the charges against her and her husband, tempting him with a plea bargain so that his story would not be told in court. Since Elizabeth's defence relied on reference to Thomas's story which had not been told, the excuse of marital coercion did not work.

The cases against James Gardiner and Jane Harrison provide an example of how difficult it can be to understand jury decisions unless the narrative evidence is looked at in detail rather than considering only the statistics of cases. These two were jointly indicted, capitally only, in two separate cases. The extent of their note-selling activities was considerable and the Bank was determined to have them both convicted. It had used an elaborate and financially costly entrapment procedure, involving a cheese-monger and his friends who signed on to the Bank's payroll for these cases. The defendants had the help of three counsel. Gardiner was not a poor man. He lived in a large house in Rose Street, Covent Garden, which was variously used for music and dancing, meetings of a 'painting society', concerts at which he played the flute or the violin, and a place to which men 'came with girls – it was used for such purposes'. He carried on a cautious and successful trade in selling forged notes around the public houses and clubs of Covent Garden, when he was not 'playing at concerts' further afield. Jane Harrison lived with him as his housekeeper. In both cases Gardiner was found guilty and sentenced to death, and in both cases Harrison was found not guilty. The decisions in her favour are difficult to understand since it seems that her involvement was unequivocal, and her defence – that she did not understand what she was selling – ingenuous. Evidence from the entrapment witnesses also seemed unequivocal, such as 'I delivered the copper (to pay for notes) to Harrison – Gardiner was not there'. Or,

> She asked me if I wanted to do anything that evening. I said, 'Yes, I wanted to go to work'. She asked how many I wanted. I said 'Two', and paid ten shillings. She took a piece of whitey-brown paper out of her pocket, containing a great number of notes: after looking them over on the table she picked out two for me and said 'these two are very good ones'; wrote on the front of each (a false name and address) and then delivered them to me. I conversed with her about someone else who would like some.

---

[42] OBSP, July 1811, 321–4; BECLS, M5/311, 3 July 1811; *London Chronicle*, 15 July 1811.

On another day the conversation was:

> 'Do you want anything tonight?' I said 'Yes, half a score, but I can only take five tonight'. She said, 'I will pick you out five good ones', which she did and told me they were good ones. I asked her how much they were. She said £1 and 5 shillings. I gave her that. Gardiner came in and confirmed that they were very good.

It is difficult to believe that she lacked knowledge of what she was involved in, since she repeated this kind of conversation and activity with others who, unknown to her, were working under cover for the Bank. It is likely that aversion to the entrapment of a young woman was at the heart of the jury's decision about Harrison. Defence counsel castigated the entrapment procedures, and maligned those whom the Bank was paying to do this work. The case against Gardiner was watertight: he had nothing to say in his own defence, presenting only some alibis – that he was playing his violin elsewhere at times when he was said to be negotiating with the decoys. Harrison submitted a written defence: 'My Lord and gentlemen of the Jury, I am very young, under 20 years of age. I was living with Mr Gardiner as his housekeeper and delivered out the papers without any knowledge of their being forged notes.' The jury may have wanted to believe her, particularly since the entrapment procedure had been so elaborate. Perhaps they felt the prize of Gardiner, clearly a leading player in the Bank note forgery game, was sufficient for justice. They may have thought that Harrison operated under duress from a more powerful man, but they may have been affected by her as 'an interesting looking female', as the London Chronicle reporter clearly had been.[43]

Difference in a 'different' crime

It is unfortunate that the limited number of not guilty pleas in Bank note forgery cases prevents a full exploration of the fascinating stories which forged Bank notes utterers might have told in court, and from which to tease out evidence of discretion and diversity. However, what can be gleaned from the records of the prosecution of this crime in the public arena of the Old Bailey Sessions is useful in showing that attitudes to the offence itself affected verdicts (if not sentences in this controlled legal situation), emphasising the importance of looking more closely at the variations within categories of property crime. The seriousness with which this set of crimes was regarded, the reduced opportunity for court deliberation created by the massive use of plea bargaining, the lack of personal relationship between prosecutor and accused and the efficiency of the prosecuting machine, all changed the dynamic of the trials. There was often a suggestion in not guilty pleas that it

43 OBSP, May 1820, 393–7; London Chronicle, 23 May 1820.

was the Bank of England which was on trial for its prosecution policies and its production of inferior paper money. Juries allowed the benefit of any doubt, created by the Bank's high-handedness or entrapment, to the defendant.

The dynamics were further altered by the smaller proportion of women involved. Had their proportion been as great as in pickpocketing and shop-lifting, verdicts in not guilty plea cases might have been more lenient in order to avoid sentencing large numbers of women to death. Since few stories were told in court, it is not possible to be sure that there was always little difference between men and women in their modes of operating to utter, dispose or put away forged notes. However, when stories were told in not guilty pleas, similarity of illegal activity is clearly seen. Whether transactions took place in shops, in public houses, clubs, alleys, private houses or lodgings, the task did not vary.

Although there is evidence that women were slightly more likely to be found not guilty if they pleaded not guilty, the over-riding picture is of equivocal gender distinction at this stage of the judicial process. It was only when the public exercise was over, when the relationship between Bank and prisoner was out of the public gaze, that discretion on gendered lines emerged strongly.[44]

[44] See chapter 7 below.

6

After Sentencing

When I was at the Bar my Life was then in your hands and I now feel it more acutely. Let mercy be blended with Justice – it is yet in your power to save the Life of an unhappy sufferer.[1]

To be pardoned, or not?

Being found guilty and sentenced was by no means the end of the journey through the criminal justice system for the hundreds of shoplifters, pickpockets and forged note utterers. Very many of them were now to pass through further processes of negotiation and pleading which could trigger a wide range of responses – pardons, mitigation and other merciful actions. Sometimes unexpected decisions were made about their future, and 'gender' played a further part.

This chapter starts to trace whether the sentences of the court were carried out, and, if not, which prisoners obtained a lighter deal, and why. It explains how the system of mercy, pardoning and remission of sentences operated at this time, its developing bureaucratic nature, and continues to question how the sex of the convicted criminal affected decisions. The difficult subject of gender and the death sentence is also addressed. Why were so few women executed, and what might have been the nature of those who were? Chapter 7 will elaborate on less bureaucratic, more discretionary, aspects of the final stage of the journey through the justice system. Bureaucracy and discretion added their different colours to the picture.

The men and women sentenced found that the journey through the justice system continued to twist and turn. Their post-sentencing experiences seemed as full of surprises and idiosyncratic responses as had all that preceded it. The writer of the biography of Mary Bryant, sentenced to hang for highway robbery at the end of the eighteenth century, influenced by the power of the myth of an effective, efficient and merciless 'bloody code', suggested that 'Like a protagonist in a Greek tragedy, once she had embarked on a course of action, the result was inevitable given the times in which she lived.'[2] There was nothing inevitable about what happened to Mary Bryant,

---

1 Charlotte Newman, after her sentencing for uttering forged Bank of England notes: BEFP, F25/5.
2 J. Cook, *To brave every danger: the epic life of Mary Bryant of Fowey*, London 1993, 33.

nor was there anything inevitable about what happened to the men and women tried for any serious crime at the end of the eighteenth or the beginning of the nineteenth century.

The period from the 1780s to the 1830s saw both continuity and significant change in English penal practice.[3] Much has been written on these issues and it is not proposed to engage at length with them here.[4] The later years of the eighteenth century saw the formulation of a more settled debate on the need for change, although none of the ideas was emerging for the first time. The morality, justice and efficacy of execution, the purpose, cost and efficiency of the transportation system and of imprisonment had long been subjects of dispersed discussion, if not insistent debate. Those discussions came to express a serious level of discontent with current penal practice on moral, cultural, practical and administrative grounds. By the early nineteenth century little had changed in practice. A steady stream of convicts was executed, transportation was still a well-used convenience and the role and state of prisons were rarely criticised. Administrative and political inertia can always be blamed for such a situation. However, those who influenced the justice system had a certain confidence that they had the situation under control.[5] The 'bloody code' might appear rigid and disproportionate, but judicial discretion and the apportioning of mercy and pardon provided for a situation that was acceptable to them. Yet, by the time Sir Samuel Romilly

[3] McGowen, 'Problem of punishment', provides an excellent overview and explanation of long term change; see also Beattie, *Crime and the courts*, 13–14, and 'London crime', 49–76.

[4] Among the useful works which deal with punishment and change in the penal system at the particular period are Radzinowicz, *History of English criminal law*, i, ii; L. Radzinowicz and R. Hood, *A history of English criminal law and its administration from 1750*, V: *The emergence of penal policy in Victorian and Edwardian England*, Oxford 1990, 465–79, 689–719; Ignatieff, *A just measure of pain*, and 'State, civil society and total institution'; Beattie, *Crime and the courts*, 450–616, 'Royal pardon', and *Policing and punishment*; King, *Crime, justice and discretion*; Gatrell, *Hanging tree*; Jenkins, 'From gallows to prison?'; C. Campbell, *The intolerable hulks: British shipboard confinement, 1776–1857*, London 1993; McGowen, 'Problem of punishment', 'Powerful sympathy', 'The changing face of God's justice', 'Punishing violence', and 'Civilizing punishment: the end of public execution in England', *JBS* xxxiii (1994), 257–82; J. S. Cockburn, 'Punishment and brutalization in the English enlightenment', *LHR* xii (1994), 155–79; Devereaux, 'In place of death', and 'Making of the Penitentiary Act'; A. R. Ekirh, *Bound for America: the transportation of British convicts to the colonies, 1718–75*, Oxford 1987; M. Gillen, 'The Botany Bay decision, 1786: convicts, not empire', *EHR* xcvii (1982), 740–66; R. Hughes, *The fatal shore: a history of transportation of convicts to Australia, 1787–1868*, London 1987; J. Innes, 'The role of transportation in seventeenth- and eighteenth-century English penal practice', in C. Bridge (ed.), *New perspectives in Australian history* (Institute of Commonwealth Studies, occasional seminar papers 5, 1990), 1–24; and J. Innes and J. Styles, 'The crime wave: recent writing on crime and criminal justice in eighteenth-century England', *JBS* xxv (1986), 380–435, rev. and repr. in A. Wilson (ed.), *Rethinking social history: English society, 1570–1920, and its interpretation*, Manchester 1993.

[5] King, 'Decision-makers'.

worked on law reform in the early years of the nineteenth century, judicial discretion had become an issue of concern to be dealt with. There were also other pressures at work. Since more offenders were being successfully pursued through the courts, there was a surge in capital convictions, creating fears of a threshold being passed which would bring the whole of the law into disrepute. Further, the weight of numbers of convicts, capital and otherwise, placed pressure on the state's administrative resources. Ways of coping with these demands had to be found, at the same time as preserving an effective image for the system of justice and punishment.[6]

The system for pardon and mercy

The years which have formed the basis for this study saw subtle and progressive change in the workings of the system for pardoning wrongdoers and for remissions of their punishments. A more bureaucratic system was necessarily developing in order to grant 'automatic' pardons, not only to avoid the execution of hundreds of people, but, more important, to ease the dangerous overloading of incarceration facilities. The great increase in criminal business in the courts following the end of the wars with France was also matched by deteriorating official record-keeping.[7] However, the evidence, difficult as it is to penetrate or to trust, does show how many convicts did not serve the sentences passed on them. Death sentences were remitted to sentences of transportation, or even imprisonment. Transportation was remitted to imprisonment, and prison sentences were shortened. In some cases, free pardons were granted.

The whole system of royal mercy had become more complex, handling not just appeals against execution but also against transportation, and the length of prison sentences and sentences of hard labour. This meant an increased number of stages in the convicted prisoner's journey after sentencing where there was a need for choices to be made and pre-emptive action to be taken.[8]

---

6 For arguments about the role of 'pressures on structures' and the collapse of the 'bloody code' see Gatrell, *Hanging tree*, and responses from R. McGowen, 'Revisiting the hanging tree: Gatrell on emotion and history', *BJC* xl (2000), 1–13; Hilton, 'The gallows and Mr Peel'; and Devereaux, 'Peel, pardon and punishment'.

7 This deterioration consists of very apparent failures to make entries at crucial points in the criminal registers (HO 26), Newgate calendars (HO 77) and the transportation registers (HO 11). For instance, in the criminal registers, apart from missing or inaccurate information about prisoners and offences, where decisions on their disposal from Newgate after sentencing were held back to the following month, they were not always recorded in subsequent months. The Newgate calendar lists names of people to be executed who were not executed in the end, and the transportation register shows similar inaccuracies.

8 See Beattie, *Crime and the courts*, 430–6, for details of procedure. However, since his study ends in 1800, it retains a strong emphasis on the death penalty and the appeal system that flowed from it. See also Gatrell, *Hanging tree*, 543–54.

These post-sentencing choices were widely exercised and influenced – by victims and prosecutors, by judges, by prisoners and their friends and acquaintances in deciding to appeal against sentence, and by the Secretary of State, the servants of the Home Office, the gaol and hulk superintendents and their committees, and the King-in-Council in making decisions to vary or annul sentences. The opportunities for decision and choice were legion, and there were many 'gatekeepers' to open or keep closed the barriers on the convicts' travels through the next stages of the criminal justice system.

It is noticeable that, by the early nineteenth century, the use of the royal prerogative of mercy was a more limited instrument than its late eighteenth-century full-blown discretionary manifestation.[9] Even in the earlier period, 'most sentencing and pardoning decisions were almost certainly based on universal and widely agreed criteria rather than on "class favouritism and games of influence" '.[10] The pardoning procedure in the eighteenth century was a more organised and systematic procedure than it later became, and was to a considerable extent a procedure for selecting the right men and women to be executed.[11] The decisions made later, particularly in the early decades of the nineteenth century, were about different possibilities, in a busier judicial environment. The handling of appeals against sentence became a more complex operation, less cohesive, and significantly flexible.[12] By the 1820s a more bureaucratic response had been added to the discretionary system – a system of 'automatic' pardons on grounds of time served, good behaviour and state of health. The mix of discretionary pardoning – to be begged for – and 'automatic' pardoning suggests flexibility in a system which had grown up itself in a flexible and mixed manner. What was happening was perhaps an attempt to present a more pleasing image of justice, to avoid alienating many who were uneasy about the penal regime and to create a more consensual atmosphere at a time of increasing debate about the validity and effectiveness of the judicial system.[13]

What seemed to be a lottery for defendants at the Old Bailey up to and including their sentencing in court appeared to continue as such afterwards. Nevertheless, the system had its own inner logic and rules, still based partly on common understandings of who was a 'proper object' for mercy, and partly on the pressing needs of the state to decrease the burden on institutions of incarceration. It is not possible to know, over the whole of the period, exactly how many convicts appealed against their sentences, nor how many went on

[9] See, for example, Hay, 'Property, authority and the criminal law', and Beattie, 'Royal pardon'.
[10] King, 'Decision-makers', 58.
[11] Beattie, 'Royal pardon'. His emphasis was on appeals against death sentences, using the State Papers Domestic rather than the Home Office archive, and references are to secondary works of historians who may not have used the later pardoning archive, HO 17.
[12] Devereaux, 'In place of death', and 'Peel, pardon and punishment'.
[13] McGowen, 'Image of justice', 'Making the "bloody code"?', and 'Problem of punishment'.

to serve their sentences without further judicial struggle; nor how many were let off their sentences before they were completed. In the case of those who appealed successfully, there is no clear understanding of why they should have been successful. Even so, the criteria for making decisions were becoming less opaque and there was an executive system, with rules, which reduced the need for subjective discretion. Many men and women were set free well before the expiry of the terms of their sentences, from gaols and the general penitentiary in London, on grounds of the length of time served, behaviour in confinement, good service in the gaol's employment, a good character before trial, availability of employment and the prisoner's state of physical and mental health. Home Office quarterly returns show that, due to the operation of this system, large numbers of men and boys were released from the hulks. The pressure for space was particularly great in prison areas for males, hence they benefited significantly from this strategy. The lists of convicts to be given a free pardon and discharged were accompanied by reports from the gaol keepers, or the superintending committee of the penitentiary, or the captain of the ship or the surgeon of ship or prison.[14]

The criteria for pardon were transparent, as can be seen in a request from the general penitentiary for free pardons for four women and eight men; it specified that ten of them had 'served most of their sentence' (upwards of three and a half years of a seven year transportation sentence which had already been commuted to a prison sentence), and that the state of health of the other two (women) caused concern. The penitentiary committee reported that all these prisoners were of exemplary behaviour and had friends to receive them. The paper was annotated at the Home Office: 'This appears to be all regular. Approved. All free pardoned 5th October 1829.'[15] There were many such systematic applications from the general penitentiary and other prisons. One, from Newgate gaol in December 1821, related to a group of prisoners who had been employed in the gaol, seven men and one woman, all tried at the Old Bailey in 1818 and 1819. One of the men and the woman had received sentences of fourteen years' transportation, the rest seven years' transportation. None left England. The men had been cooks in the gaol kitchen, wardsmen, a gatekeeper and a plasterer. All were said to have families, friends or employment to go to for support, all had worked well, were of good behaviour, proving their reformed natures and all were said to be of previous good character. These glowing reports may have been true, but there could have been other factors at work. Those in charge of the gaols may have had other reasons for offering their names. They could have been particularly difficult prisoners, or they could have paid well for the recommendations.[16]

Batches of letters and, later, completed *pro formas* reached the Home Office each quarter from the hulks. Large numbers of men and boys received

---

14 Throughout HO 17.
15 HO 17/50 part 1/Ho63; HO 17/58/Km4.
16 HO 17/57/Kh50.

free pardons. The letter or list heading would state: 'A List of x being two out of every hundred convicts confined on Board the xx at xxx who have served more than half their sentence, are of orderly and uniformly good behaviour, selected by the captain who makes oath to the Impartiality of his choice of them to the Superintendent as fit objects of the Royal Mercy.' The formula used here (two in every hundred on board the hulks) was usual and resulted in the release, with a free pardon, of about a hundred males every quarter. In June 1824 fourteen women, transferred to hulks in 1823 from Millbank prison to alleviate the effects of disease, were listed as 'the last remaining fourteen female convicts on board Narcissus'. All received free pardons. Most had been sentenced to seven years' transportation, reduced to four years in the penitentiary. Now, having been found homes to go to, they were freed after between eighteen months and four years.[17] For these women, the chance provided by the epidemic of infectious diseases at Millbank, was their gateway to freedom.

The fate of London and Middlesex convicts

It has been important to the approach used in this study to keep the focus on the three selected crimes and the men and women involved in London and Middlesex. Unfortunately, as they are followed through the later records of the judicial process, some of their names disappear through gaps in those records. Gaps appear as early as 1809. Carelessness, occasioned as a result of the increasing number of criminal cases handled by the courts, began to over-take the record-keepers. From about 1816 the records became even more unreliable.[18] Table 20 brings together the sentencing information for the three groups of crimes – shoplifting, pickpocketing and forged Bank note uttering. It confirms the significant numbers that had to be processed through the system. In the years analysed, over 1,300 men and women were sentenced at the Old Bailey for these crimes; 252 were sentenced to death, 834 to trans-portation, 219 to imprisonment and 21 to other punishments. Many of these sentences were not carried out, but it is not possible to be certain just how many. Certainly none of the fourteen prisoners sentenced to hang for pickpocketing was executed. Only two of the 112 sentenced to hang for shoplifting were executed.[19] Fifty-three men and at least five women were executed for forged Bank note crimes in London between 1805 and 1829,

---

[17] HO 17/53 part 2/Ik8.

[18] See appendix for details of the records used. Gaps in the national records for those sentenced for Bank note crime have been filled by use of the Bank of England records.

[19] Official statistics (for example, *Select committee on capital punishment in felonies*, PP, 1819, viii, appendix 2, pp. 135–9) show no executions in this period for either shoplifting or pickpocketing; however, there were two executions for shoplifting in London in the period: HO 26/3.

Table 20
Sentences for shoplifting, pickpocketing and forged Bank note crimes: Old Bailey Sessions in selected sample years, 1780–1834

Offence	Death		Transportation		Imprisonment		Other	
	M	F	M	F	M	F	M	F
Shoplifting (23 sample years, 1780–1823)	50	62	102	86	86	104	12	7
Pickpocketing (17 sample years, 1780–1808)	9	5	48	33	7	22	2	–
Forged Bank note crimes (1804–34)	96	30	423	142	–	–	–	–
Totals	155	97	573	261	93	126	14	7

Sources: OBSP; BECLS, M5/307–33; HO 26/1–40.

underlining the fact that the state's attitude to this crime was different from its attitude to other property crimes. It is not possible to assume that even an act as serious as an execution would always be officially recorded. However, these figures are likely to be correct.[20] From 1791[21] until about 1817 it is possible to be reasonably sure of the immediate post-sentencing fate of all but a few of London's shoplifters, pickpockets and forged Bank note utterers. However, it is not possible to know what happened finally in all cases, since early commutations of their sentences could be followed by further unrecorded mitigation. From 1817 it is unwise to rely on the official records. However, despite being cautious, it can be asserted that hundreds of convicted criminals did not hang, were not transported and served far less time in prison than their original sentence stipulated.

The study of verdicts and sentences in chapters 3, 4 and 5 of this book has shown that each of the three crimes brought diverse responses from juries and judges. Similarly, they also brought particular responses from those in a position to make, or assist, decisions which confirmed or modified sentences. The seriousness with which forged Bank note circulation was viewed by those in positions of power is illustrated by the fact that, between 1804 and mid-1817, of the twenty-six death sentences for this crime passed at the Old Bailey – eighteen men and eight women – all eighteen men were executed. However, only two of the eight women were executed.[22] There was a gendered post-sentencing response, even to this crime.

[20] Jenkins, 'From gallows to prison?'. Bank of England records (BECLS, M5/307–33) confirm this calculation.
[21] This was the first year for which the criminal register series (HO 26) was kept.
[22] HO 26/10–23, HO 77/11–19; BECLS, M5/307–20.

Table 21
First commutations of death sentences passed in shoplifting and pickpocketing cases tried at Old Bailey Sessions, 1791–1817 (selected sample years)*

Death sentence commuted to:		Men	Women
Transportation:	for life	10	16
	for 14 years	1	0
	for 7 years	3	2
Imprisonment:	for 2 years	1	3
	for 1 year	2	5
	for 6 months	0	2
	for 3 months	0	1
Army, navy, navigation		4	0
Discharge on sureties		0	2
Free pardon		1	0
To Philanthropic Society		2	0
Died awaiting decision		1	0
Total		25	31

Sources: HO 26/1–40; HO 11.

* Official criminal registers recording this information (HO 26) commence only in 1791, and after 1817 the records become unreliable. Within this period, the sample years are as shown in appendix.

The immediate commutations of the death sentences passed on pickpockets and shoplifters at the Old Bailey, where it has been possible to trace them, are included in table 21.[23] (Since attitudes to Bank note crime were so specific, reflection on it has been separated from consideration of the other two crimes.)

Instead of being executed, most of the pickpockets and shoplifters under sentence of death were transferred to await transportation. This accounted for 56 per cent of the men and 58 per cent of the women, suggesting no immediate intention to be more lenient in pardoning women than men. A few of the women (eleven) were directed towards imprisonment, for periods varying between three months and two years. Two more women were set free on sureties being offered by their friends for their future good behaviour. Among the males, a much smaller number, three only, were given prison sentences, but there was a number of other ways of dealing with these conditionally pardoned male convicts. Four were sent into armed service, two boys

[23] Some cases are untraceable at this point, even in this period (4 men, 3 women). These have been omitted from table 21.

to the care of the Philanthropic Society [24] and one was granted a free pardon. For the thirteen women and ten men who had been sentenced to death and then had found themselves, at worst, in the British army, or in prison, however unpleasant, for very short periods, or even let go free, the lottery of the journey through the justice system had surprising results – leniency abounded.

It is then possible to find in the official records what happened to the London and Middlesex pickpockets and shoplifters sentenced between 1791 and 1817 to seven years' transportation. The vast majority of the women found themselves on board transportation ships (70 per cent of them). Of the men, 25 per cent were listed on board transportation ships, with another 47 per cent on the hulks in the Thames or around Portsmouth. The rest of those sentenced to seven years' transportation were allowed other ways out of making the long voyage. Of the women, a substantial minority ended up in prison for terms of between six months and five years, a small handful were quickly given free pardons, two women died soon after initial sentencing and there are another five for whom details cannot be found. The alternative exit from transportation was rather different for the men. None of them appears to have ended up in a conventional prison. One was allowed voluntary exile, one was fined, one was freely pardoned, one was released on security for good behaviour, nine were conditionally pardoned to serve in the army or navy and there are twelve more for whom details of this stage of the journey cannot be found. [25]

However, for the men and women sentenced to fourteen years' transportation for forged Bank note crimes, there was little chance of escaping the voyage to Australia. Of the 142 London women thus sentenced, it is certain that 125 (88 per cent) set off to Australia, maybe slightly more. Of the few 'Bank women' who escaped transportation, one was pardoned after many years in the penitentiary and, in the case of the remaining sixteen or so, since delays to their planned departures were caused by illness or giving birth, it is difficult to be sure that they sailed in the end. It is certain that at least 75 per cent of the men sentenced to transportation for Bank offences sailed for

[24] The Philanthropic Society was a school charity established in 1788 'for the prevention of crime, encouragement of industry, culture and good morals among children training up to a vicious course, public plunder, infamy and ruin'. It took children of both sexes between the ages of 8 and 12, and could keep them until they were 21. From about 1810 it became difficult for the society to take girls since it was unable to separate daughters of convicts who had been merely misbehaving from girls who were themselves convicted criminals, as space did not permit. The school did not think it proper to mix the two categories: A. Highmore, *History, design and present state of the various public charities in and near London*, London 1810, 860–8.
[25] HO 11/1–8 covering 1787–1832; HO 13/25–8 covering Nov.1813–Mar.1816; HO16/1–5 covering 1815–34; HO 26/1–40 covering 1791–1834; HO 26/56 covering 1792–3; HO 77/1–41 covering 1782–1834; BECLS, M5/307–33 (1802–34); BEFP, F25/1–13 (1797–1834).

Australia. Of the rest, one remained in prison and one on the hulks since they were deemed too old to go to the other side of the world and one boy of fifteen whom the Bank had prosecuted by mistake was sought a place in the Philanthropic Society. There were delays and uncertainties about the remaining 22 per cent of the men, but it is likely that most of these made their way to New South Wales.[26] Here is further evidence that the nature of the crime and of the prosecutor affected the exercise of discretion and that gender played a somewhat different role in decision-making. Overall, however, the flexibility and responsiveness of the system of pardoning, and the 'new' bureaucratic discretion, created through overload in the post-sentencing system, allowed many convicts to escape through 'doors' which in an earlier period might have been closed to them.

Gender, transportation and imprisonment

The evidence discussed previously emphasised the role of transportation as the main secondary punishment for the three crimes at this time, although by no means all those sentenced or commuted to transportation left the shores of Britain. The significance of transportation as the main residual punishment for felony in this period bears strongly on the choices made by the decision-makers in the justice system. Its use has also to be seen alongside the evolution of methods of prison discipline and the growing importance of incarceration, particularly by the later years of the period. Further, it became impossible for the Home Office to avoid both the pressures to 'manage' the choices of punishment for convicts, and to be the centre of the debate about those pressures.[27] Such developments necessarily diminished the operation of discretion based on elite views of the character and behaviour of those who had committed crimes. The fates of men and women awaiting punishment increasingly depended on the pragmatic decisions of government, coping with the needs and problems of the time.

Transportation was a magnificent way of exporting problems, a way of ridding the country of undesired and dangerous low-life. Transported criminals would never be seen again on these shores, and the administrative problems they created would be dealt with by someone else.[28] The evidence for transportation to New South Wales points to a policy of ridding the nation of problems, rather than to a grander strategic imperial project.[29] The heterogeneity of the transportees, particularly in the early phases of the Australian venture, the dominance of urban men and women and their lack of skills for

---

[26] BECLS, M5/307–33; BEFP, F25/1–13.
[27] Atkinson, 'State and empire'.
[28] Innes, 'Role of transportation'.
[29] Gillen, 'Botany Bay decision'; Innes, 'Role of transportation'; Atkinson, 'State and empire'. Contrast with these A. Frost, *Convicts and empire*, Melbourne 1980.

creating a penal society and a convict economy were obvious. 'But, suited for Australia or not, they were at least out of England.'[30]

The imbalance in the numbers of men and women, and the 'type' of woman arriving in the penal colonies of New South Wales and Van Diemen's Land was a matter of constant irritation, both to those administering the colonies and those in the Home Office charged with the despatch of convicts. The parliamentary select committees on transportation (1812, 1838) were much exercised by the issue. From a very early stage Governor MacQuarrie of New South Wales deplored the lack of suitable female convicts arriving there. In 1810 the colony reported that there were 2,734 male convicts there and 1,266 females, an undesirable situation.[31] In 1810 MacQuarrie required the government to send him as many male convicts as possible, 'the prosperity of the country depending on their numbers; whilst, on the contrary, female convicts are as great a drawback as the others are beneficial'. His objections were to the quality of female transportees, to their 'depraved' sexual behaviour, their unsuitability for work as servants and, frequently, to their poor state of health. Yet women were needed to assure the future of the colony and enough of them to control the men's sexual behaviour.[32] The dilemma was unresolved by the end of this period. By 1821 the imbalance was worse, with 12,608 male convicts to 1,206 female convicts in New South Wales. The British government's policy for selecting transportees was explained:

A selection is in the first instance made of the male convicts under the age of 50, who are sentenced to transportation for life and for 14 years; and the number is filled up with such from amongst those sentenced to transportation for 7 years, as are the most unruly in the hulks, or are convicted of the most atrocious crimes; with respect to female convicts, it has been customary to send, without any exception, all whose state of health will admit of it, and whose age does not exceed 45 years.[33]

Such a policy could hardly have assisted the administration of New South Wales. The government justified its selection policy (or lack of it), admitting to the pragmatism of its dealings:

they are aware that the women sent out are of the most abandoned description, and that in many instances they are likely to whet and encourage the vices of the men, whilst but a small proportion will make any step towards reformation; but yet, with all their vices, such women as these were the mothers

---

30 Innes, 'Role of transportation', 20–1.
31 W. C. Wentworth, *Despatches and papers relating to the settlement of the states: a statistical account of the British settlements in Australia*, i, 3rd edn, ed. G. B. Whittaker, London 1824, 481, giving details of the 1810 muster.
32 *Report from the select committee on transportation*, PP, 1812, ii. 341; Wentworth, *Despatches and papers*, 482–5.
33 *Select committee on transportation*, PP, 1812, ii. 341, p. 8.

of a great part of the inhabitants now existing in the Colony, and from this stock only can a reasonable hope be held out of rapid increase to the population . . . The supply of women to the colony must, however, be materially diminished by the proposed system of employing convicts in Penitentiary Houses.[34]

Thus a difference in policy towards female convicts was driven by the needs of the state and by developments in penal policy in England, especially the development of penitentiaries – and, in New South Wales, by the establishment of the female factory at Paramatta.[35] Transportation, the gendered selection of transportees – however crudely made by the Home Office – and the growing role of the penitentiaries, especially for women, have to be added to the complex equation of decision-making about punishments.

It is reasonable to believe that transportation was a worse punishment for women than for men. All, male and female, endured appalling conditions on board the transport ships. They were usually confined in irons, with inadequate food and medicine, coping with extremes of heat and cold, while disease spread easily in such cramped, ill-ventilated environments. Children, other than babies at the breast, had to be left behind. For mothers, who had had the care of their young children in prison, the burden of abandoning them, never to see them again, must have been particularly distressing. Babies being weaned went with their mothers on the ships, and coping in such circumstances must have been daunting.[36] The fitters-out of the convict ships had given no thought to women who might give birth on the ships; this they did on filthy shelf 'beds', in chains. On board ship the women were generally regarded as prostitutes, and many were used as such by the ships' officers and crews. On arrival in the colony, the women, grossly outnumbered by men, lived crude, brutalised lives in consequence. Transportation was not a lenient sentence for any convict; for women it was exceptionally severe.[37]

One of the more significant differences between male and female convicts in England was the use of the conventional prison for women – the house of correction or the penitentiary. Many of their prison sentences were accompanied by hard labour and gendered discretion was exercised here. Women were not thought capable of the type of physical work handed out to men. They

---

[34] Ibid. p. 12.
[35] Earl Bathurst (from Downing Street, London) to Governor MacQuarrie, 3 Feb.1814, and MacQuarrie to Bathurst, 7 Oct.1814, in *Historical records of Australia (HRA)*, 1st ser. viii (1813–15), Sydney 1916, 134, 312.
[36] 1820s reforms outlawed confinement in irons, allowed children up to the age of seven to accompany their mothers, and embarkation of women with very young babies was delayed until the child was weaned: A. D. Smith, *Women in prison: a study in penal methods*, London 1962,114; Zedner, *Women, crime and custody*, 174–5; Hughes, *Fatal shore*, ch. viii.
[37] W. Tench, *A narrative of the expedition to Botany Bay*, London 1789, and *A complete account of the settlement at Port Jackson in New South Wales*, London 1793; Smith, *Women in prison*, 113–17; Hughes, *Fatal shore*; Oldham, *Britain's convicts*; P. Clarke and D. Spender (eds), *Lifelines: Australian women's letters and diaries, 1788–1840*, St Leonards, NSW 1992.

did not go to the mainstream hulks. For a short while two hulks were used as an extension of the general penitentiary at Millbank.[38] One of the problems for women in prison was a lack of work by means of which either to earn small amounts to supplement their gaol allowance or to keep occupied. When work was made available, it was of a type thought suitable for women – patchwork items, knitted socks, clothes for the army and navy. From 1810, when the first women were moved from Newgate to Millbank, they were fed a worse diet than the men, which made them more susceptible to ill-health and disease, such as the epidemic of scurvy, dysentery and diarrhoea of 1822–3. This epidemic, affecting women worse than men, led to their evacuation from the prison to the hulks.[39]

Being sent into military or naval service was generally welcomed by younger men as an alternative to transportation or prison. They frequently requested this and their friends and relations sometimes saw it as a 'respectable' outcome with potential to 'save face'. When the many forms of punishment are considered, degrees of leniency are difficult to classify. Different treatment of men and women was often intended by those with the ability and power to make decisions about the disposal of convicts, but those decisions were largely the result of practical political priorities which had to be observed.

The shadow of the gallows

Some of London's convicted felons did not have the options of freedom or lesser punishments allowed to them. It is important to examine why their journeys ended in death on the gallows. Historians considering the impact of capital punishment in the eighteenth and nineteenth centuries work with imprecise statistics. Henry Hobhouse of the Home Office reported to the select committee on the criminal law in 1819 that the statistics he produced were 'very imperfect', even for London and Middlesex. The Old Bailey Clerk of Arraigns, Thomas Shelton, said that records were getting better, but much of what he had produced was 'generality'. There had been the greatest diffi-

---

38 Campbell, *Intolerable hulks*, 99–100; Smith, *Women in prison*, 87. As part of the evacuation of Millbank prison because of scurvy, parliament (4 Geo 4. c.82) authorised removal of female prisoners to two hulks, the *Narcissus* and the *Heroine*, at Woolwich, in order to recover their health. (Other women were sent to the Royal Ophthalmic Hospital in Regent's Park, which was empty at the time.) The first women went aboard the hulks on 16 Aug. 1823. The epidemic continued on board and there were problems of discipline. Pardons were granted to all the women, as soon as homes were found for them. The Home Office corresponded with all the women's relatives and friends to secure places for them. By February 1824 no woman was left on the hulks.
39 Smith, *Women in prison*, 87.

culty in producing statistics on the precise crime for which an execution had taken place, and the official statistics must be regarded with caution.[40]

It is likely that there were just over 1,200 executions of men and women who had been sentenced for all capital offences at the Old Bailey Sessions between 1781 and 1834, an average of twenty-three a year. These deaths represented about a quarter of those executed in the whole of England and Wales. During the eighteenth century there had been significant annual fluctuations in the number of executions. Between 1701 and 1750, five or six people a year had been hanged in London, but as many were hanged there in the 1820s as in the 1790s. Twice as many hanged in London in the thirty years 1801–30 as in the fifty years 1701–50.[41] About 20 per cent of those executed in London in the eighteenth and early nineteenth centuries had been tried for murder, together with a small additional proportion for attempted murder, for rape and for sodomy. The majority (about two-thirds) was executed for property crimes – burglary and housebreaking, robbery, stealing horses, sheep or cattle, and a substantial proportion for forgery of various types, uttering forged Bank notes and for counterfeiting coins. The remainder of those executed had committed piracy, offences at sea, offences against the Post Office and other types of fraud.[42]

Amongst these executions, the proportion of women was small. Of 1,232 people hanged at Tyburn between 1703 and 1772, it is likely that only ninety-two were women (7 per cent of the total executed). Of fifty-nine people executed in London between 1827 and 1830, three were women, all for murder – a similarly low proportion.[43] There is no certainty about the exact number or names of the women who hanged, even in the period from 1780 to 1830. There are the celebrated cases, which Gatrell exploited at length in his fascinating, provocative and emotional study of the gallows at the centre of English, especially London, life. Such micro-histories help bring to mind the barbarity of the gallows. However, what surprises is the obscurity of most of those who hanged in the metropolis; most of them were the poor of

[40] *Select committee on capital punishment in felonies*, PP, 1819, viii.19–22. There are major discrepancies for London and Middlesex if the statistics seen by the select committee are compared with names counted in HO 77/1–25, or in statistical presentations in newspapers. J. H. Capper of the Home Office was unable to explain the difference between his statistics and Bank of England statistics for 1817, because there was 'some reservation of judgement at the end of the Sessions'. R. W. Rawson, 'An inquiry into the statistics of crime in England and Wales', *Journal of the Statistical Society* ii (1839), 316–45, tried to show that men and women commit different crimes and claimed that no woman had been committed for 'robbery in dwelling-houses accompanied by violence' or 'administering unlawful oaths'. Study of the evidence in OBSP and in newspapers shows that not only were they committed but they were hanged for such crimes.
[41] Figures evaluated from *Select committee on capital punishment in felonies*, PP, 1819, viii. 25–39, 146–51, HO 77/1–37, and Gatrell, *Hanging tree*, 7 and appendix ii.
[42] HO 26/8–36; HO 77/9–37. These records are not trustworthy. Newspaper reports of executions in London show different figures.
[43] Gatrell, *Hanging tree*, 8.

London.[44] This is particularly so in the case of women. Some are a little more celebrated – Eliza Fenning, the poisoner, and Phoebe Harris, Margaret Sullivan and Catherine Murphy (*alias* Christian Bowman), who were staked and burned between 1786 and 1789 for coining offences. Maria Theresa Phippoe *alias* Mary Benn (1797) and Elizabeth Fricker (1817) were seen as notorious freaks of ferocious womanhood. Ann Hurle (1804), who forged bank transfers, was seen as a scheming deceiver and Esther Hibner merited many lines in the Complete Newgate Calendar and the newspapers for the murder of a workhouse child in 1829.[45] Otherwise, the majority of poor women were executed with little interest taken by the newspapers in their individual cases.

It has been possible to trace, in the official records, the Complete (or New) Newgate Calendar and newspapers, the names and some details of forty-three women hanged in London between 1780 and 1832. Since the fates of these women are unusual, it is worth looking for features reported about them which might have caused the decision on execution to go against them. It is immediately noticeable that the largest group of executed women (fourteen individuals) were those who had defrauded their victims – four by counterfeiting coins, six by uttering forged Bank notes, and four by serious fraud, deceit and impersonation. Another group of executed women (twelve) was hanged for theft – robberies and burglaries – accompanied by violence. There was another distinct group (nine) executed for murder or attempted murder; a group (four individuals) who stole from dwelling houses, using no violence or force, but where they were servants, and four who were involved in the London riots of 1780 and the unfeminine and violent act of ransacking and stealing from Lord Mansfield's house. There was nothing specifically 'female' about any of these crimes. They are the same crimes for which men were executed, although men committed a further range of other capital crimes to which women were not attracted. The crimes for which women hanged may have been seen as deserving death in order to protect society from danger from women who acted like men. Besides murder, always the worst of crimes, these executed women had attempted to prevent men being able to inherit or keep their property in safety. They had been fraudulent in the male world of trade; they had collapsed trust between a man and his servant; they had been violent and unruly.[46]

44 P. Linebaugh, *The London hanged: crime and civil society in the eighteenth century*, London 1991, 74–111.
45 Fenning: *The Times*, 27 July, 1, 3 Aug.1815; Harris: *The Times*, 22, 23, 27 June 1786; Sullivan: *St James's Chronicle*, 24/26 June 1788, and *The Times*, 24–7 June 1788; Murphy/Bowman: *The Times*, 19 Mar.1789, and *The Gentlemen's Magazine* lix/1 (1789); Phippoe: *The Times*, 12 Dec.1797; Fricker: *The Sun*, 5 Mar.1817, and *The Times*, 6 Mar.1817; Hurle: *The Times*, 8, 9, 13 Feb.1804; Hibner: *The Times*, 14 Apr.1829.
46 For an interesting discussion of women and homicide, particularly murder, and the likelihood of execution of such women, in comparison with men, in early modern England, see Walker, *Crime, gender and social order*, 113–58.

However, this is not a sufficiently satisfactory explanation, since other women committed the same categories of crime and were not hanged for them. There can be little doubt that the state had an aversion to executing women. Yet, for all the discussion by historians and contemporary commentators on the meaning and effect of the gallows, little has been said about executions of women – as to why they were not common, or, conversely, as to the reason for executing the few. 'An often instinctive chivalry, or if you like embarrassment',[47] sounds like an excuse for avoiding examination of the reluctance to execute women. Nor do suggestions that women posed a lesser threat to order in society, or that the state thought it unwise to execute those who might excite pity provide a satisfying answer either.[48] Gatrell gave this issue extensive thought, moved perhaps too much by the few individual women with whose stories he had become acquainted. There may at times have been strong sympathetic responses from powerful males to 'the wronged woman, particularly if she was of inseminable age and fetchingly vulnerable to male wiles'. However, Gatrell also considered some stories of less physically attractive women and admits that females could receive no better treatment than men, whether in prison or on the scaffold, sometimes worse.[49] There appear to be few examples, other than those cited by Gatrell, where sympathy for executed women was expressed in newspaper reports. Accounts are chillingly matter of fact, following stereotyped formula.

The end of the eighteenth century may have marked a watershed in attitudes to the execution (and other physical punishment) of women. 'Anxiety about executing women, about burning their bodies . . . or about whipping them . . . now tended to be activated by the sense that even at their worst women were creatures to be pitied and protected from themselves, and perhaps to be revered, like all women from whom men were born.'[50] A few well-publicised female executions caused revulsion. The hanging spectacle often provoked unease. Anxiety grew about extreme punishments for women 'who by being the weaker body, are more liable to error, and less entitled to severity'.[51] However, newspaper reporting of the execution of women hardly supported a sense of real anxiety. With a few exceptions, the executions of London women were marked more by silence than by many words. Although Gatrell made extensive use of the few cases of executed women which attracted attention in print, he also admitted that, 'executions take up a few passing lines in pages given over to healthier doings'.[52] The 'few passing lines'

[47] G. R. Elton, 'Crime and the historian', in J. S. Cockburn (ed.), *Crime in England, 1550–1800*, 13,
[48] Beattie, *Crime and the courts*, 436–9; F. McLynn, *Crime and punishment in eighteenth-century England*, Oxford 1991, 128–9.
[49] Gatrell, *Hanging tree*, 335–6.
[50] Ibid. 337.
[51] *The Times*, 24, 25, 26, 27 June 1788 on the execution of Margaret Sullivan for coining.
[52] Gatrell, *Hanging tree*, 55.

were, sadly, the usual response to hangings in London, whether of male or female. The cursory mentions suggest either a matter-of-fact acceptance, or the need to hide the horror from the public in order to retain the acceptability of the death sentence.[53] Reports, more often than not, were of the following nature: 'The following malefactors [list of names including one woman, Mary Gardener, a rioter] were carried in three carts from Newgate to Tyburn where they were all executed according to their sentences. They all behaved very penitent.'[54] Or the following: 'Yesterday morning at 8 o'clock Richard Cowling alias Jones, for personating a seaman and receiving his wages, and Melinda Mapson for robbing the houses of her master, Mr Digham, grocer of New Street, Covent Garden, were executed opposite the Debtors door at Newgate.'[55]

Sometimes the woman's name would not even be mentioned.[56] Reports often showed more interest in other issues – among them pickpockets operating in the watching crowd,[57] the collapse of a scaffold holding 200 spectators,[58] seventy spectators crushed to death,[59] reversion to the use of the cart instead of the new drop at the gallows[60] and the precipitation from the scaffold of the Ordinary (the clergyman attending the condemned person) when the executioner removed a spring too early.[61] These reports seem to avoid the main issue. With significant exceptions, executions of men and women were presented as inevitable and unexceptional. When this was the tragic end for so few women, the lack of outrage and emotion is extraordinary.

This was a period of contradictory pressures on the decision-makers. On the one hand, current constructions of femininity emphasised women's weaknesses, their specific design and calling to domesticity, wifehood and motherhood, and their moral superiority.[62] On the other hand, those responsible for order in society were dealing with what they saw as an epidemic of crime in

53 McGowen, 'Civilizing punishment', supports a view that keeping horror from public sight was a strategy of those who favoured the retention of hanging.
54 St James's Chronicle, 21/23 Nov.1780, which was a copy of the report in the London Evening Post, 22 Nov.1780.
55 The Times, 14 June 1810.
56 Jane Vincent and five men executed with her were not mentioned by name in The Morning Chronicle and London Advertiser, nor in The Morning Herald and Daily Advertiser, 7 June 1781.
57 This was reported at the execution of Jane Vincent: Lloyds Evening Post, 6/8 June 1781; also at Charlotte Goodall's execution: London Chronicle, 15/17 Oct.1782.
58 This was reported at Charlotte Goodall's execution: London Chronicle, 15/17 Oct.1782.
59 This was reported at the execution of Elizabeth Godfrey and two men: The Times, 24 Feb.1807.
60 This was reported at the execution of Ann Hurle with one man: The Times, 8, 9, 13 Feb. 1804.
61 This was reported at the execution of Mary Parnell: The Times, 14 Nov.1805.
62 See, for example, Barker and Chalus, Gender; Fletcher, Gender, sex and subordination; Hill, Women, work and sexual politics, Hitchcock, English sexualities; Honeyman, Women, gender and industrialisation; and Shoemaker, Gender in English society.

which women were playing a significant part. The judicial system still had to punish, control and rid the nation of those who undermined social order. To support an image of the criminal justice system as a process which worked fairly, some women had to pay the full penalty. Dualistic notions about women perpetually fed the state's dilemma. A writer to the *Gentleman's Magazine* in 1795 thought:

> Softness, delicacy, benevolence, piety, and, I may add, timidity (the guardian of virtue) are the natural characteristics of women. Such endearing qualities touch the heart of the hero, awe the profligate, and extort respect from the most abandoned; whilst she in whom they are wanting creates only disgust; she appears to be an unnatural and monstrous being, and instead of love and the softer passions, she excites only contempt, and meets but with neglect. No man who sincerely respects the female character would wish to see their amiable qualities and natural sensibility annihilated; and it is with sincere regret that their best friends observe, among the ladies of the present day, a tendency to masculine vice which is of the worst consequence.[63]

The biological and symbolic centrality of the woman's body to execution, by whatever method, is stressed by Naish in her study of judicial killings of women from the fifteenth to twentieth centuries. She suggests that it is the female body itself that poses the problem: 'There is something repugnant about destroying a body which gives life, even when strict egality requires that women should be punished just as men.'[64] Deep fears about the female body which holds ultimate power over the human future and the male's ability to procreate and dominate were expressed in a letter to *The Times*, putting arguments against execution for stealing 'a little piece of silver'; the writer casually emphasises such fears about killing those who are to be the child-bearers: 'Is it not possible that those nations which condemn to death a young woman of 18 years of age, who might be the mother of five or six children . . . should have sufficiently meditated on the tables of the probabilities of human life which they have so learnedly calculated?'[65]

No doubt there were deep-seated male anxieties about executing, burning and whipping women, and these may partly account for the use of discretion to save many of them from the gallows. It is then all the more difficult to understand why the women who were executed did not merit this discretion. Zedner, for a slightly later period in the nineteenth century, suggests that growing anxieties about the perceived undermining of hierarchical relations caused by industrialisation, the disintegrating effects of urbanisation and the growing irreligion of the urban poor, were palliated to some degree by elevating the concept of 'the family' and the idealised role of the woman as

63 *The Gentleman's Magazine* lxv (Feb.1795), 102–4.
64 C. Naish, *Death comes to the maiden: sex and execution, 1431–1933*, London–New York 1991, 251.
65 *The Times*, 30 Oct.1788.

mother, with her superior morality.[66] Women seen as fulfilling these roles were irreproachable and untouchable. Women were judged against complex, constructed, notions of ideal womanhood. Labouring and plebeian folk were measured by these ideals which they neither created nor subscribed to. A criminal woman represented a negation of imposed ideal femininity. 'The angel in the house' had a mirror image in the plebeian woman – degraded, brutish and immoral. In the latter half of the eighteenth century the image of plebeian women suffered, as the picture of their industriousness and productivity was replaced by one of immorality and criminality through growing unemployment and urbanisation. They were regarded as responsible for swelling the ranks of thieves, beggars and prostitutes. They were no longer even deserving of paternalistic sympathy.[67]

Maria Theresa Phippoe, executed for murder in London in December 1797, was described as 'a ferocious female', 'a woman of masculine behaviour and of a daring disposition'. Esther Hibner was hanged in April 1829 for murder of her little apprentice girl in a violent and cold-bloodedly cruel way. The judge sentencing her said, 'Although you have been the mother of a child yourself, you saw her [the dead child's] sufferings without any of that feeling which one would imagine could never have been absent from a female breast.' Pictures were constructed of women who were not 'real' women, creatures devoid of physical weakness, moral sensitivity, maternal and gentle disposition.[68]

London women hanged for Bank note offences

Returning to focus on the specific crime of forged Bank note uttering, it is useful to take a closer look at the five women hanged in the period for this activity in London and Middlesex.[69] The perceived seriousness of their offences was undoubtedly the primary reason for their executions. Mary Parnell (hanged in 1805), Ann Lawrence (1817), Charlotte Newman (1818), Harriett Skelton (1818) and Sarah Price (1820) leave slight evidence of this tragic end to their lives. For Mary Parnell, there are merely official registry entries and a brief report of her trial at the Old Bailey. There

---

66 Zedner, *Women, crime and custody*, 13–18, 28–30, 62–8.

67 Clark, *Struggle for the breeches*; Kingsley-Kent, *Gender and power*.

68 The publication in which these stories appear drew on the accounts of the Ordinaries of Newgate, based on their visits to condemned prisoners and their last moments with them at the scaffold. They depended on information in OBSP, chapbooks and broadsides, and became substantial productions, with different titles. They are printed in A. Knapp and W. Baldwin, *The complete Newgate calendar*, 1826 edn, iv–v, ed. G. T. Cook, London 1926. Esther Hibner's case was further embellished in *The Times*, 14 Apr.1829.

69 One woman (Elizabeth Brown) was hanged (in 1798) for uttering forged Bank notes earlier during the period of suspension, which was outside the scope of the study of forged Bank note crimes in this book.

are hints in the trial report as to why she would not have impressed as a feminine, weak, woman. She was 'very joking, as if in liquor', her face was 'painted', she had only one eye, and described herself as 'an unfortunate girl'. Her case dates from early in the period of 'suspension', before public unease had surfaced about the high number of prosecutions, transportations and executions. Parnell's life-style and the image of womanhood she projected may have been sufficient, in addition to the seriousness of the crime, to make her one of the exceptions to the exercise of merciful discretion.[70]

Ann Lawrence (*alias* Woodman) worked with a group of men and 'carried on an infamous traffic in forged notes', around the public houses of Whitechapel. She was described in a newspaper report of her trial at the Old Bailey as a young woman, well-dressed, who begged the gentlemen of the jury to recommend her to mercy for the sake of her *seven starving and unprotected babies* [reporter's italics]. All the men she worked with were executed (including the father of her children) but she was again pregnant and successfully able to 'plead the belly', thus putting off her execution. Lawrence made no further appeals and the prison visitors, Elizabeth Fry and her workers, were greatly distressed about her. Fry's record states that she was executed a few weeks after the birth of her child. The Bank had invested a good deal in breaking up the gang to which Lawrence belonged, and it may have been her expertise in crime over a long time which allowed no mercy.[71]

Charlotte Newman, executed in February 1818, was another woman who came within the orbit of Elizabeth Fry's concern. Her letters of gratitude to Mrs Fry shortly before her death are models of calmness, submission and serenity inculcated by the nurture of Fry and her helpers with their assurance of the boundless mercies of God. She wrote an equally moving letter to the Bank of England to beg for forgiveness and for their last-minute support in her appeal for her life, to which came the unemotional reply: 'I received your letter but cannot interfere on your behalf. The Governors and Directors of the Bank have considered your case, and they also decline to interfere.' Newman had been tried with her male companion, George Mansfield, who was found not guilty of uttering forged notes. They had been on a tour of London, spending forged notes in wine vaults and liquor houses. A large amount of 'bad' money was found in her apartment. Her husband had been previously transported for housebreaking.[72] There is sufficient evidence to permit understanding as to why Newman should have been selected, or

---

[70] BECLS, M5/307, 11 June 1805; OBSP, July 1805, 393–9; HO 26/11 (exec.13 Nov.1805).

[71] BECLS, M5/318, 3, 17 Oct, 7, 26 Nov.1816; OBSP, Oct. 1816, 466–8; *The Times*, 6 Mar.1817; F. Fry and R. E. Cresswell (eds), *Memoir of the life of Elizabeth Fry with extracts from her journal and letters, edited by two of her daughters in two volumes*, London 1847, 263, 275, 279.

[72] BECLS, M5/319, 13 Nov., 4, 11 Dec.1817; OBSP, Dec.1817, 22–4; BEFP, F25/5; *Memoir of the life of Elizabeth Fry*, 309–10; HO 26/24, HO 77/25.

allowed, to hang. Her connections were bad, she was a major utterer and she was regarded as responsible for leading Mansfield astray.

Harriett Skelton was the subject of energetic, but unavailing, petitioning by Mrs Fry. This case appears to defy reasoning about leniency shown to women. Fry appealed to the duke of Gloucester, to Lord Sidmouth, the Home Secretary and to the Bank directors, since she was convinced that there were extenuating circumstances:

> Harriett Skelton; a very child might have read her countenance, open, confiding, expressing strong feeling, but neither hardened in depravity, nor capable of cunning; her story bore out this impression. Under the influence of a man she loved, she had passed forged notes; adding one more to the melancholy list of those, who by the finest impulses of our nature, uncontrolled by religion, have been lured to their own destruction.[73]

Skelton appeared to have been on a strange forged note-spending spree which had included the purchase of three Twelfth Night cakes, each costing half a guinea, a pound of tea, 18s.-worth of flannel and two pelisses. She said the notes came from her husband or brother. Unfortunately, her brother was a well-known trader in forged notes. Harriet's case aroused interest, and she had many prison visitors – 'dwellers in palaces and lordly halls were to be found in her desolate abode'. She wrote a long letter to the Bank to explain the false opinions passed about her, which she thought had led to its lack of sympathy towards her. She had been told that there was no hope of her sentence being changed to transportation for life:

> as my character is considered as particularly bad and my case very flagrant . . . Guilty as I am, and deservedly involved in disgrace, I am not guilty to that extent which is supposed . . . I never lived in any house of ill fame kept by my brother or anyone else . . . Part of my time was employed at my business of doing upholstery work of the house which was furnished by my brother . . . I confess that my motive was not the good of the public but to gratify a desire of revenge on the part of my brother whose advice I sincerely regret that I followed . . . I hope these few remarks will convince you that I am not so abandoned a character as you suppose.[74]

The view of Skelton held by Elizabeth Fry and others at Newgate was at variance with the view that the Bank and the judiciary held of her:

> She was ordered for execution – the sentence was unlooked for – her deportment in the prison had been good, amenable to regulations, quiet and orderly; some of her companions in guilt were heard to say, that they supposed she was chosen for death, because she was better prepared than the rest of them.[75]

---

73 *Memoir of the life of Elizabeth Fry*, 312.
74 Ibid. 313.
75 BECLS, M5/320, 5, 26 Feb., 12, 19 Mar.1818; OBSP, Feb. 1818, 155–6; *Memoir of the life of Elizabeth Fry*, 314; BEFP, F25/5; HO 26/24.

Sarah Price refused the Bank's offer of a plea bargain, pleaded 'not guilty' to the capital charge, thus ensuring that, if she were found guilty, she could expect no mercy from her prosecutor. Her evidence at the Old Bailey had been confused. She said she received the notes from two women who bought a mattress and six chairs from her second-hand goods shop. Then she said that her husband had received them in his wages and unknowingly had given them to her to spend. The report of her execution, in December 1820, said that she was one woman among five men, that they were all 'respectable, more so than usual' and that their behaviour was exemplary. There was an 'immense crowd' at the hangings because of the 'great public feeling excited by this extensive exercise of the severity of the law after all that has been said and written on the necessity and propriety of the amelioration of our penal code and more especially as these individuals were none of them old or hardened offenders'. The London sheriffs had tried hard to prevent these executions, but the Secretary of State had rejected their appeals.[76]

The stories of these five women may not provide a model for the sort of women whom the state determined to hang. The perceived severity of their crimes is likely to have been the reason for their execution. It is easier to suggest reasons why women, as women, were not often executed than to understand why the selected few died in this way. Old Bailey trial reports, newspaper reports and the language of appeals suggest that female criminals were seen as less of a threat to the order of society: 'Humane feelings prevail when their costs in terms of security or comfort are bearable; when they can be productively acted upon; and when they bring emotional and status returns to the "humane".'[77] It is perhaps not difficult to be lenient to those you do not fear. Yet the powerful were, unsurprisingly, inconsistent and contradictory in their decisions. If the powerful, and those with the opportunity to be 'humane', did not fear women, why did they ensure that they executed some of them? It is possible that they did indeed fear women who did not behave as women 'should', thus threatening their security and the order of society.

The Bank of England, as an institutional powerhouse and prosecutor, was able to protect security through its bureaucracy and its outward show of impartiality. A decision, once taken, stood. Business could not be conducted otherwise. The women executed as the result of its prosecution found no public expression of humanity from the Bank which could save them from the gallows. Its humanity was shown in less public ways. It is important, therefore, not to over-generalise. The mix of motives in decision-making about criminals was complex. However, the contradictions are not unexpected. If the end of the journey was execution, gender played a major role in the final decision, negative or positive. Moreover, the decision could be the

[76] BECLS, M5/324, 13 July, 27 Sept.1820; OBSP, Sept.1820, 524–5; HO 26/26, HO 6/5; *The Times*, 14 Dec.1820.
[77] Gatrell, *Hanging tree*, 12.

result of contradictory assessments. The decision might be that the weak, unfortunate female body which safeguarded the future of the nation, should be saved and reclaimed. On the other hand, a dangerous or 'unwomanly' woman should be disposed of – because she was feared. This apportionment of the ultimate sanction also provided a means of fulfilling the need to show that justice was being evenly applied to men and women. There is little doubt that women were much less likely to be hanged at this period, but the decisions are puzzling. Final judicial decisions puzzled observers at the time:

> I am shocked by the inequality of punishment. At one time a man[78] is hanged for a crime . . . because there are few to be hanged, and it is some time since an example has been made of capital punishment for his particular offence. At another time a man escapes for the same crime . . . because it is a heavy calendar, and there are many to be executed. The actual delinquency of the individual is comparatively little taken into consideration. Extraneous circumstances determine his fate.[79]

Others made similar observations, but at the top of the decision-making tree, with the King-in-Council, no public sign of disquiet was expressed. 'Secrecy kept the law's private parts decently veiled.'[80]

If the end of the journey was not execution, the role of gender was less obvious. The needs of the state dominated when it came to transportation, and the decision to imprison depended on the availability of space in appropriate institutions. Women were proportionately more likely to be transported to meet the demand for female services.[81] However, pragmatic considerations came to require that many of them, deemed unsuitable for life and work in New South Wales, should not be sent there. A new prison discipline was needed to contain them. Men were more likely to be used in public works at hard labour from the hulks or to be dispersed into military service. Later, the numbers of men transported continued to be significant. Decisions on the disposal of men and women convicts were gendered and made complicated by the political and practical needs of government.

---

[78] I take the use of the word 'man' here to mean both men and women, as fitting the context.
[79] Colchester, *Diary*, entry for 28 June 1828, 154–5.
[80] Gatrell, *Hanging tree*, 549.
[81] D. Beddoe, *Welsh convict women: a study of women transported from Wales to Australia, 1787–1852*, Barry 1979, supports a view that women were more readily transported.

7

Gendered Appeals

youre Moste humbill peticiner was in the gretest Distress and Could get no work to do that was the cause of me pawning the things and I had no friends neaer me youre humbil peticiner has been Informed it is in your Lordships power to send me to the penitentiary it will be the prayers of a poor Old Coupil my aged Father and Mother me being theire only Child.[1]

A more discretionary face of the criminal justice system lay behind the developing bureaucratic operation described in the previous chapter. After these conditional pardons and mitigations of sentence had been awarded, further negotiations could be pursued towards lesser sentences or even to freedom. Consideration of this late stage in the system of criminal justice, well away from the public setting of the courts, allows the uncovering of the significant role played by 'gender', both in the language and the forms of appeals for mercy and the responses of the decision-makers.

This more private world will be explored through the evidence provided by two distinct and rather different collections of documents. One is the little used part of the Home Office petition archives, collected together from 1819, in which appeals from Londoners are to be found. This large collection has been barely touched since the papers were bundled up and tied with pink ribbon nearly 200 years ago. It contains hundreds of letters and petitions from convicts to the Home Secretary on their way, the petitioners hoped, to the king, pleading and seeking leniency from the royal seat of mercy. The factors and the language which men and women used in these appeals are evidence of their use of the 'gender card', sometimes perhaps deliberately and sometimes unknowingly.[2] The other collection of papers, by way of contrast, is the previously unexplored records of the solicitors to the Bank of England, containing letters and appeals to the Bank, the 'generous prosecutor' from 'its' prisoners as they waited for their sentences to be effected. These writings, and the responses to them, provide a remarkable view of gendered discretion in the application of favours and merciful actions.[3]

---

[1]   From the petition of Eleanor Savory, sentenced at the Old Bailey, Dec.1830, to 7 years' transportation for stealing two pillows; her petition was marked in Home Secretary Peel's hand '2 y Penity' and in his clerk's writing 'Ord^d to Pen^y 1 Decr 1831': OSBP, 9 Nov.1830; HO 17/54, part I/Iq25.
[2]   HO 17 covering 1819–39. HO 17/1–5/Ah–Ao, 15–19/Bh–Bz and 25–131/Ch–Zz contain petitions for England. For full details of the bundles consulted within these files see appendix.
[3]   BEFP, F25.

Londoners and their appeals

In the late eighteenth and early nineteenth centuries, pardons were granted to the majority of capitally convicted people, generally on condition that they were transported for life. Much has been written about this aspect of the pardoning procedure.[4] However, less has been heard about the more extensive procedure of pardoning and commuting sentences which resulted in many transportation sentences not being carried out, and in prisoners being moved from one type of punishment to another. This extended system of pardoning and mitigation affected many of the men and women convicted at the Old Bailey.

Unfortunately, until 1819, very few of the petitions from the men and women of London and Middlesex, convicted and sentenced at the Old Bailey, were kept in the Home Office petitions archive. The archives containing pre-1819 papers produce rich information which comes largely from cases outside London and include the reports of judges who had been requested to pass their opinion on the substance of the appeals. These earlier papers allow a good understanding of the factors mentioned in appeals which might have achieved a successful result.[5] However, the proximity of the Old Bailey to the decision-takers, to the Home Secretary and to the king meant that, usually, the judiciary's views on pleas for pardon and remission were given orally in London and Middlesex cases.[6] It has been estimated that, between 1786 and 1815, only about twenty non-capital appeal cases a year from London and Middlesex were referred on appeal to the judiciary.[7] However, the post-1819 collection of petitions material, including a high proportion from London and Middlesex, demonstrate how much the appeals business had increased commensurate with the increase in volume and efficiency of prosecution in the criminal courts following the end of the French wars. At the same time, government administration itself was becoming more efficient, orderly and bureaucratic.[8] It was also handling a greater volume of appeals, not against the gallows, but from transportation, hard labour and

---

4 See, for instance, Beattie, *Crime and the courts*, and 'Royal pardon'; Gatrell, *Hanging tree*; and Hilton, 'The gallows and Mr Peel'.
5 These papers are contained mainly in HO 6, HO 42 and HO 47.
6 For a detailed and sensitive explanation of the appeals and pardon system for London and Middlesex see Devereaux, 'Peel, pardon and punishment'. The reports of the Recorder of London, produced and read at the meeting known as the 'Recorder's report', were given orally; no written copies survived for the early nineteenth century. No one appeared to know where the custom of the 'Report' originated, and why London was so different from the rest of the country, where the assize judges prepared lists of people sentenced to death whom they intended to be spared execution; these lists were accepted without further discussion: Beattie, *Crime and the courts*, 431–2. For the origins of the 'Report' see Beattie, *Policing and punishment*, 346–62.
7 Devereaux, 'Criminal branch', 285–6 and table 10.2.
8 Ibid. 281–3

long prison sentences.[9] From 1819 the Home Office handled several hundreds of requests each year. The volume of business makes it difficult to know the result of appeals, in the way it was possible for an earlier date and with out-of-London material. The immediate response to petitions was recorded, but in many cases this was merely a note that a decision had been deferred. Where the record showed a decision, a further decision taken a few days or weeks later might not be shown.[10]

Well over one-fifth of the petitions in the post-1819 collection came from prisoners convicted at the Old Bailey. The rest came from every part of England, Scotland and Wales, and a few from Ireland. Appeals on behalf of males dominate the total archive. Among the lesser number of female appeals, the women of London and Middlesex were prominent.[11] Dossiers for male petitioners, who had easier access to the support of employers and other suitable acquaintances, often contained many letters from a variety of sources. Female petitions were usually no more than one simple letter, written by the prisoner herself, or by her parents or partner. Often turnkeys or other semi-literate gaol servants would earn themselves a little money, obliging a prisoner who had little other help, with a crudely written, deferential, letter.

Even the immediate results of most of these appeals are uncertain. In some cases the Secretary of State or an under-secretary wrote instructions on the papers, such as 'The law to take its course', 'Refused', 'To General Penitentiary' or 'Prepare a free (or conditional) pardon'. Often the word written was 'Nil'; it might be assumed that this meant 'refused', but this was not necessarily so, as records made later show that the appeal may have been successful.[12] Frequently nothing was written, and sometimes: 'Report in Council', with the date of the next Recorder's report at the meeting of the King-in-Council.

Factors in appeals: what men and women said

The appeal letters and papers are public documents, written by, or on behalf of, the powerless to the powerful. The language is deferential, tactical, often desperate. They are not carefully crafted narratives. They do not tell a story, but are special pleadings and protestations of good personal characteristics. Most are direct and unsophisticated, and many are semi-literate. They are

---

9   HO 17/1–131.
10 HO 19/1–4.
11 See appendix for details of the archive analysed and the relative numbers of men and women. Although appeals in the sample on behalf of females were only 9% of the national total of all sampled petitions, nearly 50% of those female appeals followed sentencing at the Old Bailey; they amounted to 20% of all petitions from London and Middlesex cases.
12 These can be found in HO 19.

Table 22
Factors mentioned in petitions from prisoners convicted at Old Bailey Sessions, 1820s–1830s*

Factors mentioned	Males	Females
Previous good character	49	59
Youth	29	25
No previous conviction	33	41
Post-crime destitution	26	13
Post-crime distress of parents	26	20
Possibility of innocence, malicious prosecution	29	30
Drawn in by others	29	23
Previous military service	10	0
Prisoner or family respectable	59	34
Old employer gives good character	33	13
Employment available	16	14
Pre-crime destitution	16	25
Crime not violent	6	1
Insane or drunk at time of offence	1	9
Old age	0	9
Physical factors	0	27
Reformability/ reformed**	10	21
Mentally handicapped	2	4
Others (positive)***	38	24
Total factors mentioned	412	392
Total of petitioners	136	134

Source: HO 17/25, 35–58.

* For details of sample see appendix.
** Since so many of the petitions spoke of work and behaviour in prison, this has been included as evidence of 'reform'.
*** This category is overloaded. It includes such mentions as 'contrition' and, for men only, assistance to the prosecution in Bank of England forged note cases.

representative of a strategy much used by the poor as they wrote to the charitable and humane in society.[13] In London, few convicts had, or used, educated or wealthy friends or patrons to present their cases. There are many pleas which, on the face of it, might have softened the hardest heart, and provoked the operation of the 'good mind' in the decision-maker, to allow mercy and amelioration of an appellant's situation. By the early nineteenth

13 See D. Andrew, ' "To the charitable and humane": appeals for assistance in the eighteenth-century London press', in H. Cunningham and J. Innes (eds), *Charity, philanthropy and reform from the 1690s to 1850s*, Basingstoke 1998, 87–107; Hitchcock, King and Sharpe, *Chronicling poverty*; and T. Sokoll (ed.), *Essex pauper letters, 1731–1837*, Oxford 2001.

century, the decision-makers were no longer choosing an occasional object for mercy, to be spared from the gallows. They were selecting an occasional example of terror. To petition was almost a matter of course. Support for a petition was not difficult for most prisoners to find. The words of the poor are clearly heard in the petitions, saying what they believed the decision-makers needed to hear.

Table 22 presents the result of an analysis of the factors mentioned in their appeals by men and women sentenced at the Old Bailey between 1817 and the late 1820s (and appealing for changes in sentence through the Home Office in the 1820s and 1830s) – factors which they thought the recipients would wish to know and which would prove favourable to them. This analysis builds on the work done for a slightly earlier period by Peter King.[14] Since the focus in this book is on London and Middlesex, information about which of the factors mentioned were regarded favourably by the decision-makers cannot be included because appeals dossiers rarely contained reports from the judges who tried them. Uncertainty about the final result is a further drawback to providing anything approaching a complete picture of the comparative success of the factors mentioned in the appeals. Nevertheless, a systematic 'factors mentioned' approach like this is worth attempting, since it avoids the temptation merely to pluck quotations from petitions. Dividing the factors by gender has provided some additional important insights, producing evidence of different ways of petitioning between men and women. Of course, the appeals archive contains complex documents which need to be treated with care, since they were couched in terms that the supplicant thought would be effective, rather than being documents purporting to reflect the truth. However, it is possible to use them to make a quantitative approach to understanding more about the pardoning system. The overall conclusions reached are similar to King's, and similarly challenge analyses which stress 'respectability' and neglect issues of poverty and distress. Separating male and female factors produces interesting differences which can be linked to wider discussions about gender and sentencing.[15]

For men, the factor of greatest importance was 'respectability', usually the respectability of their parents and close family. Few of the London and Middlesex petitioners were supported by the great and the good, the gentry or the clergy. The words in letters and petitions were those of urban neighbours, tradespeople and friends in lowly stations in life. The notion of respectability which prevailed was that of a stable family life, having lived at one address for many years, of parents who had brought up their families to respect God and be deferential to those in authority. The respectability of the petition writers, rather than of the prisoner for whom they appealed, was an important feature. On occasions, the Home Office set out to verify the backgrounds of

---

[14] King, 'Decision-makers', and *Crime, justice and discretion*, 297–325. He used papers in HO 47 for 1787 and 1790.

[15] See appendix for the selection of the sample of petitions.

the presenters of the petitions. Where the father of the prisoner was a former soldier, this was emphasised by the petitioner. Respectability was important to women too, although when Mary Ann Bacon's prosecutor and neighbours said 'she has the most respectable character for honesty and industry in servitude', it is not clear whether this was a factor of respectability, or of good character.[16]

The question of whose respectability was at stake was an issue often raised. The Home Office received a letter on behalf of Sarah Gilman, sentenced to death, from a gentleman, Richard Bellamy, which said nothing at all about Gilman, but related:

> her parents lived with Lord Sydmouth and his sister, Mrs. Goodenough, and were his servants for eight years while he was Speaker of the House of Commons; her mother, when widowed, went to Cheltenham with Mrs. Goodenough and Miss Addington (who married Judge Bragger). Mrs Goodenough and Mrs Gilman had very friendly talks. I believe her (mother) to be a very honest and deserving woman. Another reason is that the sister has been in my service for 18 years.[17]

Views on respectability varied. Elizabeth Emma Guy's gaoler described her as 'a loose character', but her supporters said she was the daughter of a master builder, who entitled himself 'esquire'. She had been deserted by her husband, left in great distress, had a previously unblemished character and used to move 'in circles of the utmost respectability in Derbyshire'.[18] Eliza Smith's mother wrote to tell the Home Secretary that she – the mother – was the daughter of a Mr Powers of Niagara, 'who lost £5000 in property at the conflagration of that Town by the War with the United States in the Year 1812. And also Three Vessels lent to Commodore Brisbane in the Year 1778'. Moreover, she said, Eliza was a girl of unblemished character, whose state of health required a mother's care; but the gaoler had written on the petition: 'Prostitute, married, one child'.[19]

For females, the main factor mentioned was previous good character, with a claim that this was their first offence. Men were more likely than women to have their former employers give them a good character reference. Women's employers (often the mistress of the house in which they worked) sometimes gave good references, even when the prisoner was convicted of theft from the house. Women's petitions often tell of their shame following the offence. They had, they said, told no-one what had happened, ending up in court without friends or character witnesses. They certainly would not tell their

---

16 HO 17/35/Eo1 (July 1829). For the 'elastic' quality of 'respectability' see King, *Crime, justice and discretion*, 308–9.
17 HO 17/25/Ch27. The papers (June 1821) were marked 'report requested', but the report is not with the papers.
18 HO 17/40/2/Fn11 (Apr.–June 1828); her papers were marked 'Nil'.
19 HO 17/37/Es57 (May 1833); her papers were marked 'Nil'.

mistress if the crime had been committed beyond the confines of the house. Mary Clarke, sixty years old, who had worked all her life as a respectable ladies' maid and housekeeper, was out of work, ill and in extreme want when she stole from her lodgings. She said she was ashamed and had not told her friends. She therefore had no 'character' at her trial.[20] Sarah Leggatt, sentenced to transportation for a similar offence, said that her mother had respectable friends who would have spoken for her at her trial, but she was too ashamed to ask. Despite her mother's respectable friends, including her prosecutor and the chaplain to the Spanish embassy, vouching for her good character, respectable family and her delicate health in their petition, her papers were marked 'refused'.[21] Nursery maid Ann Shuttleworth said she was so full of shame, sorrow and remorse, her reputation 'for ever blasted', that she had pleaded guilty to stealing from her employer. He made an impassioned plea for her, saying he never intended to get her transported. He had thought she would go to prison for a first offence and there her character could be 'reclaimed'.[22] Men did not appear to experience shame in the same way as women did, or, at least it was not a sufficiently masculine sentiment to mention in petitions.

Often the impression was given, for males and females, that offenders were misguided, unfortunate, but essentially gentle and public-spirited individuals, lacking much agency of their own. Parental appeals dominate the London and Middlesex cases. Even when the prisoner was a young or even middle-aged adult, parents strove to emphasise youth, good upbringing, a mistaken prosecution, an ill done to their offspring and frequently a sense of disappointment at what had come to pass despite all their efforts at good parenting. An example of exasperated parenthood was James Farquhar's 'poor, distracted, broken-hearted widowed' mother. Farquhar was young, his sentence for stealing handkerchiefs already commuted from death to life transportation. The Newgate gaoler knew him from a previous sojourn in the gaol. His mother pleaded for him to be sent to the penitentiary, for she had: 'toiled both early and late to bring up this undutiful child in the paths of rectitude and virtue which at an evil hour was departed from . . . he will bring down my poor grey hairs in sorrow to the grave. O God, give me strength to bear so severe a trial'. However, a mother's pleading could not over-ride the eminent suitability of a young man for life in Australia, and his papers were re-marked 'transport'.[23]

One of the marked differences between men and women was the frequency with which physical ill-health symptoms were referred to. Obviously pregnancy was a female prerogative, but that was rarely, if ever, a factor

[20] HO 17/43/Fx32 (Jan.1837); her papers were marked 'Nil'.
[21] HO 17/44/2/Gl5 (Oct.–Nov. 1825).
[22] HO 17/45/1/Gn48 (May–July 1828); her papers were first marked 'Nil' but a month later 'To Penitentiary'.
[23] HO 17/57/Kl32 (Feb.1826).

taken into account for discretion. Judging from the lack of preparation made for women about to give birth in prison and on ships, this significant event in a convict woman's life was of little interest to men of power and influence. However, the ill health of women was a frequently mentioned factor, which men did not cite. This may say much about the realities of the lives of plebeian women, or about their willingness to discuss their state of health. It is also noticeable that women tended to be age conscious, calling themselves old or well-on in years, whether they were in their seventies or as young as thirty-eight. The phenomenon of women being able to talk or write more of their problems, about what troubled them, to be less guarded on personal issues, is marked in the appeals papers – something noted in modern criminological research.[24] It saved a considerable number of women from transportation.

Petitioners on behalf of women frequently asserted that they would be reclaimed or reformed if they were allowed to go to the penitentiary rather than have to endure a harsher sentence. This fitted with a stereotypical view of women's behaviour. Women convicts, when petitioning on their own behalf, took a practical view of their possibilities of reform. Many had little children. They asked not to go to New South Wales, since, they argued, it would be better if they stayed in England to look after and be responsible for them. This they could do from the penitentiary. They could be 'useful' to those who ran the prison and earn their keep. Many mentioned the work that they already had done while serving their sentences so far – cooking, sewing and as wardswomen and teachers.

Mary Hart's mother made an ambitious plea as to the reformability of her fifteen-year-old 'gall' who was 'farley duped by the Other Gall that was with her', and was 'raley sorrey for hir past transgrations', a 'sincer Penetant', who 'will for the feuter become a member of his Church, a frind of Sober Secoitey A Comfourt to hir poor widowless mother and A Criditt unto hirselfe'.[25] Female reformability, frequently mentioned by petitioners themselves, was commented upon by officials and officers. A combination of female gender and youth featured in the cases of eleven-year-old Mary Hughes, Mary Louch, aged fifteen, and Sarah Lander, aged eighteen. Their gaoler's written comment was: 'dishonest and loose' and, in respect of Hughes, 'Bad, but only 11 years old'. The judge felt differently:

> The two eldest are soldiers' and sailors' prostitutes, living a very wretched and disorderly life, and ought to be removed from their relations and present haunts as I think their youth may induce a hope that they may reform, and their appearance may lead one to imagine that they may become respectable wives and mothers *alio sub sole*. The youngest may be reformed by educa-

24 Daly, *Gender, crime and punishment*.
25 HO 17/49/1/Hh9 (July–Nov.1821).

tion and good habits forced on her at the Penitentiary. But I believe that a short imprisonment and then turning her loose . . . will be to her anything but mercy.[26]

Men and women equally blamed others for their plight. Men were as likely to blame women, as women were to blame men. Ann Lutman's successful appeal told of how she 'was lead into Error by the bad counsel and participation of her husband'.[27] Mary Mitchell asserted that her husband was the cause of her offending. He had ill-used and deserted her and their eleven-year-old child: 'no one transaction of her life could ever give cause for, or justify such a mode of procedure equally unfeeling as a husband, as a Father and unbecoming as a man' [petitioner's underlining].[28] Martha Lucas insisted that she uttered forged Bank notes 'at the instigation only of her husband', but she was to receive no response to her petition for a reduction of her life sentence, and in the end, it was illness and good behaviour which helped her (*see* chapter 8).[29]

A successful petition on behalf of Sarah Hooker was the only one found in the sample of women's petitions which alluded distinctively to marital coercion in the committing of the offence. Hooker had been the receiver of property stolen by her husband. He was in the habit of 'brutally ill-using and threatening his wife . . ., she was compelled through fear to do whatever he required. Yet the natural feeling evinced by a wife towards her husband prevented her from giving him into the hands of Justice'. Her papers were marked, 'Free pardon prepared 24 October 1832'. In an earlier unsuccessful petition, she had invoked the whole gamut of factors which might work in her favour: she had never offended before, she supported her aged mother and was concerned about what would happen to her, she would reform, she had previously had a good character, she had been forced by her husband, and she was full of contrition. It was only when the Old Bailey judge reported that, in the meantime, her husband had himself been prosecuted for the theft that the decision turned in her favour. This demonstrated the need to put the right argument, get the right support and to be persistent.[30]

Women who blamed their men were matched by men who blamed their women. John Hiett, 'who entered into a marriage before the years of maturity to a female of bad character was through her persuasions and her acquaintance led to fraud'.[31] John Boyce married an 'unfortunate woman', was accused of robbing a client she had brought home and said it was all her fault.[32] William Garton's supporters insisted that he had not pursued a criminal course until he married his current wife, who 'turned out to be a most

[26] HO 17/43/Fy18 (Jan.1838).
[27] HO 17/25/Cm41 (Jan.–Mar.1827).
[28] HO 17/40/2/Fp39 (Oct.1830) (misfiled in box 45/2 as batch Hp39).
[29] HO 17/34/Eh27 (Aug.1820); HO 17/44/1/Gk22 (May 1824).
[30] HO 17/46/1/Gq34 (Sept.1831–Oct.1832).
[31] HO 17/50/1/Hp39 (Sept.1830).
[32] HO 17/50/Ho6 (Sept.1829).

wicked and base woman and it was through her influence that he was prompted', and that 'she is now living in whoredom and insensible and unconcerned about the awful situation of her unfortunate husband and it was solely through the Influence of this wretched woman' that he was led into crime. These words were strongly pencil-marked in the margins by a Home Office official as if importance might have been attached to them, but Garton was not successful in his appeal against the death sentence.[33]

Nevertheless, the overwhelming relationship of men and women, spouses and partners appears to have been mutually supportive, out of economic necessity and often from affection and friendship. This makes many of the petitions moving to read. Although such sentiments might have had little effect on the outcome, their lack of formulaic repetition of demands for discretion presents a genuine picture of the dreadful situation in which these unfortunate people found themselves. Economic responsibility for the family was frequently shared between the partners. Mary McCarthy, aged forty-four, awaiting a fourteen-year transportation sentence for receiving stolen money, had a 'poor old disconsolate husband' lacking the use of his limbs. They had ten children living, five of whom were under ten years of age, and she was yet again in an advanced state of pregnancy. She was the family's breadwinner.[34] Mary Smith, aged forty-five, was already on board ship for a seven-year transportation sentence for stealing a child's clothes. She appealed desperately on three occasions, explaining that she had had fifteen children, eight of whom were alive, three of them under seven and that they were all entirely dependent on her since her husband, to whom she had been married for twenty-seven years, was sick and infirm and unable to provide for them.[35] Jane Taylor, serving a one-year sentence for manslaughter, had seven children under fourteen dependent on her, as her husband was ill.[36] None of these petitions received a positive response.

The gender card implicit in motherhood and daughterhood was frequently played, but was matched equally by the obligations of fatherhood and sonhood. To lack a father's care was considered a serious matter for children of any age and aged parents depended on a son's care and earnings. The importance of the mother to the family was a strong petitioning factor, as was the importance of a daughter to her mother. One petition tells of a family 'in great want of a tender mother'; of infants 'at an age when a mother's parental affection is needed', 'a daughter who needs a mother'; of the 'filial feelings of an affectionate daughter to her aged mother who has seen better days' and of 'mutual utility if they are able to console each other'.[37] Husbands appealed for their wives – 'affectionate partners and mothers'. But they could some-

33 HO 17/49/1/Hh6 (Sept.1821).
34 HO 17/36/Ep1 (late 1830).
35 HO 17/36/Ep49 (late 1830).
36 HO 17/36/Er7 (early 1832).
37 HO 17/42/Fv48 (May 1838).

times sound more like aggrieved and disappointed parents. Ann Perrin's husband begged that his wife, to whom he had been married for twenty-nine years, should not be sent away from her six children. He called her 'my unfortunate and erring partner' and explained that she, 'decoyed' by an 'evil association' had been stopping away from home and her wifely duties, and was tempted to steal from a shop.[38] Sarah Martin's husband of twenty-five years sounded disappointed and peevish. His wife had gone to see their daughter at Knightsbridge, stayed until midnight and on her way back had got into conversation with a medical student in the Strand, and was charged with picking his pocket after he had taken her for a drink. Her husband said, 'I know her well, and a small amount [of alcoholic drink] can make her intoxicated.' He maintained she was innocent of robbery, but guilty of idle conversation and drinking when she should have been at home. He finished by pointing out that it had been a lesson to her and she would not be doing anything like that again.[39]

Responses to petitions

The discretionary pardoning process was based on a complex interplay of attitudes and interests. The long eighteenth century may have been the golden age of discretionary justice, particularly in relation to property crime, and the pardoning system may have 'created a finely tuned field of discretionary justice'.[40] This may have remained true of the public face of justice in prosecution and trial options in the early decades of the nineteenth century. However, by the 1830s, in the more 'behind the scenes' pardoning arena, changes were taking place and the practical needs of the state were playing a significant role, affecting the way in which discretion was exercised. Towards the end of the eighteenth century it might still have been appropriate to see the operation of 'the good mind and the bad mind' on those with the power to make decisions. Henry Fielding had argued that the 'good mind' of the decision-maker – that prevalent tendency to be affected by stories of destitution, misery, necessity and youth – was repugnant, since it led to the wish to mitigate sentences to a dangerous degree. Reason should overcome this 'good mind', because only severity, through the operation of the 'bad mind' would deter others from committing crimes.[41]

The way in which records were kept makes it difficult to know how successful were the men and women who appealed directly to the Home Secretary in the first instance, without being, at that point, part of any automatic pardoning deal. It is also almost impossible to know the reason for the

---

[38] HO 17/38/2/Ez45 (about Oct.1838).
[39] HO 17/48/2/Gx37 (Feb.1837).
[40] King, Crime, justice and discretion, 355.
[41] The concept of 'good mind' and 'bad mind' is presented and expanded ibid. 325–33.

responses made to their petitions. Of the 134 women included in table 22, there is reasonably clear evidence in the official records that thirty-two were 'successful', securing a mitigation of their sentences. Of the 136 men, there are nineteen cases where success appears certain. There is every reason to believe that there was a much higher success rate than this for both men and women, but the records require further lengthy scrutiny to establish this. The 'successful' men had invoked a wide range of factors in their appeals, most frequently good character, youth and pre- and post-crime destitution. The 'successful' women had invoked the factors of good character and youth. However, where things differed significantly for the 'successful women' was in the categories of 'physical illness', 'reformed/reformable behaviour' and 'good work in prison', provided that they had already served a substantial proportion of their sentences. These same factors ranked highly when women were being considered for 'automatic' pardoning.

These factors also rated highly in decisions about men, although men were not so frequently said to be unwell. Women's ill health was a distinctive factor which worked to their advantage in the last stages of the criminal justice system. When sixteen-year-old Elizabeth Stevenson appealed against her sentence of transportation, her parents described her as sickly, delicate and needing their care. Her papers were marked, 'Does her health render her unfit for transportation?' The reply to this question resulted in a second marking, 'Refused'.[42] It is interesting that men did not try to appeal on these grounds. It is, therefore, likely that gender played a strong, but indirect, role in judicial discretion at this point in the justice system. The 'good mind' of the decision-makers may have been triggered by the playing of a gendered card.

Discretion and compassion from the Bank of England

The story of the Bank of England's compassionate and generous treatment of some of 'its' prisoners, mitigating the effects of their sentences, is relatively unknown.[43] The exercise of the 'good mind' of this great institutional prosecutor provides a remarkable example of the operation of discretionary gendered paternalism, hidden from view by the autonomy of an autocratic, wealthy corporation, which brushed aside questioning of its motives and policies. As they waited in prison for their sentences of transportation to be put into effect, men and women convicted of Bank note offences wrote copiously to their prosecutors.[44] Their letters provide a contrasting picture of how a mighty institution dealt with its criminal business in a cool, organised, prag-

---

42 HO 17/44/ 2/G19 (Jan.1825, but more likely to be Jan.1826).
43 See D. Palk, ' "Fit objects for mercy": gender, the Bank of England and currency criminals, 1804–33', *Women's Writings* xi/2 (2004), 237–58.
44 See J. Slinn, *A history of Freshfields*, London 1984, for the association between the Bank

matic, yet discretionary, way. However much the Bank came under pressure from the weight of currency forgery business or from the opprobrium heaped on it for the extent and severity of its prosecution enterprise, it maintained a careful, reasoned policy towards 'its' convicts. This policy changed from time to time, depending on the progress of note forgery activity and the escalating costs of prosecution. However, it was an extraordinary mix of cold, arrogant distance and calculated, yet profligate, compassion, with a deeply gendered texture.

Petitions and letters begging mercy and charity poured in to the Bank from prisons and hulks all over England and Wales, couched in both formal and informal terms. In all cases, there is annotated evidence of how each request was dealt with.[45] The correspondence between the convicts, especially the female convicts who were multi-letter writers, and their 'generous prosecutors'[46] built up into an unexpected relationship, which gave financial and moral hope to those spending many months in grim prison conditions, awaiting a terrifying voyage into the unknown. Most letters came from men and women in the London area. This confirms the existence of 'know-how' and networks within Newgate, especially on the Women's Side, and the ease with which letters could be delivered by hand, or by two-penny post, to the Bank's solicitors around the corner from the prison. A few special cases aside, it was only when women from the provincial prisons met up with the women from London as they went to the transport ships, that they realised they had missed the opportunity for a beneficial relationship with their prosecutors.

The Bank's response to the requests from convicted prisoners was deliberate and rational. To those, male or female, who were condemned to die, it would make only the cold response that it was not its business to interfere. Nor would it support others petitioning the Home Secretary or monarch. Having gone through the expensive and difficult process of prosecuting capitally those it believed to be a serious threat to the nation's, and its own, security, it stood back, justified in its actions. On the other hand, the Bank showed tolerance towards those who were going to be removed from the country. It had done its duty in prosecuting, even offering the chance of a guilty plea to the non-capital offence of possession, which allowed it to assume an appearance of generosity from the start of the relationship. The relative status of the indebted, convicted prisoner and the benevolent offended party was clear in the correspondence. Unless constrained from time to time by the governor's and directors' concerns at the immense cost of conducting forgery prosecutions, the Bank was willing to respond with generosity to women convicts while they remained in prison and when they went

---

of England and its solicitors from 1743 to 1983 which is crucial to this discretionary episode.
[45] BEFP, F25; BECLS, M5/307–33 for 1804–34.
[46] Term first used by Ann Haynes alias Foss, Newgate, 22 Oct.1804, BEFP, F25/1.

on board the transport ships. In general, it responded favourably to requests from women, and unfavourably to requests from men, so it is little wonder that, *pro rata*, petitioning and corresponding was a female activity in London.

The archive contains letters or petitions from more than 350 men and more than 200 women. Since the proportions of women convicted of forged note offences were much lower than those of men, it is clear to what extent the letter-writing was a female enterprise. Women were also more likely than the men to write more than one letter, presumably because of the more positive response they received; some carried on a written relationship over several years. More men wrote from outside London than from within London. On the other hand, more than three times the number of women wrote from London than those outside London. In fact, of the London-based prisoners, 92 per cent of the women prisoners wrote, compared with 26 per cent of the London men.

Men and women asked for different things in their letters and petitions. This may have been because their needs were different, or because they knew how to be successful at invoking favours – or both. In the unhappy circumstances in which these men and women found themselves, any strategy was worth trying. Analysis of the letters written from prisoners in London gaols show that about 95 per cent of the women were seeking pecuniary relief, whereas just over a quarter of the men sought such assistance. The largest proportion of the men (well over a third) was seeking advantages of all sorts in exchange for giving information to the Bank which might lead to other forgers and utterers of notes being apprehended. Otherwise the men's requests were spread over a wide range of favours – pleas for mitigation of sentence, for their spouses and children to accompany them to New South Wales, for the return of money taken from them on apprehension, for relief for their family, to arrange their own exile, to delay or hasten transportation, to give messages to friends. The very small proportion of women's requests which were not for pecuniary relief included a handful of offers of information on forgers, and a couple to delay or hasten transportation. In all, requests diverged significantly according to sex.

If pecuniary relief was what the women most desired, this was what they got in abundance. Men who were seen as relatively more independent financially than the women were, tended not to beg for small amounts of money and probably knew that it was unlikely they would be successful. The Bank made clear its attitude to men who requested financial relief; in 1818, when eleven men in Newgate, about to be despatched to a transport ship, asked for 'that Donation which we understand as generally been bestowed to the unfortunate culprits who have been convicted by your honourable Company', their petition was annotated 'These are Male'. No payment was made, no reply offered.[47]

[47] BEFP, F25/6.

Requests from women for pecuniary assistance were recorded as early as 1799, when a Bank prisoner, Mrs Row, was paid a guinea.[48] Another, Mary Burn, was to be paid half a guinea a week from June 1806 'until she is sent away'.[49] This generous amount of money became the 'standard' weekly payment to women petitioning in the early years of forgery prosecutions, perhaps before anyone realised just how long convicts would be confined, awaiting space on a transport ship. From 1810 it dropped to 7s. a week. From 1813 until 1822, when the Bank intended to cease the practice,[50] payments were 5s. a week for childless women, 7s. 6d. for women with one child, and sometimes 10s. 6d. for those with more than one child. Until about 1824 nearly all women were given £5 each on embarkation for New South Wales. This applied equally to the women from provincial gaols if they applied, having met up with the women from London and learned what might be on offer.[51]

The Bank records suggest that it exercised genuine compassion compatible with the paternalistic outlook of the middling and professional classes. There were also strong political motives behind the compassion, since the Bank was subject to enormous pressure from various quarters for its conduct of the paper money supply and of criminal prosecutions. The Bank had little idea of the huge amount of prosecution business it was going to handle over the twenty years of 'suspension', nor of the effect of a plea bargaining system, which was to leave so many men and women waiting for ships to take them to New South Wales. For the most part, it had caught, not the forgers themselves, but poor people, engaged in what they must have thought was petty crime. The significant number of women, many of whom were very poor, was also not what had been expected.

When requests were received, the Bank sent investigators to Newgate to report on their genuineness – whether prisoners were truly in distress, without friends, pregnant, had recently given birth, ill and so on. Sometimes they accepted the views of Brown, keeper of Newgate, with his jaundiced

---

48 BEFP, F25/1.
49 BECLS, M5/307, 26 June 1806.
50 When the period of suspension ended in 1821, the Bank did not plan to continue its previous level of prosecution and, concerned at the vast expense of the prosecution enterprise, curtailed expenses, decreasing rewards and signing off its retained investigators and unofficial police. The batch of women it was then paying in prison was not due to sail until Jan.1822; the Bank agreed to pay until then (BECLS, M5/325, 12 Mar., 26 Sept., 14 Nov., 19 Dec.1821). The last recorded payment of relief to a woman in prison was in Sept.1824 (M5/327, 1 Sept.1824).
51 It is difficult to establish the comparative values or generosity of the Bank's payments. In comparison with poor relief payments made both in or near London and in other parts of the country, the amounts were high, at times double the relief that would be paid to a single woman. For examples see Hitchcock, King and Sharpe, *Chronicling poverty*, and *Essex pauper letters*. Elizabeth Fry, describing the work of women prisoners in 1818, stated that 'The earnings of work, we think, average about eighteen pence per week for each person': *Memoir of the life of Elizabeth Fry*, 317.

attitude to the women he was holding. Sometimes a Bank representative would check Brown's views, with kinder results. There were signs that these representatives of the Bank were concerned at the conditions which many of the women endured during their long waits in prison.[52] The fact that the relief payments to the women while in prison were not automatic, and that decisions were recorded, allows some understanding of the discretion used by the Bank, and why this was so openly gendered.

Larger payments were made to a very few women during their wait in prison and on embarkation, and it is reasonable to assume that these were for information and assistance given to the Bank. Amongst a group of four 'Bank women' going on board the *William Pitt* in June 1806 was Ann McCarthy. The Bank wished to give the captain some money for the three others, but, for McCarthy, there was a payment of £15. This was to be used by the captain to buy items for the comfort of McCarthy and her child, with the remainder to be given to her on arrival at 'Botany Bay', since she had conducted herself with propriety since her conviction. The captain was also requested to give her protection. McCarthy's three letters to the Bank from prison make it obvious that she had been informing. She was desperate to get on the transport ship to:

> avoid reflection which unthinking and ill-natured people cast on me . . . The noble gentlemen can understand the anxiety which persons experience in a prison especially when they keep themselves select from the Lower Orders of Society . . . they are saying I caused the death of the men who suffered the sentence of the law last Thursday and they say that when I get on the ship I shall be treated with the greatest severity and likewise abroad. I was indiscreet but I do not know the men, so when your man comes will he speak for me to Mr Kirby and stop their ill usage of me.[53]

When money was paid weekly to women, the reasons given for doing so were distress, hunger, little children to support, lack of clothing, no husband or friends to give support, no one to visit them. Men were not so likely to be in this condition, or so the Gentlemen of the Bank believed. Jane Williams was a profuse writer on her own and others' behalf, organising petitions and thank-you letters, since she was able to write herself. Her letters sum up what the relationship with the Bank came to mean to many of the women. Williams started writing when she was committed to Newgate before her trial in August 1818, complaining that she had only bread and water, requesting the Bank send her 'the smallest trifle'. Her next letter, after her conviction, thanked the Bank, and asked for more, since she observed their 'charity extended to some of my fellow prisoners'. This letter was marked: 'Mr Christmas to give her 5/- and to report further as to her situation'. Further

---

[52] BECLS, M5/318, 26 Sept.1816; M5/320, 29 Oct.1818, 25 Feb.1819; M5/322, 28 Apr.1819; M5/323, 9 Feb., 1, 8, 15 Mar.1820; M5/324, 11 Oct.1820.
[53] BEFP, F25/1.

letters expressed thanks, and upbraided the Bank for 'getting into arrears' with payments which had clearly become expected. In April 1819 Williams wrote for 'the Bank Prisoners in Newgate':

> We for the last time beg leave to Address you and return you Our Sincere Thanks for the Charity extended towards us which has been the means of sup-porting Ourselves During our long and tedious Confinement and Farther Entreating your Charity to be Extended towards us on our leaving our Native Country for Ever so that we may be enabled to Go with Some Degree of Com-fort During our long and perilous voyage as we are ordered for Embarkation on Wednesday or Thursday morning. Honorable Gentlemen we beg leave to Subscribe Ourselves with Humble respect your Obliged and Humble Servants and Prisoners.

Not content with this, Williams, with seven other women, had a final claim on the Bank's charity, writing a few days later as they left Newgate that, 'We have contracted a few debts in prison – please allow us The Usual Stipend.'[54]

Such relationships – of humble supplicant and charitable donor – were a normal part of the life of some poor women. The words and sentiments used and the donor's check on the truth of the claims was a standard ritual. This strategy of supplication, rewarded by a generous response, was perhaps to be expected. Charitable compassion was a mark of the donor's power as well as a responsibility. There were contrary views – that charity of this kind was feeding poverty rather than aiding the poor. One of Elizabeth Fry's assistants directly confronted the Bank with such views.[55] However, although the rela-tionship of the Bank and its female prisoners fitted well with the charitable perception of the time, it was hardly usual in its setting, commencing with capital prosecution of a serious felony, costing the institution a huge amount of money and bringing it under public ridicule, where people's lives had been put at risk. Nor was it a publicised relationship, other than through the prison networks. Further, the highly gendered response, whereby men were largely excluded from this 'charity', suggests that this was not a 'normal' response to distress and poverty.[56]

There were women to whom the Bank refused relief, even the frequently paid money for the voyage. A few women, whose husbands were still in the country, but incarcerated, awaiting transportation themselves, were refused until the men sailed, since a husband was supposed to support his wife, despite his imprisonment. Some women, who had been notorious, persistent, major forged note utterers, were refused, as were those who continued the trade in prison. The Bank was desperate to get rid of such women, petitioning

---

54 BEFP, F25/5; F25/6; F25/7.
55 Letter from Mrs Pryor, 6 Feb. 1821, BEFP, F25/9.
56 Andrew, 'To the charitable', 87–107, and 'Noblesse oblige: female charity in the age of sentiment', in J. Brewer and S. Staves (eds), *Early modern conceptions of property*, London–New York 1994, 275–300; Hitchock, King and Sharpe, *Chronicling poverty*.

the Home Secretary to bring forward the order for them to join their ships. Some of these were not even paid the money for the voyage.[57] The Bank did not wish to make payments to Hannah Polley, whose case resulted in censure of the Bank from the Prince Regent for its attempt to manipulate the court by getting her to plead guilty to a capital charge, promising life transportation in return. The judge had refused to be manipulated and she had been sentenced to death. Polley wrote many times and, after being in Newgate, a 'gloomy Weary prison', for fourteen months, described herself as an aged woman (she was fifty-one) in poor health, whose husband was in the poor house. The Bank relented and sent £2 to the keeper to buy food for her.[58] Similar refusals were experienced by women who did not accept the offer of a plea bargain, although they invariably received money for the voyage.

When there was concern about legal costs in 1820, the Bank became more careful about its charity. A group of seven women, claiming severe distress, petitioned for relief. The Bank responded by requesting an investigation of their situations. The Newgate keeper reported 'that they were all women of the worst description, unworthy of the Bank's bounty, and to give them anything would be a kind of encouragement, that they are all employed at work and received a proportion of their earnings every Saturday'. Relief was refused.[59] Another four women made the same request, and the Bank investigator reported that all had jobs and some had earnings every Saturday. Moreover, they had no children except one, who had an infant of five months, and although her journeyman husband came to visit her, she was to be paid 5s. a week, the others nothing.[60] From about 1813 a pattern was established of not paying women without children, women with friends visiting who could give a little support, those who gave a false account of their situation, 'bad characters' and those who continued criminal activities. Nevertheless, all but those in this last category received £5 on sailing.

By the end of 1821, at the conclusion of the 'suspension' period, the Bank hoped that the need for its charity would also end, but transportation ships were still taking a long time to make ready to sail. Four of its female prisoners were still in Newgate, all of whom had been receiving weekly either 2s.6d. or 5s. for over a year. The Bank resolved that assistance should cease from January 1822, despite the fact that the women were certain to be in Newgate for another six months. It refused all new requests from women in Newgate. It still paid £5 on their joining the ship, but made it sound as if this was a special favour.

The men to whom the Bank gave support or payments were few, underlining how gendered was this discretion. Far from seeing male convicts as distressed, poor, ill and deserted, as they saw the women, they saw the men as

---

57 BEFP, F25/3.
58 BEFP, F25/6; F25/7.
59 BECLS, M5/323, 1, 8 Mar.1820.
60 BECLS, M5/323, 15 Mar.1820.

independent and self-sufficient, with enough means or prison work to get them by. Where men received payment, nearly all were engineered in response to the assistance they gave, leading to apprehension of other forgers and utterers. Michael Gerain, who helped the Bank to bring capital charges against his elderly wife, received 5s. a week for two years.[61] The result of John Sly's informing was a reluctant one-off payment of £5 while he was on the *Zealand* hulk.[62] William Henningham informed from Newgate, and requested relief for the distress of himself, his wife and children. He was awarded 7s. a week, and his wife, who was not implicated in the forgery business, was paid £5.[63] Charles Games, a substantial informer, obtained permission from the Home Secretary to take his wife and children with him on the ship to New South Wales, and, ostensibly for this reason, the Bank paid him £10 on his departure at the end of 1813.[64] Richard Walker petitioned for his wife who was paralysed with rheumatism and gout. There were several payments of £5 to her. Other prisoners alleged that the couple was being maintained by the Bank for the steady stream of information forthcoming.[65] A handful of other men can be added to this list, but most who applied were ignored.

This remarkably gendered response by the Bank of England is a note-worthy example of elite discretion in practice. There was, of course, much more to the motivation behind this exercise of generosity than can be written about here.[66] The women prisoners were seen as a different class from the men – the Bank observed the greater physical needs of women, their lack of support, their childcare responsibilities and their lesser ability to earn money from work while in prison. These women were also likely to have started from a point of greater need when they committed their crimes, although not all of them were in a state of deep distress. Some were reasonably educated, could read and write and showed signs of being worldly-wise, able to make the best of the situation they found themselves in. Here, outside the public space of the criminal justice system, a national institution, run by men of the professional classes, wedded to a particular view of womanhood, showed care, generosity and compassion to the unfortunate and underlined the gendered discretion available within the workings of the criminal justice system, and the essential link between paternalism and power.

[61] BECLS, M5/309,12 May 1810; M5/312, 10 June 1812.
[62] BECLS, M5/309, 27 Sept., 8 Nov.1809, 14 Feb.1810; BEFP, F25/1.
[63] BECLS, M5/311, 19 Feb.1812; BEFP, F25/1.
[64] BECLS: M5/314, 1 Dec.1813 (mistakenly called George); BEFP, F25/2.
[65] BECLS: M5/314, 22 Dec.1813; BEFP, F25/2.
[66] Palk, 'Fit objects'.

8

Gendered Behaviour, Paternalistic Justice and Political Necessity

This book has explored some of the experiences of the men and women of London and Middlesex whose activities brought them before the judges and juries at the Old Bailey for three capital property crimes. Questions have been asked about how they carried out their offences, who they were, what they stole and how they stole, how each category of crime differed from the others, and how the decision-makers responded to them. They have been followed through each of the stages of the criminal justice system, from apprehension to final punishment, first to discover the nature and extent of the influence of gender in their encounters with the system and the decisions taken about them, and then to try to find reasons for the different ways in which the authorities dealt with them. Throughout, the challenge of remaining systematic, of using both qualitative and quantitative data, of attending to the ways in which different forms of illegal appropriation were undertaken and organised, of considering what was stolen, how it was stolen and what was done with the stolen property, and of locating the study within the history of law enforcement has been taken up and met, so far as it has been possible.[1]

It is hardly surprising, on such a bewildering journey through the criminal justice system, that the effect of gender emerges in complex and uneven ways. Rarely have overt explanations for the discretionary use of gendered treatment been uncovered. When the forces affecting judicial decisions were openly discussed or written down by contemporaries, gender was not one of them. However, the experiences presented show that gender was a strong force at work in judicial decisions, but that it pulled in different ways at different points in the system. Judicial and penal decisions were being made in a society fundamentally organised and ordered in a gendered way. Such decisions were not necessarily consistent, although they were, at most times, rational. The effect of gender is one of the keys to understanding that rationale. How men and women acted, and how they were judged and processed through the system, was gendered at all stages, but at no stage was the effect entirely predictable. Females were not always favoured, nor were they always disfavoured. Contemporary notions about masculinity and femininity could

---

1   These are the directions for research proposed by Innes and Styles in 'Crime wave'. See also appendix below.

exert contradictory pressures. Most important, the needs of the state had to be met, and the public's perception of specific crimes had also to be fed into the equation. The strongest proposition about the effect of gender on the application of justice which emerges is that the criminal act was gendered before it came within range of the justice system. This in itself might be sufficient explanation for the apparent leniency shown to female defendants, certainly for the different ways in which they were treated.

This concluding chapter considers some of the complexities and uncertainties which arise in the search for the operation of gendered discretion, together with a further reflection on the lives of the men and women whose journeys have been followed in order to recollect their reality as human beings and not as mere statistics. The diverse evidence about their journeys through the criminal justice system can then be brought together and be seen through the filters of three main themes which have emerged strongly during this enquiry. The first theme is of gendered behaviour on the part of those committing serious offences – the proposition is that what they did, or did not do, was already gendered before their encounter with the justice system – and this necessarily influenced the decision-makers' choices, and the verdicts, sentences and final outcomes for offenders. The second theme is that of decision-making in a society where gender was a basic organising category.[2] This is an important theme for any study located within the criminal justice system, since the law itself enshrined the precepts at the heart of a patriarchal society.[3] The third theme is that of the needs of the state – a complex area to consider. Changes in penal ideology, in the economy of deterrence and the need to invest in different approaches to policing and punishment in the early nineteenth century were having their effect on what happened to prisoners and convicts in the latter stages of their journey through the judicial system. However, put simply, the state needed to disperse the 'criminal' population to particular places, in specific ways, at different times. The bureaucratic decisions taken to effect both ideological and pragmatic policies involved a gendered component.

Gender and justice: complexities and uncertainties

Statistical evidence provides reasons for the assertion that women were more leniently treated than men at all stages of the criminal justice system, particularly at the point of sentencing. So frequently do historians and criminolo-

---

[2] J. Scott, 'Gender: a useful category of historical analysis', in her *Gender and the politics of history*, 30.
[3] P. Lawson, 'Patriarchy, crime, and the courts: the criminality of women in late Tudor and early Stuart England', in Smith, May and Devereaux, *Criminal justice*, 16–57, a rare attempt by an historian to tackle the effects of patriarchy and paternalism in the criminal justice system.

gists make such statements that it is possible to overlook how puzzling are such conclusions. They may be based on simple, bulk statistical evidence, which seriously mismeasures justice since the disparities lying behind judicial decisions are left unquestioned. The conclusion that gender plays a large part in informing the decision-makers remains without context, since there is no explanation of how or why it plays this distinctive part. Disparity and difference – in activity, in story, in judicial decisions, in strategies and responses – have been the persistent focal points in this study. Exploration of these disparities and differences has required oscillation between the uncovering of new sets of statistics, and the use of narrative modes of description and reasoning. Both the quantitative and qualitative approaches have been necessary in order to understand the disparities in the lives and activities of men and women and in the judicial responses to them.

It is not easy to draw conclusions, either from quantitative or qualitative material, about the nature and extent of the role of gender. Even when modern researchers are able to question magistrates' sentencing rationale and the effect of gender on their thinking about crime, offenders and sentencing, their findings beg many questions. However, their research provides hints about the operation of gendered attitudes and concludes that differences in the sentencing of men and women are not a consequence of anything as simple as deliberate gendered discrimination:

> If that were true one would expect the statistical exercise to show women consistently receiving different sentences to men. But they do not. For example, they stood an equal chance of going to prison for a first violent offence, whereas among repeat offenders, women were less likely to go to prison. And among drug offenders, women recidivists were as likely as men to be imprisoned, but first timers were not . . . Sentencing decisions are the outcome of the interactive effect of a number of factors. The most important of these is the nature of the offence. However, the offender's circumstances, the way the other participants in the courtroom portray the offence and the offender, the offender's appearance and behaviour in court . . . Together these factors shape the court's perception of an offender as essentially troubled or troublesome, and this in turn determines whether help or punishment is at the heart of the court's response.[4]

I reach a similar overall conclusion. In many different ways, sometimes slight and puzzling, sometimes covert and indirect, sometimes overt and direct, decisions were prompted or affected by notions about gender. The focus in this book on three capital property crimes, held systematically through as much of the criminal justice system as possible, highlights the importance of attention to the detail and the distinctiveness of each criminal activity, each verdict, each sentence and each act of pardon, and commutation. Attention to detail is necessary, since each of these activities resists uniform classifica-

---

4 Hedderman and Gelsthorpe, *Understanding the sentencing of women*, 56.

tion and quantification. Even so, such examination and analysis can only yield hints and suggestions which might explain why men and women were treated differently by the justice system, and how or whether the gender card was played.

Historians who have worked in this area have carried out some of the burdensome task of classification and quantification.[5] Their labours show that justice and discretion have a gendered face. They appear to suggest that, in general, women were more leniently treated by the courts and the penal system. However, sustainable arguments for why this should be so have not usually been produced. It has been suggested that women were seen as less of a threat to order in society since they were less violent, inherently less criminal, less active, less professional, the helpers of men; or that, in accordance with some constructions of femininity and masculinity, women were the weaker vessel, vulnerable and easily led astray, and to be helped rather than harmed; or that they were reformable and pliable, so certain types of punishment were more suitable. These suggestions depend on over-generalised patriarchal or paternalistic notions of womanhood and femininity. Attempts to analyse and question the statistics of judicial leniency in context have more recently been made, together with a challenge to the historiography that sees women's crime as less serious than men's, or as a mere shadow of 'real' male crime.[6] If 'like' is compared with 'like' and if research and analysis is specific and contextual in relation to women's lives, not only can it be seen that the experience of men and women is truly incommensurable, but there is little evidence that women were more leniently treated.[7] The close focus of this book upon three specific crimes, and the longer view taken through the whole of the justice system, show that gendered treatment results from a much more complex mix of motives – as one might expect.

The poor who offend

The short period in which this study has been set – the 1780s to the 1830s – is often seen as a time of significant change and upheaval in most areas of English life: a time of social and political change, changes in trade, industry and work patterns, in medicine and science, and, most pertinently, in administrative functions. It was the final period of the 'old regime', before the main

5   In particular this has been done by Beattie, 'Criminality of women', and *Crime and the courts*; King, 'Female offenders', and 'Gender, crime and justice'; Lawson, 'Patriarchy, crime and the courts'; and, to a lesser extent, Walker, 'Women, theft and stolen goods', and *Crime, gender and social order*; Wiener, 'Sex roles and crime'; Emsley, *Crime and society*; and Sharpe, *Crime in early modern England*.
6   Walker, *Crime, gender and social order*, passim, esp. pp. 4, 5, 22, 113, 158–89, 208, 270–9. Unfortunately, she terminates her research at the sentencing of offenders and does not enquire further into the judicial system.
7   Edwards, *Sex and gender*, 363.

repeal of the 'bloody code' and the introduction of professional preventative policing.[8] The core of the 'golden age' of discretionary justice in England remained[9] but was changing in nature.

The constant theme of anxiety about the perceived lawlessness of the lower and (by definition) poorer classes took on a new intensity in the late eighteenth century as the ruling classes felt their understanding of order being threatened. Crime and the criminal carried their fears about social change itself, encompassing all those reluctant to take on disciplined and controlled work and those who dissented or were excluded from the consensual norms of society. From the 1780s criminal activity came to be seen more as an 'important problem' rather than as the outcome of personal depravity. Sensibilities were touched. Changes in the penal regime were discussed and implemented. Prosecutors, judges and juries were gradually becoming more chary of the death penalty for many offences. The loss of the facility to transport convicts to America necessitated hard thinking about suitable replacement secondary punishments. Crime began to be seen in materialist terms, rather than as the result of sin; and as a social issue arising from the squalor of the growing great cities. The fear of revolution, following events in America and France, introduced urgency to debates on the increasing insubordination and presumed politicisation of the poor.[10]

Those who were instrumental in reinforcing social discipline and those who saw how such reform would defend the order they desired would have been conscious of the changes taking place in the justice and penal systems. How far the poor were similarly conscious of change, or consented to or resented it, is less clear. Comparison of the experiences of a London shoplifter of the 1790s with those of one of the 1820s would show that continuity in her life, needs and attitudes would be the more likely keynote, rather than change. Some of the men and women whose stories have been followed belonged among 'the labouring poor', although many more of them were to be found amongst the even less articulate minorities who, by definition, leave few records of their own. For this reason, many historians of the labouring and working classes have avoided engagement with the full range of the plebeian majority. The poor are 'difficult' to study, to hear. Historians of women seem to have even greater difficulties finding the words of poor women; their writing on 'the working class' tends to be about more articulate

---

8   Styles, 'Emergence of the police'; A. T. Harris, *Policing the City: crime and legal authority in London, 1780–1840*, Columbus, Ohio 2004; Hay and Snyder, 'Policing'; Gatrell, 'Crime, authority and the policeman state'; C. Emsley, *The English police*, London 1991.
9   King, *Crime, justice and discretion*, passim; Brewer and Styles, *Ungovernable people*, 11–20. Specific developments in the administration of criminal justice are dealt with in Devereaux, 'Criminal branch', 'In place of death' and 'Peel, pardon and punishment'; Hilton, 'The gallows and Mr Peel'; Atkinson, 'State and empire'; Ignatieff, *Just measure of pain*; and McGowen, ' The image of justice', and 'Powerful sympathy'.
10 Ignatieff, *Just measure of pain*.

subjects.[11] However, it is possible, through written sources – of the judicial system, and contemporary letters, appeals, texts, ballads and poetry, written by, for and about the poor – to recover much of their personal histories and environment.[12]

Life on the margins changed little, particularly for poor women. Continuity in their work opportunities, their way of economic survival and their standard of living is striking over very long periods. There are places where the voices of such people can be directly and clearly heard, although they were communicating in ways which they believed would favourably impress their audience. The petitions and letters in the Home Office appeals archives, and the correspondence of the 'Bank of England prisoners', are valuable examples of the words of the poor. They can help us understand the experience of poverty, exclusion and marginalisation; and the strong sense of a customary right to relief, from the rich to the poor. Overall, when their voices are heard through these documents, the continuities of their lives come through strongly.

Reviewing the factual evidence

When shoplifters and pickpockets were tried at the Old Bailey between the 1780s and 1820s, women were more often in the dock than men. Not guilty verdicts went more in women's favour in both crimes, more so in the case of pickpocketing. Death sentences were passed equally on men and women shoplifters and pickpockets, although it must have been common knowledge that it was unlikely that any execution would be carried out. Where partial verdicts were returned, men were more likely than women to be sentenced to transportation for seven years, much more likely in the case of pickpockets. On the other hand, women were more likely to be sentenced to imprisonment than men. However, prosecutions for offences against the Bank of England in the first three decades of the nineteenth century showed different decision-making patterns. Few defendants were found not guilty. The dominant plea bargaining system determined the sentencing. Men and women chose equally to refuse the offer of a plea bargain and, when they did refuse, women were more likely to be found not guilty than men. In sentencing, both capitally and for transportation for fourteen years, the balance of men and women was about equal. So, overall, at the end of the public trial stage of

---

[11] For instance, Clark, *Struggle for the breeches*, passim, whilst understanding the heterogeneous nature of a 'working class', still writes about a more politicised, respectable, employed section of the labouring class.

[12] See, for instance, all contributions to Hitchcock, King and Sharpe, *Chronicling poverty*; T. Hitchcock and J. Black (eds), *Chelsea settlement and bastardy examinations, 1733–66*, London 1999; *Essex pauper letters*; Palk, 'Fit objects'; Hitchcock, *Down and out*; and Gatrell's use of convict petitions, ballads and broadsides in *Hanging tree*, 109–75.

the criminal justice process, women gained the advantage at many of the decision points, but this was not an advantage which operated consistently. At the next stage of the journey through the justice system, none of the death sentences for pickpocketing was carried out, and two men only were hanged for shoplifting – men with an unusually violent record.[13] The picture was different for forged Bank note crime. Over half of the males sentenced to death were executed whereas less than a quarter of the women so sentenced were executed.

When death sentences for all three offences were commuted at the first stage of the pardon and remission process, men and women were equally likely to be selected for the secondary punishment of transportation. More women than men were selected for the secondary punishment of imprisonment. Since other secondary punishments were available for men, such as service in the armed forces and forced labour on the Thames navigation, there was little difference in the quality of intended punishment for the men and the women who had been sentenced to death.

When it came to the death sentence, a very small proportion of women was executed. The final outcome for all those sentenced for the three crimes cannot be securely ascertained. The first award of a commutation of sentence or a conditional pardon was, in very many cases, not the end of the story. As most of those sentenced to death were not executed, so large numbers who had been sentenced or pardoned to transportation did not leave the country. Many prison sentences were shortened, sometimes drastically. The appeals archives provide examples of this, and, where it was possible to follow the names of London convicts through the records, punishments were found to have been diluted as the offender progressed through different stages of the system.

Where a significant number of women appeared in court for a particular crime, the effect of gender in judicial decisions worked in their favour overall, but inconsistently and unevenly. It is vital to look more closely at the individual offenders' stories emerging at and after trial and at the environment in which their prosecutors or other decision-makers operated. Focusing on three property crimes rather than on many allowed this to be done.

As Kermode and Walker have suggested:

It is becoming increasingly apparent that qualitative material can tell us far more about the activities and attitudes of ordinary people than can aggregates of litigation alone . . . the reconstruction of recorded words and actions is an important preliminary to deciphering the encoded social, cultural and individual meanings which informed court actions.[14]

13 The choice of these two property crimes – shoplifting and pickpocketing – tends to predict this outcome; other crimes, such as burglary and highway robbery, resulted in a higher rate of executions.
14 Kermode and Walker, *Women, crime and the courts*, 9.

Attention to the detail reveals a different, women's, world: in shops, where rustling, swirling gowns and cloaks, and suddenly enlarged bellies hid appropriated goods; and where unremarkable wives and mothers bought tea, sugar and ham for the family's sustenance, using forged bank notes; on the night streets, in back alleys and dark lodgings, where women of all shades of talent and beauty variously negotiated with unwise men and divested them of their possessions.

A systematic approach to qualitative, as well as quantitative, evidence also allows a view of varying public perceptions of the three crimes. Private stealing was always viewed as a mean sort of crime. However, despite the complaints of shopkeepers, and newspaper reports which suggested that shoplifting was a common activity in any town of reasonable size, few prosecutions were brought to court from the time it became a capital offence in 1699. The overwhelming majority of cases nationally were brought in London, but these represented the tip of a large iceberg. Prosecutions were not good for business. They required expenditure of much time and trouble, with the likelihood of failure in court. In London, by the early nineteenth century, shopkeepers were reluctant to prosecute under the capital statute.[15] Shoplifting was seen as a petty offence. Most offenders were casual, occasional, small-time operators. Some may have been 'in the habitual practice of it', but many 'were not persons who are regular traders in thieving, but are persons in better circumstances, especially the women'.[16] Although the prevalent view was that some women were regular shoplifters, it was not perceived as a dangerous, organised crime, involving gangs, although, as the Old Bailey records show, women often operated in pairs. Overall, it was not a crime that frightened the public or the courts sufficiently for them to pursue use of the death penalty.[17]

Similarly, pickpocketing was an activity much written about in the newspapers. Common and difficult to prevent, pickpocketing was not often pursued in court, largely because of the technical problems surrounding the proving of the case. Most of the men who suffered losses at the hands of women on the London streets did not take the matter further, because of their personal need to maintain anonymity and propriety. It was mainly women, however, who, in London, were left to face prosecution, but judges sometimes made it clear that they had little sympathy with the male prosecutors of these women.[18] Sometimes bystanders preferred to administer their own rough justice to a pickpocket in the street.

Criminal activity involving forged Bank of England notes was perceived differently. Prosecutions during the period of 'suspension' were numerous and the numbers of men and women hanged were significant. It was an offence

---

15 *Select committee on capital punishment in felonies*, PP, 1819, viii. 60.
16 Ibid. viii. 27.
17 Beattie, *Crime and the courts*, 179–80.
18 Ibid. 180–1.

that was seen to strike at the heart of the commercial economy. Those in authority, such as members of parliament, were easily persuaded to uphold and press for the death penalty. Public feeling was sometimes ambivalent about this crime in the early decades of the nineteenth century. There was revulsion at the attack it represented on the well-being of the nation but, at the same time, there was antipathy towards the Bank of England for its failure to produce satisfactory bank notes, for its failure to reinstate payment in gold and for its arrogant attitude to the prerogative of the judiciary. The public mood swung at times between 1797 and 1834, depending on the numbers of prosecutions. In 1823 parliament was told that 'in the course of the last ten years, no capital punishment had so excited so much odium, and rendered the administration of public justice so unpopular as that in the cases of forgery'.[19] Different perceptions about different categories of crime may also explain diverse verdicts and sentences, adding further complexity to decision-making.

Of the three main explanatory themes that have emerged in this book – gendered behaviour, decision-making in a patriarchal environment and political necessity – the first is perhaps the most significant.

Gendered behaviour

This asserts that criminal activities were 'gendered' before the offender entered the justice system. The narratives which have emerged have, in many cases, although by no means all, highlighted the differences in the ways that men and women behaved in committing their illegal acts. This understanding provokes the obvious question as to whether differences in court verdicts and sentences resulted from the decision-makers' responses to the different behaviours they heard about at the trial. Differences were clearest in pickpocketing cases. The numbers of female defendants in court were greater than the numbers of men and, among the women, a particular life-style and way of operating on the streets of the metropolis predominated. In shoplifting cases, although the differences in the ways of carrying out thieving activities were not as great as in pickpocketing cases, the presence of so many women, in a women's world, suggests that considerations of different behaviours would influence judicial decisions. Similar distinctions were not apparent in forged Bank note crime in London and Middlesex. London was not a centre of mechanical forging activity – a largely male activity in other parts of the country – and the men and women of London and Middlesex were involved in selling, uttering and possession of notes in ways that resembled the activities of each other. The number of women in court charged with these crimes was proportionately smaller than in the other two crimes. This fact alone may

19 J. Mackintosh, speech in House of Commons, *Debates of the House of Commons*, n.s. ix, 1823, 412.

have produced different decisions particularly if there was a 'not guilty' plea which allowed the jury to hear the prosecutor's and the prisoner's stories.

However, it is important not to see women, or men, as homogenous categories. Their social and legal status also affected the making of decisions. It would not be useful to base explanations of differentials – either of motivation, behaviour, or of court decisions – only on the sex of offenders. The narratives of these cases certainly do not show women as passive and men as assertive. There is no evidence of assumptions that women were less criminally dangerous, the accomplices of men, stealing items of less value, less violently, and thus receiving more generous treatment from the courts. The stories presented in court, and the words of the convicts later in their journey, show that not only did some women receive more severe treatment, but that they were not more likely to work with men, steal less valuable items or behave in a more becoming fashion than men. However, they were likely to have operated in a different way on many occasions, and to such an extent that their crimes could be seen to be different in kind from men's. Examination of who the women were, what they stole and exactly how they went about infringing the law has demonstrated the gendered differences in the committing of these three crimes.

Differences in treatment arise from the roles and status of these men and women in contemporary society, roles which were, in themselves, gendered. The records give at least a partial view of the people involved in the trials.[20] Many of the men were occupied in the expected activities of London males, in trades and crafts of various kinds. The indiscriminate term 'labourer' was often used, but there were handfuls of those who earned a living at sea, soldiers, weavers, shoemakers, watchmakers and jewellers, gold and silversmiths, butchers, tailors – and parish paupers. To these can be added other trades and occupations – carpenters, coachmen, a fishmonger, wheelsmith, painter and paper hanger, potter, gentleman's servant, printer, gardeners, hairdressers, a chimney sweep, a blacksmith and a feathermaker. There were a few examples of men whose means may have been more substantial: a farmer, an attorney, some clerks and a few men of independent means.

As usual, it is difficult to establish female occupations: official records rarely describe them, other than by a sporadic entry as to their marital status, and the stories told in the Old Bailey sometimes provide a little information about occupation and life-cycle. Apart from explicit descriptions of the trade in sexual services – the full or part-time occupation of the majority of female pickpockets – other female offenders represented the expected range of mantua-makers, staymakers, potscourers, washerwomen, fruit and watercress-sellers, market traders and housemaids, all of them in and out of work. If

[20] OBSP; HO 26/1–11. Only between 1791 and 1805 was information given about occupations of males and, sporadically, about the status of females.

property offences were committed by men on the breadline, the financial needs of female offenders were even more pressing.[21]

It is not possible to be sure to what extent destitution was the motivation for crime on the part of many of the defendants, since they said little directly about this in their defences. Later, in the letters of appeal on their behalf, seeking pardon or commutation of sentence, poverty as a motivation for the offence was more frequently mentioned by women. Many women were the focus of the economic survival of a family. Urban women had particular difficulties in holding their family economies together in the bad years of the economic cycle. For single women, with or without children, the problem would have been particularly acute. The tendency has been noted for the age of female offenders to be slightly higher than their male counterparts, evidence of the varying and continuing needs of the female life cycle – family responsibilities combining with the difficulty of obtaining and maintaining paid employment. Urban women had particular difficulties, lacking the ability which many rural women had to exploit customary rights to ease economic difficulties. The work in which significant numbers of women were involved allowed them access to goods which they could easily pawn through the city's well-developed network for receipt of stolen goods. Both factors – family responsibilities and marginal work situations – are also marks of continuity in the lives of poor women. The 1820s showed little difference from the 1780s in this respect and both demonstrate strong similarities with periods of very recent history, where women predominate in the older age groups of offenders and are more widely spread over the whole age distribution.[22]

In London, shoplifting was perceived as, and, so far as indictments were concerned, certainly was, a largely female crime, particularly in times of war.[23] Pickpocketing, as seen by the court in London, was also a female dominated crime.[24] Juries were used to seeing females in court for these offences but found many more females than males not guilty of the charges. The chance to exit, at the trial stage, from the criminal justice system was given to 29 per cent of female shoplifters, and 50 per cent of female pickpockets, compared with 16 per cent and 30 per cent respectively of men. Whatever the motivation of juries in reaching these decisions, they were presented in court with stories which described gendered worlds of different male and female activity. It is not surprising that they distinguished, consciously or subconsciously, between men and women, in making the first crucial decision about guilt. As so often, women were seen to have committed more trivial, less threatening, offences. They were seen to be struggling with economic demands, more 'troubled' than directly undermining public order. Once the

---

21 King, 'Female offenders'.
22 D. Farrington, 'Age and crime', Crime and Justice: a Review of Research viii (1986), 189–250.
23 See table 1 above; Beattie, 'Crime and inequality'.
24 See table 9 above which contrasts with Beattie, Crime and the courts, 91, 180.

jury had decided that a defendant was guilty, distinctions between males and females were not as clear. For shoplifters, a fully guilty verdict, resulting in an automatic death sentence, was applied equally to males and females. For pickpockets, such a verdict was rare, and rarer for women than for men.

Crimes prosecuted by the Bank of England provide a useful counterbalance to this tale of difference between men and women, both in their criminal behaviour and in the responses to it. They confirm the importance of looking at specific categories of crime in order to give better definition to broad statements about leniency in the sentencing of women. Public perception of forged currency crime contrasted with a growing tendency to see private stealing as more and more of a trivial offence, when considered against its prescribed end at the gallows. However, juries did not hear many accounts of uttering, selling and possession of forged Bank notes because of the massive plea bargaining system in effect. Verdicts and sentencing were thus out of the hands of the court and in the hands of the prosecutor. Discretion operated only later, when appeals were handled and petitions made for relief. So far as this group of offences was concerned, in the London metropolis men and women operated in similar ways, in shops, public houses, streets and coaches in uttering and selling notes, and possessing them secreted in the chimneys and wainscoting of their lodgings, and the verdicts and sentences against them did not vary as greatly as those for the other offences.

In shoplifting cases, witnesses recalled women hiding their booty under cloaks – a significantly female form of attire – cloaks being lifted or flung aside to reveal stolen goods, cloaks rustling suspiciously, bulging shapes under cloaks, cloaks tangling together or being passed over the face. We have a picture of a female world of flowing clothes, rustling skirts, concealing movements and adjustments of dress; a world where shopkeepers reached under petticoats and prodded padded bosoms to reveal swathes of textiles in secret hiding places. The male shoplifting world was perhaps more open, direct and prosaic, lifting their takings on to their shoulders, tucking it under their arms or dropping it into their hats. It is likely that such different worlds and ways of operating affected juries' responses and verdicts.

Juries were interested in the type and value of goods which shoplifters stole. Women did not steal goods valued in the lowest range. They were charged with stealing mainly in the range above 10s. and below £5, not a trivial amount. It is possible, of course, that women stealing items valued at less than 10s. did not reach the Old Bailey; they may have been discharged by magistrates, tried for simple (non-capital) larceny, or their victims may have been unwilling to prosecute. Men stole mainly in the range below 10s. value, but significantly in the range above £5. The jury would have seen high value theft as a more serious offence. The only shoplifting convicts on whom the sentence of death appears to have been carried out were male members of a gang that stole highly valued jewellery. There were more significant differences in what men and women stole, and the gendered meanings of the items. Household and clothing textiles, and small items of clothing were the most popular goods for both sexes to steal. Women had a greater propensity than men to steal in these categories. They stole goods of which they had knowledge, in shops which they might be expected to frequent and for which they had the means and networks of disposal. They preferred items which could be made into clothing, sold on market stalls or taken to pawnbrokers. Some historians have dismissed female theft of textile and clothing as a petty crime, born of the need only to clothe herself or her family, or just because she liked to be ostentatious. However, the high value of the massive yardages or types of clothing stolen belies such a view. Both were valuable commodities and could fetch a thief a good income.[25]

Distinctive male and female behaviour was even more in evidence amongst those appearing in court for the offence of pickpocketing. It may be a gross over-simplification to say that the vast majority of the women were prostitutes. Nevertheless, most carried out their thieving as an adjunct to the offer of sexual activity or other 'treats', or they were working on the streets of London in the dark hours. The court records show that 76 per cent of female pickpockets could be described in this way, whether it was a full-time way of earning a living, or whether a make-way, or literally 'moonlighting'. Others were in trades which were typical of the marginal, insecure world inhabited by urban women. This difference in male and female occupation is clearly underlined in the place and time at which these private thefts took place. The evidence, discussed in chapter 4, begs the question as to whether the same offence was being committed by men and women. We might conclude that it was not and hence we should not expect any parity of treatment at trial. The enclosed, private and dark places in which women successfully operated are in almost total contrast to the busy, public, day haunts of the male pickpocket.

Decision-making in a patriarchal environment

The profoundly gendered and patriarchal nature of the law of England and its paternalistic expression provides the second theme for explanation of judicial decisions. Men's defence of their power and possessions – whether land, capital, goods, chattels, children or wives – was justified by and enshrined in the law. In practice, such a seemingly monolithic and logical structure was breached and qualified many times over. The understanding behind it was multi-layered and its impact was uneven. Women of property found many ways of evading and ameliorating the legal structure to their own advantage.[26] For plebeian men and women, this property-based edifice had little

---

[25] Walker, 'Women, theft and stolen goods', 88–99, and *Crime, gender and social order*, 159–89; Weatherill, 'Consumer behaviour', 298.

[26] Finn, 'Women, consumption and coverture'; Bonfield, *Marriage settlements*; Staves, *Married women's separate property*; Erickson, *Women and property*.

practical relevance. In relation to the criminal law, and serious property crimes, the concept of the *feme covert* was of limited application. If the circumstances were right, a married woman could attempt to use the excuse of marital coercion in abatement of the offence. This was infrequently appropriate and rarely successful.[27] Men and women did not often operate together in the crimes studied here, with the exception of Bank note crimes. If married couples did operate together it was unlikely that the woman would be found to act both under the 'influence and compulsive force' of her husband and within his sight. Nevertheless, the mere existence of these doctrines is suggestive of a deeper wish to protect women from full application of the criminal law. Patriarchal notions, resulting in paternalism or 'judicial chivalry',[28] could and did work in women's favour in criminal law courts.

It is difficult to settle on a point of attack on the question of the meaning of judicial attitudes towards women. Are they an exercise of superficial deferential behaviours and social courtesies (which might be called judicial chivalry), or of power relationships, reflecting women's social and legal inferiority, resulting from their weakness and their need to be supported and protected? It seems inappropriate to equate paternalism with lenient judgements (towards women and children). It could have been seen as more effective to sentence them more harshly, in order to ensure their protection and to bring greater benefit to the proper ordering of society in the longer term. Such judicial protection might, however, have been contingent upon females behaving in a way appropriate to the norms set by a patriarchal society – to be weak, poor, deferential and caring for dependants. On the other hand, should a female demonstrate lack of these 'feminine' traits, she could receive harsh treatment.

If the cases of Charlotte Newman and Jane Harrison, prosecuted by the Bank of England (discussed in chapter 5), are compared, the contrast is stark: Newman, an 'unfortunate woman', who was to die on the gallows, and the 'interesting looking', twenty-year-old Harrison, housekeeper to a leading player in forged note selling, twice prosecuted capitally by the Bank, twice found not guilty.[29] The reasons for the juries' contrasting verdicts in these cases must have lain in their perceptions of the two women as they stood before them. Newman was lame, had been married to an already transported housebreaker, was known to be a major trader in forged notes and had, according to witnesses, lured her accomplice (whom the jury found not

[27] King, *Crime, justice and discretion*, 285, states that between 1750 and 1800 'a considerable number of Essex wives' obtained acquittal on the strength of the judges' understanding of this principle. Examination of the detail of the cases would be needed to establish whether this might be the result of application of principle or whether other defences were successfully mounted, or whether decisions were made purely on the strength of judges' paternalist feelings.
[28] Daly, 'Rethinking judicial paternalism', 10 and passim.
[29] OBSP, Dec. 1817, 22–4; May 1820, 393–7, 402–4; BECLS, M5/319, 13 Nov., 14 Dec.1817; HO 26/23, 26; 77/25.

guilty) away from his pregnant wife to live with her. Her behaviour and appearance did not commend itself to the men of the jury for its appropriate femininity and the extent of her crime and her previous associations could have prompted them to find her guilty. On the other hand, Harrison was young, a servant led astray by a powerful master, pleading becomingly in court of her innocence. Newspaper reports described her as 'interesting looking' – no doubt pretty and sexually wholesome. In all, the evidence showed her youth, proper femininity, deference and weakness. Perhaps the apparent contrast between these two women and the contrasting views which the men of the jury had of them, provides a useful picture of a fundamentally male view of womanhood, a view which is inevitable when men of a comfortable class pass judgement on women in trouble with the law.

Among the few women who were executed in this period, the court evidence suggested how a significant number of them had been violent, abusive and operating in a 'masculine' manner. The contrasting definitions – 'troubled' and 'troublesome' – are often applied to deviant female behaviour by decision-makers in today's courts.[30] These definitions may assist in explaining much of the paternalistic decision-making in cases analysed in this book. Placing female law-breakers in one or other category provides a way of categorising and judging their behaviour which otherwise the decision-makers and the system they operate within can neither fully comprehend nor engage with.

If patriarchy describes a relationship between men and women (and children) which expects the exercise of male power and control, and of female dependence, it will, as with all relational dimensions, operate in a variety of different ways. It will not keep women in unvarying subordination or oppression. Nor would it necessarily function to shape and control the behaviour of women. In respect of the criminal justice system, patriarchal law is as likely, more likely perhaps, to shape and control the behaviour of men, since that is better understood by the male law-makers and decision-takers, and more feared. The law embodies male standards. Women frequently collude and co-operate with the patriarchal system. This aspect of their agency contributes to the strength of patriarchy.[31] The language of female appeals, and the deferential language expressive of an inferior relationship of the female 'Bank prisoners' with their prosecutors, bears this out beyond doubt. Responses from the decision-makers often – though not always – acknowledged the effectiveness of these gendered appeals. The response of the Bank of England to women who demonstrated their destitution, their responsibilities for child care, the lack of men to support them, the unavailability of work in prison and their contrite and reformed natures, was deeply paternalistic. This was expected by those who made the appeals as they manipulated the accepted

---

[30] Hedderman and Gelsthorpe, *Understanding the sentencing of women.*
[31] Ibid. 18. My argument is the opposite of Lawson, 'Patriarchy, crime and the courts', who argues that the law shapes female behaviour.

relationship in society between powerful men and apparently 'weak' women. Women who continued their criminal activities in prison, unreformed, uncontrite, who lied, who had not accepted previous offers of merciful dealing, or who were of doubtful sexual morals, were ignored, along with most of the male convicts who were expected, as was proper for men, to fend for themselves, with work, money and food.[32]

Shifts and changes in patriarchal attitudes and their operation in private and public spheres have been seen as critical in this period.[33] Many historians have seen the period as a time of crisis in men's control over women. They relate this to new thinking and knowledge about gender and sexual differ-ence emerging in medical and philosophical circles. Investigation of women's bodies resulted in assertions of their inferiority. Cartesian thought about the separation of body and mind encouraged understandings of separation between men and women in a way that older humoral theory had not done. With distinct anatomy and physiology, governed by feeling, not reason, and with distinct moral qualities, women were separate creatures who must inhabit a different world.[34]

It is unlikely that changing constructions of masculinity and femininity, or discourse on men's domination of the public sphere and women's retreat to the privacy of the home, would have been a concern of plebeian life. Putting 'separate spheres' into practice was a class privilege denied to working men and women, and certainly to out-of-work women and men. Plebeian men had little power, except over their women and children. Plebeian women had to get out of the environment in which they lived and into locations in which they could earn a living. London was a place in which men and women, plebeian and working-class, jostled for space. Sharing of crowded space makes the separation of public and private impossible. There was no comfort-able private world of home to retreat to, and men and women sought refuge in the pleasures of public life, in public houses and spirit cellars. Plebeian women often shocked observers of the middling sort with their enjoyment of public life, so different from the increasing seclusion of ladies in the private world of the home. Although, in their language of judicial appeal, they used definitions of respectability, these differed greatly from those of the middling sort. They were still much less free than plebeian men since their respect-ability was more fragile, based on sexual reputation, rather than skill.[35] The poor did not accept paternalistic offerings on the donor's own terms. They

---

32 Palk, ' Fit objects'.
33 Walby, 'Women's employment'.
34 Hitchcock, *English sexualities*; Hitchcock and Cohen, *English masculinities*; Barker and Chalus, *Gender*; Barker-Benfield, *Culture of sensibility*; M. LeGates, 'The cult of woman-hood in eighteenth-century thought', *Eighteenth-century Studies* x (1976), 21–39; von den Steinen, 'Discovery of women'; Jones, *Women in the eighteenth century*; Fletcher, *Gender, sex and subordination*; Shoemaker, *Gender in English society*.
35 Clark, *Struggle for the breeches*, 35–8.

might show deference, they might couch their requests in the right terms to get what they wanted, but the deference was mainly an illusion. They knew each other, recognised each other, they were fellow travellers through a life which was impervious to most of their choices. The distance between polite and plebeian cultures was immense. The workings of the criminal justice system, a terrifying institution of the patriarchal state, did not favour the poor, male or female.

Yet, the stories of the property offenders who journeyed through the criminal justice system demonstrate that the voyage could be negotiated. The powerless and the powerful negotiated, the young with the old, and, perhaps most successfully, the female with the male. Although convicts did not usually come from a class where the language of patriarchy, of public and private, or of masculinity and femininity, had conscious purchase, yet they understood the rules and, in many cases, secured benefits for themselves which made their punishments shorter, or more tolerable.

There was no obvious reluctance to punish women, but there was obvious reluctance to bring them to the gallows. It is strange that contemporaries did not remark in public on this, or comment profusely on the hanging of women. Only a rare record comments that a reprieve from hanging has been granted because of a woman's sex.[36] Although deeply involved with the emotional and psychological issues, Gatrell found only fragmentary evidence of discussion on the inappropriateness of hanging women. Lord Ellenborough's diary references, although they mention the woman 'spared on account of her sex, (although) she was the most guilty of all', are more concerned with the inequality of treatment of felons in general, rather than women in particular.[37] The reluctance to execute women cannot be placed entirely at the door of a patriarchal mode of thinking, nor be attributed to paternalistic and chivalrous concerns. The strategic needs of the state to maintain the acceptability and legitimacy of the death penalty would have been brought into disrepute by the sight of too many female bodies on the gallows. There was public outrage at the burning of women in the 1780s, but this seems to have been mainly because it was seen as an unjust punishment, more severe than for men in similar coining (treason) cases.[38] Gatrell's claim that the specific campaigns around the executions of a few attractive, 'wronged' women mobilised 'opinion' most effectively against 'harsh law' is difficult to substantiate. Had this been so, there would surely be more evidence of this in public debate and record. The claim that 'the critique of the law was mobilised less through reasoned argument about legal systems than through identification with the plights of women wrongly condemned, around whom luxuriant sentiment and sentimentality might flow' seems to

36 King, *Crime, justice and discretion*, 282 and n. 55.
37 Colchester, *Diary*, 154–5, entry for 28 June 1828.
38 For instance see comment in the *Universal Daily Register*, 22, 23, 25, 27 June 1786; 24, 25, 27 June 1788.

rely too much on two sensational stories of female execution which excited interest.[39]

Understandings and images of the body have an important part to play in understanding executions – deliberate, controlled and violent deaths. Any specific interest in female executions, slight though the record is, perhaps confirms the erotic interest of the observer in the female body. Concern for modesty and decency did not mask the fact that women were seen as sexual objects. The power of the female body is a fundamental challenge to patriarchy. This was acknowledged in the stays of execution granted to pregnant women. 'There is something repugnant about destroying a body which gives life.'[40] However, it is difficult to understand decisions to execute some women. Why was paternalism and judicial chivalry unable to save them? A 'projective' theory of punishment may apply, whereby those tendencies most feared in ourselves are projected on to the offender. She is punished not so much because of what she has done, but because she represents the unthinkable possibility that the rest of us might do the same. Some of the executed women were murderers, violent robbers, burglars and rioters, just like the men who were executed. If women are 'people', just like men, and can do what men do, the law, which exists to control men, can equally and deservedly be used to control them.

Political necessity

The third theme is the pragmatic and political needs of the British state which significantly affected the choices made about the lives of men and women once they had been convicted of serious crimes. The development and implementation of penal policy in the years covered by this study were, not surprisingly, a piecemeal and reactive business. The needs of the state were often the over-riding factor in decision-making, whatever the criminal activity, whatever the verdict, sentence or appeal of the convict, and whatever his or her gender.

For instance, the debate about the use and purpose of transportation during the whole of this period exemplifies the changing needs of the state. Shifting language was used to characterise it. Sometimes it was seen as a deterrent, sometimes as an opportunity for the exercise of mercy, sometimes it was seen to offer the possibility of reform, sometimes a way of suitably peopling a new colony and frequently as a means of ridding English society of undesirable citizens. These varying views had their effect on the number and gender of those shipped to Australia. In the early decades of the nineteenth century, decisions were increasingly being made for political and pragmatic

---

[39] Gatrell, *Hanging tree*, 339–60, telling the stories of Sarah Lloyd and Eliza Fenning.
[40] Naish, *Death comes to the maiden*, 251.

reasons. The Secretary of State and his servants at the Home Office sought to prop up a collapsing capital code as a deterrent to crime, while trying to avoid alienating the growing numbers who wanted reform. They were not driven by humanity but by the need to make it appear that the state had crime under control. In promoting transportation in 1824 as a deterrent form of punishment, Peel spoke against a background of public opinion which thought that life in Australia was so developed that transportation would be an inducement to crime. He was able to justify both his transportation policy, and the high rate of pardons and discharges from prisons because of the pressures on capital punishment and the overcrowded gaols in London.[41]

The attempts in this period to establish a national penitentiary system were driven by the same pragmatism. The 'temporary' expedient of the hulks had been an obvious practical means of meeting immediate pressures, particularly in London, and a policy of hard labour for strong men (women and weak men were excluded) had gone with it.[42] Expediency continued throughout the period to dominate the way in which male and female convicts were disposed of. When needs for resources in the armed forces were pressing, many more men served their sentences in the army and navy, than in the hulks or in prison.[43] This is not to suggest that the period from the 1780s to the 1830s was different in nature from previous periods. Decisions made by governments are frequently based solely on the need to relieve administrative dilemmas.[44]

However, during these years, the operation of a system of 'automatic' and bureaucratic pardons was required in order to find an administrative solution to difficult, if not dangerous, situations and to cope with the overload in various places of confinement – hulks, prison ships and prisons. The need for individually exercised discretion was minimised. Prison and penitentiary keepers had only to calculate the length of time a prisoner had served, verify reasonably good behaviour and a home or a job for the released convict to go to. Hulk superintendents had a quota of 2 per cent of prisoners who could be released each quarter. If specified bureaucratic norms were fulfilled, a free pardon resulted. Sick and injured prisoners could also be given free pardons or conditional pardons which saw them removed to the penitentiary or

41 Devereaux, 'In place of death'; Atkinson, 'State and empire'; Gillen, 'Botany Bay decision'.
42 Devereaux, 'Making of Penitentiary Act'. For the complex picture of the interconnections between transportation and imprisonment with or without hard labour see also Beattie, Crime and the courts, 520–618; Ignatieff, A just measure of pain, 80–2; and Devereaux, 'In place of death'.
43 Devereaux, 'Making of Penitentiary Act', 424, table 1. See also King, 'War as a judicial resource'.
44 See Devereaux, 'Making of the Penitentiary Act', 414 and n. 39, on the large numbers of pardons issued in early 1776. These were not discretionary or based on considered responses to appeals to the monarch, but were solely to relieve an acute administrative problem, and were dealt with administratively and bureaucratically.

hospital. Individual discretion is never absent from a state's justice system, but at this point in England it was becoming a less significant instrument.

A bureaucratic system does not operate in an ungendered way. It is apparent that more women than men achieved pardon, a shorter sentence or service in the penitentiary on grounds of dreadful ill-health, much of which seems to have been traced to child-bearing, or to long-term illness and disease which had never been treated. Their lesser ability to earn wages in prison meant that they would have been less likely to look after themselves, or indulge in activity which might have improved their lot. Many fewer men were freed from the hulks because of illness. Fewer jobs for women in prison meant that they could not score so highly in calculations of good behaviour, although many prison keepers and superintendents remarked on their reformed demeanour. The prison keepers' reports show, however, that it was difficult for them to fulfil the criterion of having a job to go to which often delayed their discharge where pardons had been granted.

They 'have conducted themselves extremely well'

The experiences of four Londoners, two apparently married couples, Martha and George Lucas, and Sarah and William Payley, who were all tried at the Old Bailey for uttering forged Bank notes provide a final informative view of the quite rational workings of the justice system and the evident but patchy effect of gender on decisions.

The Lucases were apprehended in November 1819 for each uttering a forged Bank of England £1 note. They were known to be routinely involved in this type of activity but the evidence at this time was slight so the Bank offered each of them a plea to a lesser charge of possession of forged notes. George accepted the offer and was sentenced to fourteen years' transportation to New South Wales. Martha Lucas on the other hand decided to take a chance on being seen as a woman under the power of her husband, refused the plea bargain offer and pleaded not guilty to a capital charge of uttering. Her gamble failed as the Bank of England produced witnesses to spoil her attempt to plead 'marital coercion'. Among them, the grocer she had attempted to trick insisted, 'I never saw her in company with a man except at the police office'; his wife added 'she was quite alone – I do not know that she is married'. Martha stated, 'I know nothing of this. I had it from my husband and acted under his direction.' As the jury found her guilty of uttering, the judge had no choice but to sentence her to death. At the end of the sessions, in an application of paternalistic chivalry (or perhaps an attempt to keep the gallows decently veiled), the judge remitted her death sentence to a sentence of transportation for life.

The Payleys came before the Old Bailey court a month later, charged with uttering notes of much higher value. Here there was evidence to prove serious offences. The Bank split their prosecution decision by gender, preferring an indictment against William for the capital offence only. Sarah was offered a plea bargain, which she accepted, together with her resulting sentence of fourteen years' transportation. William put in a plea of not guilty but, seeming to be in a state of confusion about the nature of the charge and its punishment, asked if he could change his plea to guilty. The judge asked him not to do this. William insisted, saying no-one had persuaded him to do so. He was executed early in 1820.

So Martha Lucas and Sarah Payley found themselves together in Newgate gaol waiting for the ship to carry them to the other side of the world. A ship was ready in April 1820 and the 'compassionate gentlemen' of the Bank of England made available £5 to each of them, along with fourteen other women, as the order came for them all to embark. On the day of transportation, both Payley and Lucas were said to be unwell and unable to sail. Then began their letter writing to the 'Gentlemen' at the Bank. At first Payley, claiming her extreme distress and illness, was refused pecuniary relief, since Brown, the Newgate keeper, described her as a woman 'of the worst description, unworthy of the Bank's bounty', and stated that to give her anything would be a kind of encouragement; she was employed in prison and received a proportion of her earnings every Saturday. However, a Bank investigator sent to check on the situation reported that she was indeed in great distress and the Bank started to pay her 5s. a week. They continued to do so for two and a half years. Martha Lucas wrote in October 1820 and she too was paid 5s. a week for over two years. Her letters emphasised her delicate state of health and that she had a child with her to support in gaol. Both Payley and Lucas were described as still being too unwell to sail later in 1820 and all through 1821. It is highly likely that the keeper of Newgate was finding them extremely useful as wardswomen. From the beginning of January 1822, the Bank decided it would no longer go on paying these women; it was, it felt, entirely the government's fault that the provision of ships for women had been delayed – a sailing was not envisaged until at least June 1822. The Bank had done enough and it was apparent that these two women had become trusted servants of the gaol and were being paid for their work.

Lucas had also petitioned the Home Secretary on at least two occasions. Her first petition, in March 1820, appears to have received no reply. Her second, in 1824, shows all the features of a woman's petition: the petitioner had not intended to offend, she was of previous unblemished character, she had uttered notes at the instigation only of her husband, her mother was a respectable nurse now afflicted by rheumatism and deprived of her daughter's care; neighbours said they would have her in their service, and that nothing bad was known about the family. The keeper of Newgate added a report about her excellent service as a wardswoman. It is unclear what effect this petition might have had on the decision-making process. In May 1824 Payley and Lucas were included in a list of females submitted by the keeper of Newgate at the request of the Home Office in which he noted, 'Have conducted themselves extremely well'. Lucas he recommended for pardon and Payley for transfer to a house of correction for a 'short term'. In the event, as the Home Office noted on the list, there was 'No room in the H of C', but Payley's fourteen-year sentence was reduced to seven years, of which she had already served well over four. Lucas, noted as having a means of earning a living, and being 'becoming and orderly' had her life transportation sentence reduced to fourteen years' imprisonment.[45]

In the journeys of these four people through the justice system, some short, some long, the flexibility and diversity of that system can be clearly seen, as well as the rational nature of the judgements and choices. The differing decisions made about men and women are also obvious, as are the gendered strategies used by the women – in telling their story in court, in petitioning and presenting their case for mercy. After sentencing, the stages of the journey through the justice system show a judge's ability to 'save' a woman from execution; how illness featured so centrally in the women's lives, how decision-makers responded differently to them as women; and, in the end, how decisions were taken which met the needs of the state to manage its convicts.

The end of the journey through the criminal justice system for many of the men and women convicted of shoplifting, pickpocketing and forged note crimes in London and Middlesex cannot be known for sure. However, the evidence and analysis in this book show the frequent significant differences in male and female behaviour in the carrying out of illegal activities which influenced verdicts and sentences. It shows the important effect of paternalism and judicial chivalry, exercised usually to the benefit of women, but not consistently so. Even when judicial decisions were taken bureaucratically and administratively, women could still be dealt with differently, because of their life experiences as women. Discretion, informed directly or indirectly by the gender of the offender, operated at many different levels and strengths of consciousness. A system of justice suffused not just with discretion but with gendered discretion.

---

[45] OBSP, Dec.1819, 29, 35–6; Jan. 1820, 114; BECLS, M5/323, 25 Nov., 9 Dec. 1819, 1 May, 12 Apr. 1820; M5/324, 5, 13 July, 4 Oct.1820; M5/325, 12, 19 Dec. 1821, 2 Jan.1822; BEFP, F25/8, F25/9; HO 17/34 Eh27; 17/44/1 Gk22, 32; 26/26.

APPENDIX

Sources and Methodology

Main sources

The main sources for the research for this book were the records of the English criminal justice system. Evidence for trials at the Old Bailey Sessions, and the verdicts and initial sentences passed, was drawn mainly from the so-called Old Bailey Sessions papers which record in more or less detail all the hearings in this court. Research on the development of the sessions papers, from pamphlets sold on the street or in clubs to their use as factual background in appeal cases, suggests that, by the period studied, a good deal of weight can be placed on their accuracy in reporting what occurred in court. Since the late seventeenth century, every trial which took place was reported in pamphlets, collected and bound in annual volumes: *The whole proceedings of the king's commission of the peace, oyer et terminer and gaol delivery for the City of London and also the gaol delivery for the county of Middlesex held at the justice hall in the Old Bailey.* These narrative accounts, recorded in short-hand by an officially appointed publisher who paid a licence fee to the Lord Mayor of London, were an early species of periodical journalism, 'true-life' stories of crime and criminals. They went on sale on the streets within days of the end of the sessions, providing interest and amusement for a lay reader-ship. The emphasis on the factual detail of the stories told by witnesses for the prosecution and by the defendants makes this an important source. The sessions papers may be of little use to lawyers since they omit much of the interaction of judge and jury. On the other hand, they are reliable to the extent that if they record that something was said, it was; the writer never fictionalised. The quasi-official status of the sessions papers from an early stage required from their publishers a duty of 'completeness'. This complete-ness was important, especially from the last decades of the eighteenth century when the sessions papers were used to assist decisions made on London and Middlesex convicts' appeals for clemency in capital cases. Naturally, in an adversarial system of justice, the stories told by the various participants in a trial cannot be taken at face value as 'true' accounts, as each had her or his own interests to defend. However, it is the undisputed detail about lifestyle, methods of going about the town and the attitudes expressed in court which provide such uniquely valuable material about the activities of offenders and the gendered nature of crime.[1]

---

1 Devereaux, 'City and the sessions papers', and 'Recorder's report'.

For the post-sentencing stage of the judicial process, the records of the Home Office held in the National Archive (Public Record Office) were used. These included: the Criminal registers (HO 26) which were started in 1791 and in which are recorded lists of prisoners committed and held for trial at the Old Bailey, the outcome of their cases, their sentences and their initial disposal on removal from Newgate; the Newgate calendars (HO 77) from 1782 which record executions; and Convict transportation registers (HO11) for London and Middlesex from 1787, recording removals to transport ships or to hard labour on the 'hulks'. None of these records can be relied on for accuracy or completeness, particularly after about 1815.

For the appeals against sentences and the responses to them, the Home Office petitions archive (HO 17) was used, from its commencement in 1819, together with its register of petitions (HO 19). HO 17 is the main archive for London and Middlesex petitions, although material before 1819 is to be found in earlier series (HO 42, 44). London and Middlesex appeals were handled differently from those from the rest of the country, for which there are rich resources (HO 42, 44) and in the reports from trial judges to the Home Secretary (HO 47). The odd London case appears amongst these, but this is unusual. London and Middlesex cases were dealt with in a more 'on the spot' manner at the 'Recorders report' – meetings which included the monarch, the Home Secretary, the Lord Chancellor and the Recorder of London. Reasons were not generally recorded for decisions made, although an interim decision was sometimes noted on the petitions of appeal them-selves and in the register books. The appeals archive (HO 17) is vast and barely touched. I have not attempted to find out how many individual cases were handled in the 131 sections of the archive from 1819 to 1839. Each of these sections contains bundles of appeal papers, 40 to 50 to each section. For instance, in HO 17/40–59, the appeals of over 5,000 appellants are bundled up. About one-fifth of these appeals come from those sentenced at the Old Bailey between about 1817 and the late 1820s. The sample of these appeal papers analysed for chapter 7 of this book was taken from HO 17/25, 35–58 covering 3,552 petitions concerned with 3,350 individuals. This selection contained cases tried at the Old Bailey between 1817 and 1823. Male peti-tioners were in the overwhelming majority (91 per cent). Because I wished to analyse only London and Middlesex petitions, and in order to have a similar number of men and women to compare for the 'factors mentioned' scrutiny in chapter 7, women's petitions only were considered in most of the sets, men and women together only in HO 17/49, 50, 57.

In addition, the records of the Bank of England were used extensively. The Bank archives provide a unique view into the criminal justice system. They include the minute books of the Committee for Law Suits (BECLS). This committee handled all the Bank's criminal business, including cases involving forged Bank notes, from its setting up in 1802 to completion of major criminal note forgery business in 1834. Decisions about all criminal cases taken by the Bank in Britain and Ireland are recorded, together with details of the results of cases, responses to appeals for clemency, and details of the apprehension, prosecution and rewards strategies of the Bank. These records, although they give only terse information to justify the decisions reached, allow an unusual sense of security in quantifying the numbers of men and women whose cases the Bank's Law Suits Committee considered for prosecution, since their accuracy is of a remarkably high standard when they are checked against records in other sectors.

In addition, the Bank's archive of miscellaneous papers was used. These papers are mainly concerned with banking matters, but also contain valuable records relevant to prosecutions for Bank note forgery. They include the papers of the Bank's solicitors (Freshfields) (BEFP) dealing with specific cases, and an unusually rich section (correspondence with prisoners) containing scores of letters written by convicts awaiting transportation or the death sentence in prisons up and down the country.

Years of specific analysis

The Old Bailey Sessions Papers were used to establish the overall picture of cases heard before that court from 1780 to around 1833. However, specific analysis was confined to a manageable number of years. For shoplifting and pickpocketing, years were chosen to cover times of war and of peace. Selection ended when each of these crimes ceased to be capital. Pickpocketing ceased to be a capital crime in 1808; shoplifting in 1823. It should also be noted that in 1821 the definition of capital shoplifting changed, with the death penalty applying only to thefts of over £15 instead of the previous 5s.[2] The years specifically analysed were 1780–2, 1789–93, 1793–5, 1798–9, 1800–8, and continuing for shoplifting, 1815–18, 1820–3. The remainder of the years between 1780 and 1823 were reviewed to discover whether broad patterns for numbers of prosecutions, proportions of men and women on trial, spread of acquittals, partial and capital verdicts, and varieties of sentencing were relatively constant.

For crimes associated with forged Bank of England notes, all years between 1802 and 1833/4 were scrutinised. The meticulous minutes of the Bank of England Committee for Law Suits were followed from 1802 until the fading out of forgery trials in 1833. (The first of the London and Middlesex trials at the Old Bailey under the Committee for Law Suits' regime came in 1804). The Bank of England archives were purged some years ago, but the Freshfields' prison correspondence appears intact. Names on letters written from prisons can be attached to most of the women prosecuted by the Bank in London. Only thirteen of their names are missing. (Of these four were executed, one was untraceable after trial, one died in prison, two were speedily moved after sentencing to the general penitentiary and one was sentenced at an early date, before the petitioning from Newgate got under way. The remaining four were sentenced to transportation and, so far, no further trace of them has been found).

Methodology

Use of quantitative and qualitative evidence

The research methodology used was prompted by the excellent summary of the field by Joanna Innes and John Styles.[3] In 1986 they suggested 'fruitful directions' for further research into crime and the criminal justice system which, despite the passing of many years, remain substantially unfulfilled. They suggested that:

> 1. more attention should be paid to the ways in which different forms of illegal appropriation were undertaken and organised; what was stolen, how it was stolen and what was done with the stolen property, with emphasis on the need for this investigation to be systematic. A systematic qualitative analysis, they believed, could offer some of the same advantages as counting crimes.
> 2. more work on the 'solidarities, attitudes and material cultures' of those prosecuted for criminal activities, such as study of age, and life history.
> 3. such study should not be separated from the history of law enforcement.

In following this strategy, the crimes selected for study were capital crimes, since this allowed the men and women who came to trial to be followed through all the stages of the justice system, from trial to final punishment or release. Different parts of the justice system could therefore be examined and the effect of gender noted in each. Pickpocketing and shoplifting were crimes about which there were strong feelings in different sectors of the elite and trading communities. There are many similarities between these two crimes, in victim and type of offender. There was a strong aversion to putting into effect the death penalty for either. Thus the two crimes can be usefully compared. Crimes around forged Bank of England notes were of a rather different order. There was significant public sentiment that these were dangerous crimes, striking at trade and commerce and the future of the nation's prosperity, and the death sentence was frequently carried out. The Bank was a different type of victim of property crime and its methods of policing and prosecution bring a further diverse dimension to the prosecution of crime, and to subsequent stages of the justice system.

In my research, I sought a 'middle way' between over-extensive use of statistics and over-reliance on individual micro-histories. Statistics demonstrate the incidence of men's and women's involvement in the three crimes

---

[3] Innes and Styles, 'Crime wave'.

and provide means of categorising and comparing the nature of criminal activity as it was carried out by males and females – their identity, their methods, and where and in what context they fell foul of the law. The verdicts and sentences passed on men and women for these offences, the subsequent changes to sentence and the approaches used in petitioning for pardon and mercy have been quantitatively treated.

Understanding how the crucial organising category of gender may operate in criminal justice history may be better served by looking closely at specific crimes, in the way presented in this book. The previous tendency of historians has been to use wide categories of crime for comparison. The treatment of fairly wide categories of property crime as if they were homogenous, for instance not considering that women very often stole different things and in ways different from men, has often meant that the full extent of the way gender worked at the heart of crime could not be explored.[4]

As to qualitative information, 'the most interesting revelations . . . lie between the lines of single cases rather than within aggregations of many – in phrasings and images which flow around a story uncensored, revealing feelings, assumptions, and attitudes which are not always conscious'.[5] The single case can be illuminating. However, it should not stand alone but should be related to others of a similar type, otherwise its energy cannot be used to throw light on wider questions. So, a qualitative approach, using some micro-histories and textual analysis, was added to the basic quantitative material. This should not run counter to a systematic approach, but should assist in reading context, feelings, prejudices and assumptions into otherwise uncommunicative statistics. The source texts used in this thesis are products of an adversarial system of justice, of prejudiced opinion, of desperate people saying what they believed would bring them relief. Because of that, they may have a major part to play in extending our knowledge of the effect of gender in the criminal justice system.

4 Walker, in *Crime, gender and social order*, has published enlightening work on women and crime. For instance, she has considered the effect of gender in theft, violence and homicide in the early modern period. This is very much in the character of research suggested by Innes and Styles, and presents an excellent dialogue between the use of qualitative and quantitative evidence.
5 Gatrell, *Hanging tree*, 614.

Bibliography

Unpublished primary sources

London, Bank of England

Freshfields papers

F2/84 Statements relating to conduct of prosecutions for forgery, 1821
F2/85 Methods of circulation
F2/86 Legal basis for prosecutions
F2/94 Case papers R *v* Frances Mackay, 1818–19
F2/108 Nos of convictions, 1791–1829
F2/110 Account of prosecutions, 1797–1818
F2/118 Prosecutions for counterfeiting tokens, 1804–11
F2/120 Names committed for trial, 1809–29
F2/127 List of those pleading guilty to capital charge and not executed, 1816–18
F2/176 Six unrelated appeals for clemency
F2/204 Correspondence on alleged libels against the Bank in '*Black Dwarf*'
F24/3–51 Case papers on individual dollar and token cases, 1811–16
F25 Prison correspondence, 1781–1844

M5/307–33 Minutes of committee for law suits, 1802–34

London, City of London Corporation Record Office
Old Bailey Sessions papers (printed series), 1780–1834
Draft of 'Return of prosecutions for forgery on bankers for ten years commencing
    with the year 1818', MISC. MSS 368.14

London, The National Archives

Public Records Office
HO 6 Judges' and Recorders' returns
HO 11 Convict transportation registers
HO 13 Criminal entry books: correspondence and warrants
HO 16 Returns of convicts for trial at Old Bailey and Central Criminal Court
HO 17 Criminal petitions: series I
HO 19 Register of criminal petitions
HO 26 Criminal registers (Middlesex and London)
HO 42 Domestic correspondence, 1782–1820
HO 44 Domestic correspondence, 1773–1861
HO 47 Judges' reports on criminals
HO 77 Newgate prison calendar

Published primary sources

Official documents and publications (in chronological order)
Report from the select committee on transportation, PP, 1812, ii
Second report from the committee on the state of the police of the metropolis, PP, 1817, vii
Third report from the committee on the state of the police of the metropolis, PP, 1818, viii
Report from the select committee on the state of gaols etc., PP, 1819, vii
Report from the select committee on capital punishments in felonies, PP, 1819, viii
Debates of the House of Commons, n.s. ix, 1823
Report from the select committee on the best mode of giving efficacy to secondary punishments, PP, 1831, vii
Report from the select committee on transportation, PP, 1837, xix
Report of the committee on the responsibility of wife for crimes committed under the coercion of her husband, 1922, vii Cmd 1677
Brown v Attorney General for New Zealand (decided case, J.C. 1898 AC)
Midland Bank Trust Co. Ltd. v Green (decided case, no. 3 1981, 3 All ER 744)

Historical records of Australia (HRA), 1st ser. viii (1813–15), Sydney 1916

Newspapers and periodicals
British Monitor, 1821
E. Johnson's British Gazette and Sunday Monitor, 1795
English Chronicle (Universal English Post), 1786
Evening Mail, 1795
Gazetteer and New Daily Advertiser, 1783
General Advertiser, 1786
Lloyds Evening Post (British Chronicle), 1781–2
London Chronicle, 1780–1832
London Evening Post, 1780–2
London Packet, 1795
Police Gazette (Hue and Cry), 1828
Public Advertiser, 1786
St James's Chronicle (British Evening Post), 1780–96
The Daily Advertiser, 1796
The Diary (Woodfall's Register), 1793
The Gentleman's Magazine, 1785–95
The London Moderator and National Advertiser, 1821
The London Packet and the Lloyds Evening Post, 1820
The Morning Chronicle and London Advertiser, 1781–93
The Morning Herald and Daily Advertiser, 1781–6
The Oracle, 1795
The Sun, 1795–1818
The Times, 1788–1832
True Briton, 1795
Universal Daily Register, 1786, 1788

Contemporary books and articles

Anon., *The laws respecting women*, London 1777

Anon., *Old Bailey experience: criminal jurisprudence and the actual working of our penal code of laws*, London 1832

Bingham, P., *The law of infancy and coverture*, London 1816

Blackstone, W., *Commentaries on the laws of England in four books* 1st edn, Oxford 1765; 5th edn, London 1773; 13th edn, ed. E. Christian, London 1800; new edn, ed. J. F. Archbold, London 1811; 17th edn, ed. E. Christian, London 1830

Bracton, *On the laws and customs of England*, trans. S. E. Thorne, Cambridge, Mass. 1968

Chitty, J., *A practical treatise on the criminal law*, London 1816

Clancy, J., *A treatise on the rights, duties and liabilities of husband and wife at law and equity*, 3rd edn, London 1827

Clarke, P. and D. Spender (eds), *Lifelines: Australian women's letters and diaries, 1788–1840*, St Leonards, NSW 1992

Colchester, Lord (ed.), *A political diary, 1828–1830, by Edward Law, Lord Ellenborough*, London 1881

Coleridge, S. T., 'Punishments: scourging females', in *Essays on his own times forming a second series of 'The Friend' by Samuel Taylor Coleridge, iii*, ed. his daughter, London 1850, 762–6

Cruikshank, G., 'Bank restriction note: a protest against the severity of the penalty for forgery', in W. Horne, *The Bank restriction barometer*, London 1818

East, E. H., *Pleas of the crown*, London 1803

Foote, S., *Memoirs of Samuel Foote, i*, London 1810

Fry, F. and R. E. Cresswell (eds), *Memoir of the life of Elizabeth Fry with extracts from her journal and letters, edited by two of her daughters in two volumes*, London 1847

Hale, M., *Historia placitorum coronae*, ed. T. Dogherty, London 1800

Hawkins, W., *A treatise on the pleas of the crown: or a system of the principal matters relating to that subject digested under the proper heads*, 7th edn, ed. T. Leach, London 1795

Highmore, A., *History, design and present state of the various public charities in and near London*, London 1810

Hitchcock, T. and J. Black (eds), *Chelsea settlement and bastardy examinations, 1733–66*, London 1999

Knapp, A. and W. Baldwin, *The new Newgate calendar being interesting memoirs of notorious characters who have been convicted of outrages on the laws of England during the seventeenth century brought down to the present time*, London 1813

—— *The complete Newgate calendar, 1826 edn, iv–v*, ed. G. T. Cook, London 1926

Merrivale, H., *Lectures on colonization and colonies, ii*, London 1841

Miller, J., *An enquiry into the present state of the statute and criminal law of England*, London 1822

Noy, W., *The principal grounds and maxims with an analysis of the laws of England*, ed. H. Henning, 3rd American edn from 9th London edn, Burlington, VT 1845

Pickering, D., *The statutes at large from the 8th year of King William III to the second year of Queen Anne, x*, Cambridge 1763

———— The statutes at large from the 2nd to the 8th year of Queen Anne, xi, Cambridge 1764

Rawson, R. W., 'An inquiry into the statistics of crime in England and Wales', Journal of the Statistical Society ii (1839), 316–45

Rickard, S. (ed.), George Barrington's voyage to Botany Bay: retelling a convict's narrative of the 1790s, London–New York 2001

Romilly, S., 'Observations on the criminal law of England as it relates to capital punishments and on the mode in which it is administered', Law Tracts 1801–2, London 1810

———— Memoirs of the life of Sir Samuel Romilly with a selection from his correspondence edited by his sons, London 1840

Roper, R. S. D., A treatise of the law of property arising from the relation between husband and wife, London 1820

Russell, W. O. and E. Ryan, Crown cases reserved for consideration, and decided by the twelve judges of England from the year 1799 to the year 1824, London 1825

Sokoll, T. (ed.), Essex pauper letters, 1731–1837, Oxford 2001

Tench, W., A narrative of the expedition to Botany Bay, London 1789

———— A complete account of the settlement at Port Jackson in New South Wales, London 1793

Wentworth, W. C., Despatches and papers relating to the settlement of the states: a statistical account of the British settlements in Australia, i, 3rd edn, ed. G. B. Whittaker, London 1824

Secondary sources

Acres, W. M., The Bank of England from within, i, ii, London 1931

Alexander, S., 'Women's work in nineteenth-century London: a study of the years 1829–50', in J. Mitchell and A. Oakley (eds), The rights and wrongs of women, London 1976, 59–111

Allen, R. (ed.), The moving pageant: a literary source book on London street life, 1700–1914, London–New York 1998

Andrew, D., 'Noblesse oblige: female charity in the age of sentiment', in J. Brewer and S. Staves (eds), Early modern conceptions of property, London–New York 1994, 275–300

———— ' "To the charitable and humane": appeals for assistance in the eighteenth-century London press', in H. Cunningham and J. Innes (eds), Charity, philanthropy and reform from the 1690s to 1850s, Basingstoke 1998, 87–107

Arnot, M. and C. Usborne (eds), Gender and crime in modern Europe, London 1999

Atkinson, A., 'State and empire and convict transportation, 1718–1812', in Bridge, New perspectives, 25–38

Baker, J. H., 'Criminal courts and procedure at common law, 1550–1800', in Cockburn, Crime in England, 1550–1800, 5–48

———— 'Male and married spinsters', AJLH xx (1977), 255–65

———— An introduction to English legal history, 3rd edn, London 1990

Barker, H. and E. Chalus (eds), Gender in eighteenth-century England: roles, representation and responsibilities, Harlow 1997

Barker-Benfield, G. J., *The culture of sensibility: sex and society in eighteenth-century Britain*, Chicago 1992

Barrett, A., and C. Harrison, *Crime and punishment in England: a sourcebook*, London 1999

Bayne-Powell, R., *Travellers in eighteenth-century England*, 1st edn, London 1951

Beattie, J. M., 'Towards a study of crime in eighteenth-century England: a note on indictments', in P. Fritz and D. William (eds), *The triumph of culture: eighteenth-century perspectives*, Toronto 1972, 299–313

―――― 'The pattern of crime in England, 1660–1800', *P&P* lxii (1974), 47–95

―――― 'The criminality of women in eighteenth-century England', *JSH* viii (1975), 80–116

―――― *Crime and the courts in England, 1660–1800*, Oxford–Princeton 1986

―――― 'The royal pardon and criminal procedure in early modern England', *Canadian Historical Papers* (1987), 9–22

―――― 'Garrow for the defence', *History Today* (Feb. 1991), 49–53

―――― 'Scales of justice: defense counsel and the English criminal trial in the eighteenth and nineteenth centuries', *LHR* ix/2 (1991), 221–67

―――― 'London crime and the making of the "bloody code", 1689–1718', in L. Davison, T. Hitchcock, L. Keirn and R. Shoemaker (eds), *Stilling the grumbling hive: the response to social and economic problems in England, 1689–1750*, Stroud–New York 1992, 49–75

―――― 'Crime and inequality in eighteenth-century London', in J. Hagan and R. D. Peterson (eds), *Crime and inequality*, Stanford 1995, 116–39

―――― 'London juries of the 1690s', in J. S. Cockburn and T. A. Green (eds), *Twelve good men and true: the criminal trial jury in England, 1200–1800*, Princeton 1998, 214–53

―――― *Policing and punishment in London, 1660–1750: urban crime and the limits of terror*, Oxford 2001

Beddoe, D., *Welsh convict women: a study of women transported from Wales to Australia*, Barry 1979

Bennett, J., *Women in the medieval countryside: gender and household in Brigstock before the Plague*, Oxford 1987

―――― ' "History that stands still": women's work in the European past', *Feminist Studies* xiv (1988), 269–83

―――― 'Women's history: a study in continuity and change', *WHR* ii (1993), 173–84

Bentley, D., *English criminal justice in the nineteenth century*, London 1998

Bonfield, L., *Marriage settlements, 1601–1740: the adoption of the strict settlement*, Cambridge 1983

Branch Johnson, W., *The English prison hulks*, Chichester 1957, rev. 1970

Brewer, J., 'This, that and the other: public, social and private in the seventeenth and eighteenth centuries', in D. Castiglione and L. Sharpe (eds), *Shifting the boundaries: transformations of the language of public and private in the eighteenth century*, Exeter 1995, 1–2

―――― and J. Styles (eds), *'An ungovernable people': the English and their law in the seventeenth and eighteenth centuries*, London 1980

Bridge, C. (ed.), *New perspectives in Australian history* (Institute of Commonwealth Studies, occasional seminar papers 5, 1990)

Briggs, J., C. Harrison, A. McInnes and D. Vincent (eds), *Crime and punishment in England: an introductory history*, London 1996

Brown, A., 'Reassessing the critique of biologism', in Gelsthorpe and Morris, *Feminist perspectives*, 41–56

Byatt, D., *Promises to pay*, London 1994

Campbell, C., *The intolerable hulks: British shipboard confinement, 1776–1857*, London 1993

Campbell, R., 'Sentence of death by burning for women', *JLH* v (1984), 44–59

Carter, P., *Men and the emergence of polite society, Britain, 1660–1800*, Harlow 2001

Chalus, E., 'Elite women, social politics and the political world of late eighteenth-century England', *HJ* xliii (2000), 669–97

Clapham, J., *The Bank of England*, i, ii, Cambridge 1944

Clark, A., *The struggle for the breeches: gender and the making of the British working class*, Berkeley 1995

Clark, M. (ed.), *Sources of Australian history*, Oxford 1957

Cockburn, J. S., 'Punishment and brutalization in the English enlightenment', *LHR* xii (1994), 155–79

——— (ed.), *Crime in England, 1550–1800*, London 1977

Conley, C., *The unwritten law: criminal justice in Victorian Kent*, Oxford 1991

Cook, J., *To brave every danger: the epic life of Mary Bryant of Fowey*, London 1993

Corfield, P. J., *The impact of English towns, 1700–1800*, Oxford 1982

Daly, K., 'Rethinking judicial paternalism: gender, work–family relations and sentencing', *Gender and Society* iii (1989), 9–36

——— *Gender, crime and punishment*, New Haven, Conn. 1994

Davidoff, L., *Worlds between: historical perspectives in gender and class*, Cambridge 1995

——— and C. Hall, *Family fortunes: men and women of the English middle class, 1780–1850*, London 1987

Devereaux, S., 'The City and the sessions papers: "public justice" in London, 1770–1800', *JBS* xxxv (1996), 466–503

——— 'In place of death: transportation, penal practices and the English state, 1770–1830', in C. Strange (ed.), *Qualities of mercy: justice, punishment and discretion*, Vancouver 1996, 52–76

——— 'The criminal branch of the Home Office, 1782–1830', in Smith, May and Devereaux, *Criminal justice*, 270–308

——— 'The making of the Penitentiary Act, 1775–9', *HJ* xlii (1999), 405–33

——— 'Peel, pardon and punishment: the Recorder's report revisited', in Devereaux and Griffiths, *Penal practice*, 258–84

——— and P. Griffiths (eds), *Penal practice and culture, 1500–1900: punishing the English*, Basingstoke 2004

Doggett, M., *Marriage, wife-beating and the law in Victorian England*, London 1992

Earle, P., 'The female labour market in London in the late-seventeenth and early eighteenth centuries', *EcHR* 2nd ser. xlii (1989), 328–53

Edwards, A. R., 'Sex/gender, sexism and criminal justice: some theoretical considerations', *International Journal of the Sociology of Law* xvii (1989), 165–84

Edwards, S., *Sex and gender in the legal process*, London 1996

Edwards, V. C., 'The case of the married spinster: an alternative explanation', *AJLH* xxi (1977), 260–5

Eigen, J. P., *Witnessing insanity: madness and mad-doctors in the English court*, New Haven, Conn.–London 1995

Ekirch, A. R., *Bound for America: the transportation of British convicts to the colonies, 1718–75*, Oxford 1987

Elton, G. R., 'Crime and the historian', in Cockburn, *Crime in England 1500–1800*, 1–14

Emsley, C., 'Repression, "terror" and the rule of law in England during the decade of the French Revolution, *EHR* xiii (1985), 801–25

―――― *Crime and society in England, 1750–1900*, 1st edn, Harlow–New York 1989

―――― *The English police*, London 1991

―――― 'The history of crime and crime control institutions, c.1770–1945', in Maguire, Morgan and Reiner, *Oxford handbook of criminology*, 149–82

―――― 'Albion's fatal attractions: reflections upon the history of crime in England', in C. Emsley and L. A. Knafla (eds), *Crime history and histories of crime: studies in the historiography of crime and criminal justice in modern history*, London 1996, 67–85

―――― *Crime and society in England, 1750–1900*, 2nd edn, London 1996

Erickson, A. L., *Women and property in early modern England*, London 1993

Farrington, D., 'Age and crime', *Crime and Justice: a Review of Research* viii (1986), 189–250

―――― and A. Morris, 'Sex, sentencing and reconviction', *BJC* xxiii (1983), 229–48

Feeley, M., 'The decline of women in the criminal process: a comparative history', *CJH* xv (1994), 235–74

―――― and D. Little, 'The vanishing female: the decline of women in the criminal process, 1687–1912', *Law and Society Review* xxv (1991), 719–57

Finn, M., 'Women, consumption and coverture in England, c. 1760–1860', *HJ* xxxix (1996), 703–22

Fitzgerald, M., G. McLennan and J. Pawson (eds), *Crime and society: readings in history and theory*, London 1981

Fletcher, A., *Gender, sex and subordination in England, 1500–1800*, London 1995

Forbes, T., 'A study of Old Bailey sentences between 1729 and 1800', *Guildhall Studies in London History* v (1981), 26–35

Garay, K., 'Women and crime in late medieval England: an examination of the courts of gaol delivery, 1388–1409', *Florilegium* i–ii (1979/80), 87–103

Gatrell, V. A. C., 'The decline of theft and violence in Victorian and Edwardian England', in Gatrell, Lenman and Parker, *Crime and the law*, 238–370

―――― 'Crime, authority and the policeman state', in F. Thompson (ed.), *Cambridge social history of Britain, 1750–1950*, III: *Social agencies and institutions*, Cambridge 1990, 243–310

―――― *The hanging tree: execution and the English people, 1770–1868*, Oxford 1994

―――― and T. B. Hadden, 'Nineteenth-century criminal statistics and their interpretation', in E. A. Wrigley (ed.), *Nineteenth-century society: essays in the use of quantitative methods for the study of social data*, Cambridge 1972, 336–96

―――― B. Lenman and G. Parker (eds), *Crime and the law: the social history of crime in western Europe since 1500*, London 1980

Gelsthorpe, L., *Sexism and the female offender*, Aldershot 1989

—— and A. Morris, *Feminist perspectives in criminology*, Milton Keynes 1990

Gillen, M., 'The Botany Bay decision, 1786: convicts, not empire', *EHR* xcvii (1982), 740–66

—— *The founders of Australia: a biographical dictionary of the First Fleet*, Sydney 1989

Ginsberg, M., 'The tailoring and dressmaking trades, 1700–1850, *Costume* vi (1972), 64–71

—— 'Rags to riches: the second-hand clothes trade, 1700–1978', *Costume* xiv (1980), 121–35

Given, J., *Society and homicide in thirteenth-century England*, Stanford 1979

Green, T. A., *Verdict according to conscience: perspectives on the English criminal trial jury, 1200–1800*, Chicago 1985

Hanawalt-Westman, B., 'The female felon in fourteenth-century England', *Viator – Medieval and Renaissance Studies* v (1974), 253–68

—— *Crime and conflict in English communities, 1300–1348*, Cambridge, Mass. 1979

Harris, A. T., 'Policing and public order in the City of London, 1784–1815', *London Journal* xxviii/2 (2003), 1–20

—— *Policing the City: crime and legal authority in London, 1780–1840*, Columbus, Ohio 2004

Harvey, A. D., 'Research note: burning women at the stake in eighteenth-century England', *CJH* xi (1990), 193–5

Hawkins, D. T., *Criminal ancestors: a guide to historical criminal records in England and Wales*, Stroud 1992

Hay, D., 'Property, authority and the criminal law', in D. Hay, P. Linebaugh and E. P. Thompson, *Albion's fatal tree*, London 1975, 17–63

—— 'War, dearth and theft in the eighteenth-century: the record of the English courts', *P&P* xcv (1982), 117–60

—— 'The criminal prosecution in England and its historians', *Modern Law Review* xlvii (1984), 1–29

—— and F. Snyder (eds), *Policing and prosecution in Britain, 1750–1850*, Oxford 1989

Hedderman, C. and L. Gelsthorpe (eds), *Understanding the sentencing of women*, London 1997

Heidensohn, F., *Women and crime*, Basingstoke 1985

—— 'Gender and crime', in Maguire, Morgan and Reiner, *Oxford handbook of criminology*, 997–1039

Henderson, T., *Disorderly women in eighteenth-century London: prostitution and control in the metropolis, 1730–1830*, London 1999

Hill, B., *Women, work and sexual politics in eighteenth-century England*, London 1989

—— 'Women's history: a study in change, continuity or standing still', *WHR* ii (1993), 5–22

Hilton, B., *Corn, cash, commerce: the economic policies of the Tory governments, 1815–30*, Oxford 1977

—— 'The gallows and Mr Peel', in T. C. W. Blanning and D. Cannadine (eds), *History and biography: essays in honour of Derek Beales*, Cambridge 1996, 88–112

Hitchcock, T., *English sexualities, 1700–1800*, Basingstoke 1997

—— *Down and out in eighteenth-century London*, London 2004

—— and M. Cohen (eds), *English masculinities, 1600–1800*, London–New York 1999

—— P. King and P. Sharpe (eds), *Chronicling poverty: the voices and strategies of the English poor, 1640–1840*, Basingstoke 1997

—— and H. Shore (eds), *The streets of London from the Great Fire to the Great Stink*, London 2003

Honeyman, K., *Women, gender and industrialisation in England, 1700–1870*, Basingstoke–London 2000

Hughes, R., *The fatal shore: a history of the transportation of convicts to Australia, 1787–1868*, London 1987

Hunt, M., 'Wife-beating, domesticity and women's independence in eighteenth-century London', *G&H* iv (1992), 10–33

Ignatieff, M., *A just measure of pain: the penitentiary in the industrial revolution, 1750–1850*, London 1978

—— 'State, civil society and total institution: a critique of recent social histories of punishment', in D. Sugarman (ed.), *Legality, ideology and the state*, London 1983, 183–209

Innes, J., 'The role of transportation in seventeenth- and eighteenth-century English penal practice', in Bridge, *New perspectives*, 1–24

—— and J. Styles, 'The crime wave: recent writing on crime and criminal justice in eighteenth-century England', *JBS* xxv (1986), 380–435, rev. and repr. in A. Wilson (ed.), *Rethinking social history: English society, 1570–1920, and its interpretation*, Manchester 1993, 201–65

Jenkins, P., 'From gallows to prison? The execution rate in early modern England', *CJH* vii (1986), 51–71

Jones, D., *Crime, protest, community and police in nineteenth-century Britain*, London 1982

Jones, V. (ed.), *Women in the eighteenth century: constructions of femininity*, London–New York 1990

Kelly, E. M., *Spanish dollars and silver tokens*, London 1976

Kent, D. A., 'Ubiquitous but invisible: female domestic servants in mid-eighteenth-century London', *HWJ* xxv (1989), 111–27

Kermode, J. and G. Walker, *Women, crime and the courts in early modern England*, London 1994

King, P., 'Decision-makers and decision-making in the English criminal law, 1750–1800', *HJ* xxvii (1984), 25–58

—— 'Female offenders, work and life-cycle in late-eighteenth-century London', *Continuity and Change* xi (1996), 61–90

—— 'Punishing assault: the transformation of attitudes in the English courts', *Journal of Interdisciplinary History* xxvii (1996), 43–74

—— 'Locating histories of crime: a bibliographical study', *BJC* xxxix (1999), 161–74

—— 'Gender, crime and justice in late-eighteenth- and early nineteenth-century England', in Arnot and Usborne, *Gender and crime*, 44–74

—— *Crime, justice and discretion in England, 1740–1820*, Oxford 2000

—— 'War as a judicial resource: press gangs and prosecution rates, 1740–1830', in Landau, *Law, crime and society*, 97–116

—— 'Gender and recorded crime: the long term impact of female offenders on prosecution rates across England and Wales, 1750–1850', ch. vi in his *Crime and law in the age of reform*, forthcoming 2006

———— and J. Noel, 'The origins of "the problem of juvenile delinquency": the growth of juvenile prosecutions in London in the late eighteenth and early nineteenth centuries', *CJH* xiv (1993), 17–41

Kingsley-Kent, S., *Gender and power in Britain, 1640–1990*, London 1999

Klein, L. 'Gender, conversation and the public sphere in early eighteenth-century England', in J. Still and M. Worton (eds), *Textuality and sexuality: reading theories and practices*, Manchester 1993, 100–15

———— 'Gender and the public/private distinction in the eighteenth century: some questions about evidence and analytic procedure', *Eighteenth-Century Studies* xxix (1995), 97–109

Klinck, A. L., 'Anglo-Saxon women and the law', *Journal of Medieval History* viii (1982), 107–21

Knafla, L. A., 'Structure, conjuncture and event in the historiography of modern criminal justice history', in Emsley and Knafla, *Crime history*, 33–44

Landau, N., 'The trading justice's trade', in idem, *Law, crime and society*, 46–70

———— (ed.), *Law, crime and English society, 1660–1830*, Cambridge 2003

Landsman, S., 'The rise of the contentious spirit: adversary procedure in eighteenth-century England', *Cornell Law Review* lxxv (1990), 497–609

Langbein, J., 'Albion's fatal flaws', *P&P* xcviii (1983), 96–120

———— 'Shaping the eighteenth-century criminal trial: a view from the Ryder sources', *University of Chicago Law Review* l/1 (1983), 1–136

———— *The origins of adversary criminal trial*, Oxford 2003

Langford, P., *A polite and commercial people, England, 1727–1783*, Oxford 1989

Lawson, P., 'Patriarchy, crime, and the courts: the criminality of women in late Tudor and early Stuart England', in Smith, May and Devereaux, *Criminal justice*, 16–57

LeGates, M., 'The cult of womanhood in eighteenth-century thought', *Eighteenth-century Studies* x (1976), 21–39

Lemire, B., 'Peddling fashion: salesmen, pawnbrokers, taylors, thieves and the second-hand clothes trade in England, c. 1700–1800', *Textile History* xxii (1991), 67–82

———— *Dress, culture and commerce: the English clothing trade before the factory, 1600–1800*, London 1997

Lerner, G., *The creation of patriarchy*, New York–London 1986

Lieberman, D., 'Mapping criminal law: Blackstone and the categories of English jurisprudence', in Landau, *Law, crime and society*, 139–61

Linebaugh, P., *The London hanged: crime and civil society in the eighteenth century*, London 1991

Lombroso, C. and W. Ferrero, *The female offender*, New York 1895

Lush, M., *The law of husband and wife within the jurisdiction of the Queen's Bench and Chancery Division*, 4th edn, London 1933

McGowen, R., 'The image of justice and reform of the criminal law in early nineteenth-century England', *Buffalo Law Review* xxxii (1983), 89–125

———— 'A powerful sympathy: terror, the prison and humanitarian reform in early nineteenth-century Britain', *JBS* xxv (1986), 312–34

———— 'The body and punishment in eighteenth-century England', *Journal of Modern History* lix (1987), 651–79

—————— 'The changing face of God's justice: the debates over divine and human punishment in eighteenth-century England', *CJH* ix (1988), 63–98

—————— 'Punishing violence, sentencing crime', in N. Armstrong and L. Tennenhouse, *The violence of representation: literature and the history of violence*, London 1989, 140–56

—————— 'Getting to know the criminal class in nineteenth-century England', *Nineteenth-Century Contexts* xiv (1990), 33–54

—————— 'Civilizing punishment: the end of the public execution in England', *JBS* xxxiii (1994), 257–82

—————— 'Forgery discovered or the perils of circulation in eighteenth-century England', *Angelaki* i (1994), 113–29

—————— 'Knowing the hand: forgery and the proof of writing in eighteenth-century England', *Historical Reflections* xiv (1998), 385–414

—————— 'From pillory to gallows: the punishment of forgery in the age of financial revolution', *P&P* clxv (1999), 107–40

—————— 'Revisiting the hanging tree: Gatrell on emotion and history', *BJC* xl (2000), 1–13

—————— 'Making the "bloody code"? Forgery legislation in eighteenth-century England', in Landau, *Law, crime and society*, 117–38

—————— 'The problem of punishment in eighteenth-century England', in Devereaux and Griffiths, *Penal practice*, 210–31

—————— 'The Bank of England and the policing of forgery', *P&P* clxxxvi (2005), 81–116

—————— 'The Bank of England and the death penalty', forthcoming

Mackay, L., 'Why they stole: women in the Old Bailey, 1779–1789', *JSH* xxxii (1999), 623–39

McLynn, F., *Crime and punishment in eighteenth-century England*, Oxford 1991

Maguire, M., R. Morgan and R. Reiner (eds), *Oxford handbook of criminology*, Oxford 1994

Massey, D., *Space, place and gender*, Cambridge 1994

May, A. N., *The Bar and the Old Bailey, 1750–1850*, Chapel Hill, NC 2003

Maynard, M., 'Beyond "the big three": the development of feminist theory into the 1990s', *WHR* iv/3 (1995), 259–81

Medd, P., *Romilly*, London 1968

Mercer, S., 'Crime in late seventeenth-century Yorkshire: an exception to a national pattern?', *Northern History* xxvii (1991), 106–19

Mies, M., *Patriarchy and accumulation on a world scale: women in the international division of labour*, London 1986

Mitchell, B. R. and P. Deane, *Abstract of British historical statistics*, Cambridge 1962

Monkkonen, E., 'Systematic criminal justice history: some suggestions', *Journal of Interdisciplinary History* ix (1979), 451–9

—————— 'The history of crime and criminal justice after 25 years', *CJS* v (1984), 161–9

Morris, A., *Women, crime and criminal justice*, Oxford 1987

Naish, C., *Death comes to the maiden: sex and execution, 1431–1933*, London–New York 1991

Newman, L., 'Critical theory and the history of women: what's at stake in deconstructing women's history?' *JWH* Winter (1991), 58–68

Nicholas, S., *Convict workers: reinterpreting Australia's past*, Cambridge 1988

O'Brien, P., 'Crime and punishment as historical problem', *JSH* xi (1978), 508–17

Oldham, J. C., 'On pleading the belly: a history of the jury of matrons', *CJH* vi (1985), 1–64

Oldham, W., *Britain's convicts to the colonies*, Sydney 1990

Oxley, D., *Convict maids: the forced migration of women to Australia*, Cambridge 1999

Paley, R., ' "An imperfect, inadequate and wretched system"? Policing London before Peel', *CJH* x (1989), 95–130

Palk, D. E. P., '"Fit objects for mercy": gender, the Bank of England and currency criminals, 1804–1833', *Women's Writings* xi/2 (2004), 237–58

Pike, L., *A history of crime in England*, London 1876

Pollack, O., *The criminality of women*, New York 1961

Pollock, F. and F. Maitland, *History of English law before the times of Edward I*, Oxford 1895

Porter, R., *English society in the eighteenth century*, London 1982

Potter, H., *Hanging in judgement: religion and the death penalty in England from the bloody code to abolition*, London 1993

Radzinowicz, L., *A history of English criminal law and its administration from 1750*, I: *The movement for reform*; II: *The clash between private initiative and public interest in the enforcement of the law*, London 1948, 1956

—— and R. Hood, *A history of English criminal law and its administration from 1750*, V: *The emergence of penal policy in Victorian and Edwardian England*, Oxford 1990

Rendall, J., 'Women and the public sphere', *G&H* xi (1999), 475–88

Reynolds, E., *Before the bobbies: the night watch and police reform in metropolitan London, 1720–1830*, Stanford, CA 1998

Rock, P. (ed.), *A history of British criminology*, Oxford 1988

Rogers, N., 'Policing the poor in eighteenth-century London: the vagrancy laws and their administration', *Histoire sociale* xxiv (1991), 127–47

Roome, H. D., *Archbold on indictments: with precedents etc., compiled from Archbold's pleading, evidence and practice in criminal cases*, London 1916

Rublack, U., *The crimes of women in early modern Germany*, Oxford 1999

Rudé, G. F. E., *Criminal and victim: crime and society in early nineteenth-century England*, Oxford 1985

Rule, J., *Albion's people: English society, 1714–1815*, Harlow 1992

Scott, J. W., *Gender and the politics of history*, rev. edn, New York 1999

Scraton, P., 'Scientific knowledge or masculine discourses? Challenging patriarchy in criminology', in Gelsthorpe and Morris, *Feminist perspectives*, 10–25

Sharpe, J. A., *Crime in early modern England, 1550–1750*, Harlow 1984

—— *Judicial punishment in England*, London 1990

Sharpe, P. (ed.), *Women's work: the English experience, 1650–1914*, London 1998

Shaw, A. G. L., *Convicts and the colonies*, London 1966

Shoemaker, R. B., *Gender in English society, 1650–1850: the emergence of separate spheres?*, London 1998

—— 'Public spaces, private disputes? Fights and insults on London's streets, 1600–1800', in Hitchcock and Shore, *Streets of London*, 54–68

———— 'Streets of shame? The crowd and public punishments in London, 1700–1820', in Devereaux and Griffiths, *Penal practice*, 232–57

Shore, H., *Artful dodgers: youth and crime in early nineteenth-century London*, Woodbridge 1999

———— 'The trouble with boys: gender and the "invention" of the juvenile offender in early nineteenth-century Britain', in Arnot and Usborne, *Gender and crime*, 75–92

Slinn, J., *A history of Freshfields*, London 1984

Smart, C., *Women, crime and criminology: a feminist critique*, London 1976

Smith, A. D., *Women in prison: a study in penal methods*, London 1962

Smith, G., A. May and S. Devereaux (eds), *Criminal justice in the old world and the new: essays in honour of J. M. Beattie*, Toronto 1998

Staves, S., *Married women's separate property in England, 1660–1833*, Cambridge, Mass. 1990

Strohm, P., 'Treason in the household', in his *Hochon's arrow: the social imagination of fourteenth-century texts*, Princeton 1992, 121–44

Styles, J., ' "Our traitorous money-makers": the Yorkshire coiners and the law, 1760–83', in Brewer and Styles, *Ungovernable people*, 127–45

———— 'The emergence of the police: explaining police reform in eighteenth- and nineteenth-century England', BJC xxvii (1987), 15–22

Summerson, J., *Georgian London*, London 1991

Sweeney, C., *Transported: in place of death*, Melbourne 1981

Taylor, D., *The new police in nineteenth-century England*, Manchester 1997

Tobias, J. J., *Crime and industrial society in the nineteenth century*, London 1967

Tozer, J. and S. Levitt, *Fabric of society: a century of people and their clothes, 1770–1870: essays inspired by the collections at Platt Hall, the Gallery of English Costume, Manchester*, Manchester 1983

Vickery, A., 'The neglected century: writing the history of eighteenth-century women', G&H iii (1991), 211–19

———— 'Golden age to separate spheres? A review of the categories and chronology of English women's history', HJ xxxvi (1993), 383–414

———— *The gentleman's daughter: women's lives in Georgian England*, New Haven, Conn.–London 1998

von den Steinen, K., 'The discovery of women in eighteenth-century English political life', in B. Kanner (ed.), *The women of England from Anglo-Saxon times to the present*, London 1980, 231–58

Walby, S., 'Women's employment and the historical periodisation of patriarchy', in H. Corr and L. Jamieson (eds), *Politics of everyday life: continuities and change in work and the family*, London 1990, 141–61

Walker, G., 'Women, theft and the world of stolen goods', in Kermode and Walker, *Women, crime and the courts*, 81–105

———— *Crime, gender and social order in early-modern England*, Cambridge 2003

Walsh, C., 'Shop design and the display of goods in eighteenth-century London', *Journal of Design History* viii (1995), 157–76

Weatherill, L., 'Consumer behaviour and social status in England, 1660–1750', *Continuity and Change* i/2 (1986), 191–216

Wiener, C. Z., 'Sex roles and crime in late Elizabethan Hertfordshire', JSH vii (1975), 38–64

Wiener, M., *Reconstructing the criminal: culture, law and policy in England, 1830–1914*, Cambridge 1991

Wilf, S., 'Imagining justice: aesthetics and public executions in late eighteenth-century England', *Yale Journal of Law and the Humanities* v (1993), 51–78

Zedner, L., *Women, crime and custody in Victorian England*, Oxford 1991

―――― 'Women, crime and penal responses: a historical account', in M. Tonry (ed.), *Crime and Justice: a Review of Research* xiv (1991), 307–62

Unpublished dissertations

Grace, S. E., 'Female criminality in York and Hull, 1830–70', PhD, York 1998

Palk, D. E. P., 'Gender, crime and discretion in the English criminal justice system, 1780s to 1830s', PhD, Leicester 2002

Short, R. M., 'Female criminality, 1780–1830', MLitt. Oxford 1989

Smith, G. T., The state and the culture of violence in London, 1760–1840', PhD, Toronto 1999

Index